VIRGIL
and his
INFLUENCE

Bimillennial Studies

Edited by
Charles Martindale

Published by Bristol Classical Press
General Editor: John H. Betts

Printed in Great Britain
by Short Run Press Ltd., Exeter, Devon

ISBN 0-86292-134-1 (hardback)
0-86292-083-3 (paperback)

First published 1984 by

BRISTOL CLASSICAL PRESS

Department of Classics
University of Bristol
Wills Memorial Building
Queens Road BS8 1RJ

This book is dedicated to all lovers of Virgil
past, present and future.

Tu se' lo mio maestro e'l mio autore
Dante, *Inferno* I.85

Fourth century A.D. mosaic pavement found at Low Ham Villa, Somerset, depicting the story of Dido and Aeneas; the Somerset County Museum, Taunton. For a full discussion, see J.M.C. Toynbee, *Art in Roman Britain* (1962) 203-205, no. 200, pl.235; in the present volume extensive reference is made to it in the piece by Stephen Medcalf, pp.234-238.

Contents

List of Illustrations
(with acknowledgements)

Preface

This volume is based on a series of open lectures given at the University of Sussex in Autumn 1981 to celebrate the bimillennium of the death of Virgil. I would like to thank Professor Geoffrey Best, then Dean of the European School, who made the lectures possible, Dr. Jeremy Lane, who organized them, and Marea Mitchell for help with the proofs.

K.W. Gransden has substituted a piece on Virgil and Milton for his original lecture, while the essays by Colin Hardie and Stephen Medcalf were specifically commissioned for the book.

The text of Virgil cited is the Oxford Classical Text by Mynors (1969), reproduced by permission of Oxford University Press. For quotation from the poems of T.S. Eliot permission has been kindly granted by Faber & Faber Ltd., from A. Mandelbaum tr. *The Aeneid of Virgil* by University of California Press, and from G. Watson Dryden: *Of Dramatic Poesie and Other Critical Essays* by J.M. Dent & Sons Ltd.; for short quotations from other works we are indebted to the various publishers who are duly cited in the respective pieces; sources of the plates are acknowledged in the list of illustrations (p.x). Contributors were asked to keep bibliographical references to a minimum; accordingly apologies are offered to those who may find that their ideas have been borrowed without specific acknowledgement.

The bimillennium has passed with less fuss than one might have hoped; we should never forget the ancient injunction *onorate l'altissimo poeta.*

Lancing
September 1982 — *Charles Martindale*

The Contributors

K.W. Gransden is Reader in English and Comparative Literary Studies at the University of Warwick. His publications include an edition of *Aeneid* VIII (1976). Further works on Virgil are to follow.

Colin Hardie was formerly a fellow of Magdalen College Oxford and Public Orator. His publications include numerous articles on Dante and the Jackson Knight Memorial Lecture, *The Georgics: a Transitional Poem* (1970).

Gabriel Josipovici, author and critic, is Reader in English at the University of Sussex. His scholarly works include *The World and the Book* (1971) and *The Lessons of Modernism* (1977).

Laurence Lerner, poet and critic, is Professor of English at the University of Sussex. His numerous books include *The Uses of Nostalgia: Studies in Pastoral Poetry* (1972), *Love and Marriage* (1979), *The Literary Imagination: essays on literature and society* (1982).

Nigel Llewellyn is lecturer in the History and Theory of Art at the University of Sussex. He is preparing a book on English Renaissance funeral monuments, and has a special interest in Italian eighteenth-century painting.

Charles Martindale is lecturer in Classical and Medieval Studies at the University of Sussex. His publications include essays on Lucan and Milton (*Comparative Criticism* 3) and Milton's similes (*Comparative Literature* 1981).

Stephen Medcalf is Reader in English at the University of Sussex. He contributed the chapter on Virgil in *The Classical World*, ed. D. Daiches and A. Thorlby (1972), and is the editor of *The Later Middle Ages* (1981).

A.D. Nuttall is Professor of English at the University of Sussex. His books include *The Winter's Tale* (1966) and *Two Concepts of Allegory* (1967).

Angus Ross is Reader in English at the University of Sussex. He has edited *Gulliver's Travels* (1972) and selections from *Tatler* and *Spectator* (1982)..

Norman Vance is a lecturer in English at the University of Sussex. He has published essays on nineteenth century literature and literary history.

R.D. Williams is Professor of Classics at the University of Reading. Among numerous publications on Virgil are editions of *Aeneid* III (1962) and V (1960), both available in reprint from Bristol Classical Press, and *Virgil: New Surveys in the Classics No.1* (1967).

Introduction

CHARLES MARTINDALE

> *Books are not absolutely dead things, but do contain a potency of life in them to be as active as that soul was whose progeny they are; nay they do preserve as in a vial the purest efficacy and extraction of that living intellect that bred them.*

This famous sentence from Milton's *Areopagitica* connects with a theme dear to a number of the poets of antiquity that the great writer lives on in his work (*volito vivos per ora virum*). Life implies growth, or at any rate change, and within any work that is still living new readers, and new generations of readers, will find new possibilities of meaning, fresh resonances and applications. A radical historicism, which insists on one historically fixed reading, brings with it a kind of death, reducing literary masterpieces to the status of exhibits in a museum. This plain truth should not be confused with its dottier modern parodies, whereby the reader becomes sole arbiter of a text's meaning, and the very idea of 'meaning' is systematically dissolved. Contempt for such aberrations must not disguise the fact that there have been quite legitimate changes in the perception of the literature of the past; hence in part the justification for a book of this kind, which explores the reception and influence of a major poet and his place in the culture of the West.

There are many reasons for such a study. First, the posthumous life of a writer's works is a valid subject for historical investigation in its own right. Virgilianism is part, and not an unimportant part, of the history of Europe. Much will be learned of what T.S. Eliot called 'the pastness of the past', the tastes, the thought processes and preoccupations of men in former ages.

Secondly, we see in action part of the workings of tradition, the creative handing down of material from one generation to another, something to which Eliot attached much importance. 'Someone said: "The dead writers are remote from us because we *know* so much more than they did." Precisely, and they are that which we know.' Otherwise we could have little hope for literature, or indeed for culture and civilisation. As Eliot claims, the literature of the West can be said to constitute a kind of unity:

> . . . the historical sense compels a man to write not merely with his own generation in his bones, but with a feeling that the whole of the literature of Europe from Homer and within it the whole of the literature of his own country has a simultaneous existence and composes a simultaneous order. This historical sense, which is a sense of the timeless as well as of the temporal and of the timeless and of the temporal together, is what makes a writer traditional. And it is at the same time what makes a writer most acutely conscious of his place in time, of his own contemporaneity.[1]

Part of the consequences of this are well described by C.S. Lewis, when telling of his early love for *Sohrab and Rustum*:

> Arnold gave me at once . . . a sense, not indeed of passionless vision, but of a passionate, silent gazing at things a long way off. And here observe how literature actually works. Parrot critics say that *Sohrab* is a poem for classicists, to be enjoyed only by those who recognize the Homeric echoes. But I . . . knew nothing of Homer. For me the relation between Arnold and Homer worked the other way; when I came, years later, to read the *Iliad* I liked it partly because it was for me reminiscent of *Sohrab*. Plainly, it does not matter at what point you first break in to the system of European poetry. Only keep your ears open and your mouth shut and everything will lead you to everything else in the end – *ogni parte ad ogni parte splende.*[2]

Thirdly, we can often provide an interesting perspective for present concerns or critical disputations. For example, it is

1. 'Tradition and the Individual Talent' in *Selected Prose of T.S. Eliot*, ed. Frank Kermode (London 1975) 37-44; the three quotations are from pp. 38 and 40.

2. *Surprised By Joy: The Shape of My Early Life* (London 1955) 56.

sometimes said that strong sympathy for Virgil's Dido is modern and anachronistic, the result of the changes in sensibility associated with Romanticism. This is implausible: evidence from antiquity is scanty, though the tears of St. Augustine (*Confessions* I.13) are not quickly forgotten, while Juvenal's picture (*Satires* 6.435) of the bluestocking who champions Dido (*periturae ignoscit Elissae*) suggests that discussion of *Aeneid* could play a part in the battle of the sexes. Certainly in the Middle Ages many were sympathetic; in Helen Waddell's words 'Dido they took to their hearts, wrote lament after lament for her, cried over her as the young men of the eighteenth century cried over Manon Lescaut.'[3] Gower tells the story of Dido and Aeneas (*Confessio Amantis* IV.77 ff.) as an example of those who wrongly delay to return to their lovers (*qui in amoris causa tardantes delinquunt*). Here we may suspect the influence of Ovid *Heroides* VII, which possibly also inspired Shakespeare's evocative lines in *The Merchant of Venice* V.i.9-12 (though some of the details seem to come from *Heroides* X, Ariadne to Theseus):

In such a night
Stood Dido with a willow in her hand
Upon the wild sea banks, and waft her love
To come again to Carthage.

But in his version of the story in *The Legend of Good Women* 924 ff., certainly based on *Aeneid* IV, Chaucer too sides with the deserted queen. He was later criticized for his partisanship by the Scottish translator of the *Aeneid* Gavin Douglas (ca. 1475-1522), whose verse prologue to the poem contains some spirited pieces of literary criticism.[4] The familiar moves are already being made: Aeneas was not 'forsworn', because he had never promised to marry Dido or stay in Carthage, and in leaving was acting under heaven's command (409 ff.). Chaucer, however, may be excused (445-9):

Bot sikkyrly of resson me behufis
Excus Chauser fra all maner repruffis:

3. *The Wandering Scholars* (1927; revised ed. London etc. 1934) Introduction xxiii.

4. For a full discussion of this translation, see P. Bawcutt, *Gavin Douglas: A Critical Study* (Edinburgh 1976).

In lovyng of thir ladeis lylly quhite
He set on Virgill and Eneas this wyte,
For he was evir (God wait) all womanis frend.

Fourthly, we may alert ourselves to aspects of a text that contemporary preoccupations and priorities may lead us to neglect or spurn. In this way we protect ourselves against cultural parochialism, against what has been called 'insularity in time.'[5] Thus Dryden and the Augustans may show us how to respond more readily to the *laudes Augusti* and the public face of the *Aeneid.* Different epochs encounter different obstacles to their enjoyment of the classics. For many readers one such obstacle may be certain aspects of Virgil's diction and of the grand style, and one of the least effective lines in the *Aeneid* may be *Aeneid* VIII.181:

onerantque canistris
dona laboratae Cereris, Bacchumque ministrant.

they load on baskets the gifts of worked at Ceres,
and they furnish Bacchus.

In other words bread and wine are served. Servius actually commends such periphrases as a way of avoiding 'mean' words (Virgil eschews *panis* altogether). In his note on *Aeneid* I.177 he comments:

fugiens vilia ad generalitatem transiit propter carminis dignitatem et rem vilem auxit honestate sermonis.

Virgil avoiding low matters has passed to a more general expression on account of the dignity of his poetry, and has exalted a low object with becoming diction.

Homer, while employing a highly stylized and poetic language, does not disdain the commonplace in quite this way: he talks without embarrassment of dung and donkeys.[6] A modern commentator P.T. Eden attributes Virgil's

5. Hugh Lloyd-Jones, *The Justice of Zeus* (Berkeley etc. 1971) 156.
6. For the material in this section I am indebted to the note on *Aeneid* VIII.181 in P.T. Eden's commentary (Leiden 1975).

fastidiousness to his 'natural delicacy', but few today will easily perceive it as a form of sensitivity. This concept of epic decorum lasted long, with results that are not always to present taste. Pope in his translation of *Iliad* XI.558 turns Homer's ass into 'the slow Beast', justifying the rather pompous periphrasis in a long and characteristically feline note. The Erasmian educationalist Juan Luis Vives (1492-1540), following Vida, criticizes Homer (*De Tradendis Disciplinis* III.7) for comparing soldiers to flies, where Virgil more decorously chooses nobler insects, ants and bees: *Vergil. decentius, qui formicis et apibus exercitus facit similes, tanto honestioribus, quam muscae sint, rebus*; for Vives the *Aeneid* is *grande opus, et plenum gravitatis ac rerum bonarum* (III.6).[7]

This is not simply a matter of style, but constitutes a sort of retreat from reality that in an extreme form can become stultifying. In his *Aeneid* Dryden often 'heroizes' the original in an unattractive way (IV.223-30):

> The glad *Ascanius*, as his Courser guides,
> Spurs through the Vale; and these and those outrides.
> His Horses flanks and sides are forc'd to feel
> The clanking lash, and goring of the Steel.
> Impatiently he views the feeble Prey,
> Wishing some Nobler Beast to cross his way.
> And rather wou'd the tusky Boar attend,
> Or see the tawny Lyon downward Bend.

Here Dryden does not match Virgil's empathy with the young prince's keen desire to shine in the hunt, raising the tone too obviously and thereby, paradoxically, vulgarizing it.[8] In the main, by twentieth-century standards, Virgil avoids, while at times pointing the way towards, the sterile side of neoclassicism. At all events there is value in seeing the matter from the rather different point of view of earlier ages, when such aspects of diction as the avoidance of particular words were one of the glories of Virgil's art and a sign of his mastery

7. See Howard Clarke, *Homer's Readers: A Historical Introduction to the Iliad and the Odyssey* (London and Toronto 1981) 116.

8. For a defence of Dryden, see Mark O'Connor, 'John Dryden, Gavin Douglas and Virgil' in *Restoration Literature: Critical Approaches*, ed. Harold Love (London 1972) 247-275.

of the principles of 'the grand masterpiece, decorum'.

In all these areas, it is worth giving attention to the translators. Few can match the iron self-restraint that Milton showed in his aggressively literal version of Horace's Pyrrha Ode, and withdraw their own poetic personalities to reveal the otherness of an alien style. Rather they display their particular interest in their chosen author, and their own beliefs about the proper nature of poetry. C. Day Lewis' failure to reproduce Virgil's verbal music, or match his elaborate rhetoric, is not merely incapacity, but reflects a mid twentieth-century distrust of such things. We can correct his response, or lack of it, with the Earl of Surrey's fine rendering of *Aeneid* II and IV which, in accordance with humanist ideals, reproduces, perhaps a trifle stiffly, in the blank verse Surrey himself invented for this translation, at least part of the diction, syntactic movement and splendid periods and paragraphs of the original.[9] However, as C.S. Lewis complained, Surrey is in a way more 'classical' than Virgil himself,[10] so that to encounter in English the colourfulness of Virgil's poetry we have to turn elsewhere, perhaps to Chaucer's vigorous adaptation of Dido's hunt in *The Legend of Good Women* (1188 ff.). But when Chaucer recounts the lovers' union in the cave (1225-8), the knowing Ovidian innuendo is wholly at odds with Virgilian *gravitas*:

> She fledde hireself into a litel cave,
> And with hire wente this Eneas also.
> I not, with hem if there wente any mo;
> The autour maketh of it no mencioun.

The swings and roundabouts continue.

The 'romantic' character of Virgil's verse, in particular the powerful evocation of the distant past, 'the dark backward and abysm of time',[11] is sometimes better captured by William Morris than by more orthodox translators. It must be admitted that the tone is often distorted by a quaint

9. See the edition of Emrys Jones (Oxford 1964).

10. C.S. Lewis, *English Literature in the Sixteenth Century Excluding Drama* (Oxford 1954) 234. (He also has [81-90] a stimulating, if idiosyncratic, account of Gavin Douglas.)

11. See on this aspect, C.S. Lewis, *A Preface to Paradise Lost* (Oxford 1942) 35-6.

Mediaevalism, with such things as 'Yea and Aeneas' very self is of their fellowship' and 'the Tyrian fellow-folk' (IV.141 and 162), which smack more of Tolkien than of Virgil. Yet Mackail's observations, if over-generous, are not wholly wide of the mark:

> In the *Aeneid* . . . the reader imputes his own qualities, but this is because Virgil's own genius is compounded of many subtly woven and far-ranging elements. For what in Virgil is most Virgilian we may go in vain to any translation: for some of his qualities, his stateliness, his rolling pomp of language, his intricate modulation, we need not go to this one: yet it sensibly, and often with great felicity, embodies certain other qualities which more fully trained translators have missed: his sweetness, his romantic melancholy, and something at least of his delicate and haunting music.[12]

Several contributors to this book have observations to make about translations of the *Aeneid*; in particular Angus Ross shows how Dryden's Virgil is a central document of English Augustanism, and its publication a highly significant cultural event.

The reader of, for example, R.D. Williams' elegant essay on responses to Virgil in this country[13] might well be tempted to conclude that such responses tell us more about Virgil's readers than about his poems. He may even despair of the possibility of there being 'true' assertions to be made about texts at all. It is of course the case, as we have already seen, that each age, and indeed each reader, to some extent appropriates a text, uses what can be used, ignores or may not even see what is less useful and what does not easily chime with current tastes and concerns, a process which is sometimes called 'accommodation'. Yet the extreme relativism that asserts that each age entirely recreates the works of the

12. J.W. Mackail, *The Life of William Morris* (London 1920) vol. I, 322.

13. 'Changing Attitudes to Virgil: A Study in the History of Taste from Dryden to Tennyson' in *Virgil*, ed. D.R. Dudley (London 1969) 119-138. For the reception of the *Georgics*, see L.P. Wilkinson, *The Georgics of Virgil* (Cambridge 1969) 270-313.

past in its own image, and which denies that there is any other steadier meaning behind the changing images, is an evasion of critical responsibilities, which conveniently sets aside the need to assess evidence. It does not allow that one of the values of reading is precisely to expose oneself to the sensibilities of another, to see with other eyes. Moreover it flattens differences between readers within any given period. Doubtless every epoch produces some readers who are conventional, flat-footed, dull, others who show individual intelligence and insight. In his study of *Paradise Lost* Christopher Ricks demonstrates how telling are many of the discussions in the eighteenth-century commentators, discussions which have not dated in the way of some of the more celebrated obiter dicta of Dryden or Dr. Johnson, and that will surely outlast many of today's wilder flights.[14]

Similarly, while some Mediaeval commentary on the *Aeneid* seems to us laboured or inept, Dante at least was an exceptionally attentive reader of the poem. It can be argued that in some measure he anticipates modern views of a divided Virgil, partly acting as spokesman for Roman imperialism and civilisation, partly meditating, with a melancholy that at times comes close to despair, on the 'tears of things'. Far from always twisting his master's work to suit his own outlook, Dante often not only saw clearly, but was moved to disagreement with what he saw. In *Purgatorio* XXX, the canto where Virgil mysteriously disappears at the coming of Beatrice, two quotations from the *Aeneid* are transferred from their original strikingly tragic contexts to celebrate Beatrice's radiant arrival (*Manibus o date lilia plenis* 21 = *Aeneid* VI.883; *conosco i segni dell'antica fiamma* 48 = *Aeneid* IV.23). Dante is perhaps hinting that Virgil's pessimistic vision is one reason why *l'altissimo poeta* is spiritually unfitted for Paradise, and why he is not included among the virtuous pagans who are redeemed. Eliot is making something of the same point when he writes 'if we are not chilled we at least feel ourselves, with Virgil, to be moving in a kind of emotional twilight.'[15] In *Purgatorio* VI Dante makes Virgil

14. *Milton's Grand Style* (Oxford 1963).
15. 'Virgil and the Christian World' in *On Poetry and Poets* (London 1957) 131.

contradict the apparent meaning of the fearful saying of the Sibyl (*Aeneid* VI.376) that the decrees of heaven cannot be swayed by prayer (*desine fata deum flecti sperare precando*). Similarly, in flamboyant denial of the implications of *Aeneid* II.426-8

> cadit et Rhipeus, iustissimus unus
> qui fuit in Teucris et servantissimus aequi
> (dis aliter visum);

> *Rhipeus too fell, who was the justest man among the Trojans and the most observant of right – to the gods it seemed otherwise*

Dante places this obscure Trojan among the elect (*Paradiso* XX). The difference between the two poets is nowhere better seen than in Dante's imitation of the Virgilian vain kiss (*Purgatorio* II.76 ff:cf. *Aeneid* II.792-4 = VI.700-2); in Virgil the feeling is of frustration, insubstantiality and sadness, in Dante of joy and wonderment.

The explanation for the shifts and complexities in the response to Virgil lies not only in factors external to the poetry; partly they result from features of the texts themselves, their complexities and even opacities. Certainly a form of impressionism is often a characteristic of Virgil's language (e.g. *stant lumina flamma*, VI.300). Instead of the sharp edges and clarity that mark some of the best Latin writing, we find something at once more blurred and more resonant, more delicately supple, more like the kind of English poetry we are most used to. Virgil likes to exploit what Jackson Knight in a happy phrase called the 'empty spaces' that many Latin works seem to have in them.[16] Thereby he extends the meaning of words, often in the direction of greater indeterminacy and suggestiveness. It is worth comparing, for example, the succession of clear though unconnected metaphors in the final stanza of Horace, *Odes* II.3

> omnes eodem cogimur, omnium
> versatur urna serius ocius
> sors exitura et nos in aeternum
> exsilium impositura cumbae

16. W.F. Jackson Knight, *Roman Virgil*, 2nd ed. (London 1944) 102; the whole section on style is suggestive.

> *we are all gathered into the same fold, the lot of all is shaken in the urn destined sooner or later to come out and put us in Charon's boat for the eternal exile*

with Virgil's predilection for language that just falls short of being clearly metaphorical.

Guy Lee gives a characteristic instance of this in the well-known lines on Lucretius (*Georgics* II.490-2):

> felix qui potuit rerum cognoscere causas
> atque metus omnis et inexorabile fatum
> subiecit pedibus strepitumque Acherontis avari

> *happy he who could get to know the causes of things and threw under foot every fear and inexorable fate and the noise of avaricious Acheron* (tr. Lee).[17]

The words *subiecit pedibus* seem to suggest trampling underfoot, but, if the idea is forced, irrationality results, since a noise cannot be trampled on. Furthermore *metus* is not a clear personification, which further deprives the language of metaphorical force. We can see more fully what is at work in Virgil's mind if we compare the Lucretian 'source', the proem of *De Rerum Natura* I, where Epicurus is praised for defeating *Religio* (62-5; 78-9). There Religion is a menacing power that stands over men threateningly (presumably in allusion to the etymology of *superstitio*), and tramples on human life, but which was defeated and in turn trodden underfoot by Epicurus. The image is clear and majestic, reminiscent (perhaps paradoxically) of the mosaic of Christ the Warrior treading on a lion and a serpent in the *Cappella Arcivescovile* at Ravenna. Virgil alludes to the passage, but retreats from its metaphoric certainty.

One could make a similar observation about many of Virgil's similes, where, to an extent unusual in his predecessors, the language used tends to blur the distinction between the two things compared. An example is the double simile

17. 'Imitation and the Poetry of Virgil' *Greece and Rome* 28 (1981) 10-22; cf. David West, *The Imagery and Poetry of Lucretius* (Edinburgh 1969) 57-63.

describing the dying Euryalus (*Aeneid* IX.433-6):

> volvitur Euryalus leto, pulchrosque per artus
> it cruor inque umeros cervix conlapsa recumbit:
> purpureus veluti cum flos succisus aratro
> languescit moriens, lassove papavera collo
> demisere caput pluvia cum forte gravantur.

Euryalus rolls over in death, and over his beautiful limbs the blood runs, and his neck sinks and collapses onto his shoulders: as when a shining flower cut at the base by the plough droops as it dies, or poppies with tired necks lower their heads, when they are weighed down by a random shower.

Some of the vocabulary used about the flowers (*languescit moriens, lasso collo, demisere caput*) could with equal appropriateness be applied to a human being at the moment of death. The pictures of the dying youth and the flowers are as it were superimposed, and coalesce into one languid image, which detracts from the sharpness with which each is separately perceived and produces what might be called a 'soft focus' (Virgil's two 'sources' *Iliad* VIII.306-8 and Catullus XI.21-4 are sharper and fresher). Lee compares a number of Virgilian imitations with their Greek or Latin originals, and concludes that they are normally 'more opulent, and more romantic', more opaque in language, and not so sharply pictorial. The elusiveness of the verbal texture is of more general significance: when the language of a work evades perspicuousness, wider evasions are likely.

W.R. Johnson suggests that twentieth-century interpreters of the *Aeneid* could be divided into two groups, styled by him the 'European school' and the 'Harvard school'.[18] The approach of the first group is exemplified in two essays by T.S. Eliot (ironically himself a Harvard man) 'What is a Classic?' and 'Virgil and the Christian World', in the opening chapters of C.S. Lewis' *A Preface to Paradise Lost*, and, at greater length, in Brooks Otis' *Virgil* (1964). A broadly optimistic account of the poem is offered, which stresses the workings of providence in history, the humane qualities of

18. *Darkness Visible, A Study of Virgil's Aeneid* (Berkeley 1976); the quotation is from p. 12. This introductory essay owes much to Johnson's stimulating work.

Aeneas, the value (despite the cost) of his achievements. Virgil's 'maturity' is praised, sometimes in contrast with the more 'primitive' Homer, and his contribution to civilisation underlined (the subtitle of Otis' book is precisely *A Study of Civilized Poetry*). Some of the exponents of such a view were of a conservative character, and several were Christians. Thus Eliot shared the belief of his admired Dante that Virgil might almost be appropriated for Christianity, since his conception of *Roma Aeterna* helped to prepare for the City of God and a united Christendom.

A very different ideology underlies the opposed 'Harvard' interpretation, which makes Virgil foreshadow the angst of the twentieth century. In writings by such critics as Adam Parry, Putnam and Clausen stress is laid on the dark side of the *Aeneid* and on (to quote Johnson) 'Vergil's infatuation with twilight moods, with blurred images, with haunted, half-enacted interviews and confrontations that disintegrate before our eyes'. In exploring Virgil's gloomy opacities critics of this group generally ignore the ebullience of episodes like the Cyclopes' forging of the thunderbolts in VIII.424 ff., a brilliantly witty and imaginative passage in a Callimachean vein, to concentrate on the lacrimose aspects of the poem. Syme's *Roman Revolution*, written during the rise of Nazism and published in 1939, may have helped to teach such critics the deficiencies of earlier views of Augustus, who was seen now not as Dryden's ideal prince, but as an ancient precursor of Fascism, seizing by revolution illegitimate power. Doubtless Virgil shared such reservations about the principate, and filled the *Aeneid* with subversive hints of his dissatisfaction with Roman achievement and the nature of things. It is worth asking whether there may not be both merit and special pleading in these two opposed readings (we should also beware of working with crude categories of optimism and pessimism). The poem may be, in the fashionable terminology, a 'dialectic', incorporating in some measure both viewpoints, and transcending both. In Borges' *Tlön,* an imaginary world made by thinkers and artists, 'a book which does not contain its counterbook is considered incomplete'.[19]

19. Quoted by Harriet Hawkins, 'The Morality of Elizabethan Drama:

The 'dialectical' character of the poem can be observed with unusual clarity in book VI. Virgil's description of the Underworld, as a number of scholars have seen, divides essentially into two parts, the first of which could be called Homeric or mythological, the second philosophical or Platonic (VI.535-547 is the transition point); a prevailing cheerlessness marks the first part, the second is (with reservations) hopeful. The Homeric Hades, in which Virgil describes what Gavin Douglas, in a superbly rolling Miltonic line, gives as 'Placis of silence and perpetuall nycht' (VI.iv.60),[20] is concerned with Aeneas' encounters with a number of people from his past who died tragically. The emphasis is on shadow, indistinctness (with particular vividness in the haunting line (VI.454) about the man 'who sees or thinks he has seen' (*aut videt aut vidisse putat*) the moon rising through the clouds (cf. Milton, *Paradise Lost* I.783 f.), on the ghostliness of the shades and the futility of their actions. Aeneas can have little confidence in the justice of what he sees (*sortem iniquam,* VI.332). Particularly memorable is the picture (VI.314), fraught with pathos, of the unburied holding out their hands in longing for the further bank (*tendebantque manus ripae ulterioris amore*), where metre and words, as Austin says, 'magically suggest the elusive distance of the shore and the pathetic longings of the ghosts'.[21] The passage, imitated by Dante in *Inferno* III, compares them to falling leaves in the first cold of autumn, that most melancholy of seasons, though there may be a hint of ultimate release in the following comparison with birds that migrate to sunny places, a rare shaft of light in the prevailing gloom.

By contrast, in the 'philosophical' Hades we find encouraging evidence of the workings of providence: an eschatological scheme of punishments and rewards; the Stoic doctrine of immanent Mind; the Platonic idea of purgation and reincarnation; the foreshadowing of Rome's achievements in the procession of famous Romans, an encouragement to fire Aeneas with zeal for his quest. There may be a further shift

Some Footnotes to Plato' in *English Renaisance Studies Presented to Dame Helen Gardner in honour of her Seventieth Birthday* (Oxford 1980) 12.

20. Bawcutt, *op.cit* (fn. 4 above) 160.
21. R.G. Austin, commentary on *Aeneid* VI (Oxford 1977) note *ad loc.*

within this Platonic section. Virgil's Elysium is initially characterized in terms of earthly beauties, streams, meadows and so forth. However, near the end of the book, Virgil describes Aeneas and Anchises (VI.887) as walking *aëris in campis latis*, 'up in the broad fields of the sky', as Milton translates in the Spirit's neo-Platonic epilogue in *Comus* (978). Commentators following Servius detect a suggestion of the view that the souls of the blessed ascend to the circle of the moon. Thus it may be that Virgil hints at more shining and incorporeal possibilities for the soul's eventual triumph. If this interpretation is correct, the atmosphere is still further lightened.

The difference in mood between the two sections of Book VI, and the adoption of first a Homeric and then a Platonic conception of what happens to the soul after death, suggest a striking disjunction in Virgil's thinking, or at any rate feeling, about the terms of life. For Homer it was this world, not the unseen place of Hades, that offered real satisfactions, but for Plato this life is the shadow of another, and it is man's quotidian, sensory existence that lacks full reality. There is no possibility of compromise between such contrary conceptions, and Virgil simply juxtaposes them, rather than attempting any resolution.

Book VI thus well illustrates the dialectical character of Virgil's imagination. However the simple contrast that has been drawn does less than justice to its full complexities. For example, there are certain shadows amid the brightness of Virgil's providential intimations. Colin Hardie notes the oddity involved in Virgil's adoption of a radical Platonic dualism and the consequent disparagement of the body, when the poem supposedly celebrates an earthly city and a man who is a kind of god incarnate (this is one of Virgil's 'errors' observed and censured by Dante). Virgil's Platonism subverts the active, this-worldly foundations of the poem. Aeneas seems to carry his dissatisfaction with life into Elysium, as revealed in his outburst (VI.719 ff.) at being shown the souls of those awaiting re-incarnation (*quae lucis miseris tam dira cupido?*), while Virgil later makes glory dissolve into tears at an unexpected moment, with the famous lines on Marcellus' early death. Furthermore, the reader's confidence in his ability to interpret may be undermined in another way by two notorious enigmas, which continue to tantalize with their ambiguities: the golden bough, a curiously sinister symbol of divine favour, and the departure of Aeneas through the ivory gate of false dreams, which could imply a measure of uncertainty on the poet's part about the validity of the whole vision.[22] Virgil artfully and unnervingly gives with one hand, only to take away with the other.

The richness in Virgil's poetry no doubt helps to explain the sense of its continuing 'relevance' that many readers have experienced, or to put the point another way the curious fashion in which the poems seem to gear in both to the experience of individuals and to what has happened in the West since Virgil's death. Gabriel Josipovici reflects movingly on the impact on him as a Jewish writer of the poet's preoccupation with the problem of displaced persons (*Eclogue* I, *Aeneid* III etc.), which has been so central to the history of our century. Helen Waddell turned to Virgil in the face of the threat to civilisation posed by Nazism:

> It was expedient that Rome should die. For one must die to become a legend: and the Roman legend was the inspiration of Europe. It is a strange thing to remember that in the meridian of her power, she herself looked back to her beginnings in a conquered city and a burning town: and the man who gave her immortality was the hollow-cheeked sad-eyed Virgil of the Hadrumetum mosaic. If all else goes from the schools, let us at least keep the second book of Virgil. I speak of it with passion, for something sent me to it on that September afternoon when the Luftwaffe first broke through the defences of London, and that night it seemed as though London and her river burned. You remember the cry of Aeneas waking in the night, the rush, arming as he went, the hurried question – 'Where's the fighting now?' – and the answer:
>
> Come is the ending day, Troy's hour is come,

22. R.J. Tarrant, 'Aeneas and the Gates of Sleep' *Classical Philology* 77 (1982) 51-55, has ingeniously suggested that Aeneas leaves by this gate because, as the possessor of a physical body, he is 'unreal' in Platonic terms.

> The ineluctable hour.
> Once were we Trojan men,
> And Troy was once, and once a mighty glory
> Of the Trojan race.[23]

We have seen how T.S. Eliot shared Dante's sense of Virgil as a significant precursor of Christianity, one who glimpsed through a glass darkly truths that would soon be fully revealed. Through the ages Christians have often felt a special sympathy with Virgil, *anima naturaliter Christiana*, as Stephen Medcalf's essay demonstrates. In the panel of the Adoration of the Lamb in the Van Eycks' Ghent Altarpiece, among the patriarchs and prophets, stands Virgil dressed in white, with a crown of laurel and a sprig in his hand, close to a figure which probably represents Isaiah with the Jesse rod. On the front of the polyptych is a Sibyl with appropriate words adapted from *Aeneid* VI.50, *nil mortale sonans afflata es numine celso.*[24] (The influence of Virgil both on iconography and on artistic sensibility is discussed in Nigel Llewellyn's essay in this book.) In particular *Eclogue* IV gave Virgil the status of a pagan prophet; its interpretation as a prophecy of Christ's birth, encouraged by the Emperor Constantine who translated the poem into Greek, was widely accepted in the Middle Ages and beyond (it was still believed by Dryden and Dr. Johnson), only eventually giving way before the historicism of the nineteenth century. On the most plausible interpretation this joyous poem celebrates the peace of Brundisium and the marriage of Antony and Octavia. It is important to see that this particular example of Christian 'accommodation' is not merely perverse. Virgil saw Brundisium and the marriage as a fresh start for the Roman world; Christians believe that a fresh start was made, some forty years later, and that the form that it took was the birth of a child. It thus became difficult for Virgil's Christian readers not to think of the Incarnation when reading *Eclogue* IV, particularly in view of the apparent similarities between some lines in the poem and passages in *Isaiah*. In the event scholarship has come to the aid of their

23. *More Latin Lyrics from Virgil to Milton*, tr. Helen Waddell (London 1976) 40 and 43.
24. See Elisabeth Dhanens, *Van Eyck: The Ghent Altarpiece* (London 1973) 52 and 59.

instincts: in a careful discussion R.G.M. Nisbet has shown that Virgil almost certainly used Greek Sibylline oracles, which in turn were influenced by Jewish apocalyptic and by material similar to that found in *Isaiah.*[25]

* * * * *

The reader of this volume will notice certain preoccupations which a number of contributors share, and I would like to mention three which concern the character of Virgil's works. The first, which has already been the subject of much of this introduction, is the presence in Virgil's poetry of a whole range of tensions, complexities, even contradictions (of the kind explored in R.D. Williams' essay). One further such tension is the tension between the 'civilised' quality of Virgil's poetry and the presence in it of barbarities (occasionally tinged with decadence), about which E.M.W. Tillyard has written, in a discussion of 'primitive feelings' in poetry:

> Virgil, a more primitive poet than Homer for all the generalisations about natural and artificial epics, is full of them.
>
> For instance, the last hundred lines of *The Aeneid* have a quality of terror that goes quite beyond the context . . . He (Virgil) chooses the supernatural mechanism of Jupiter's sending a Fury to baffle Turnus in the fight, and from the moment he describes this bird of hell till the end of the poem he is at the height of his powers. After the Fury has reached the earth, she takes the form of a little bird that men hear crying on tombs or lonely rooftops, and flies backwards and forwards shrieking in front of Turnus' face . . .

25. Virgil's Fourth Eclogue: Easterners and Westerners' *Bulletin of the Institute of Classical Studies* 25 (1978) 59-78; see also S. Benko, 'Virgil's Fourth Eclogue in Christian Interpretation', in *Aufstieg und Niedergang der römischen Welt,* ed. H. Temporini and W. Haase (2nd ser.) xxxi, part 1 (Berlin and New York 1980) 662-82; Andrew Wallace-Hadrill, 'The Golden Age and Sin in Augustan Ideology' *Past and Present* 95 (1982) 19-36.

> This idea of compressing the great Fury into the little bird crying round the tomb is one of the most terrifying in literature; it cuts through all the comforting assurances of civilised life. And when Turnus, face to face with Aeneas, answers his threats with
>
> *non me tua fervida terrent*
> *dicta, ferox: di me terrent et Iuppiter hostis*
>
> he is not Turnus speaking of the Latin pantheon, but man confronted with the terrors of a hostile and inexplicable universe.[26]

Virgil's *Dira* takes the reader into a nightmare or phantasmagoria, the world of Poe or Hieronymus Bosch, or, of more immediate relevance, the world of the Etruscan tomb paintings depicting demons of the Underworld. In the descriptions of the last hours of Dido and Turnus, death is associated with the subconscious and dreams (IV.465 ff.; XII.903 ff.), magic and the supernatural (IV.504 ff.; the *Dira*), and irrationality, those emotional extremes covered by the word *furor* and its cognates. Virgil here penetrates more perilous areas than are usually encountered in Homer, those of his (and our) deepest anxieties. Similarly his battle scenes seem more sinister than the simple cruelties of the *Iliad.* The self-indulgent description of the death of Euryalus with the double simile already discussed, a passage achingly lovely, seems to merit the description decadent. There are evident homosexual undertones in the stress on Euryalus' beauty (it is perhaps worth noticing that *flos* can be used in sexual contexts, while *purpureus* could suggest the bloom of youth), and the blending of aesthetic and erotic sensibility with blood, pain and death is a long way from the cool, straightforward, unsentimental pathos of superficially similar passages in the *Iliad.*

Secondly, there is the way that Virgil's poetry is susceptible to allegorical interpretation. A word on terminology is needed here. Many classical scholars sharply distinguish allegory, which they take to imply one-to-one correspondence and to be unVirgilian, from both typology and symbolism, which they think can be found in Virgil's poetry. But this is

26. *Poetry, Direct and Oblique* (London 1945) 52-3.

to project a crude and unhistorical view of allegory, a term which in the Middle Ages would apply to any writing that had meanings beyond the literal, and one that can only be a hindrance to an interpretation of the *Divine Comedy* or any other of the great allegories, where straightforward correspondences of this for that are relatively infrequent. Allegorizing of various kinds remains a feature of twentieth-century Virgilian criticism. For example the *Aeneid* in Otis' rather schematic reading concerns the struggle between *pietas* and *furor*, and Otis shows all the allegorist's tendency to become mesmerized by abstract nouns. A Mediaeval exegete would not have been surprised by his view that book VI concerns a symbolic death and resurrection. A.D. Nuttall notes the figural character of Virgil's imagination. In Mediaeval Biblical exegesis characters and events in the Old Testament were types, figures of those in the New; for example Jonah's descent into the body of the whale prefigured Christ's descent into hell. Each event in the figural pair had its own independent existence and reality, but there was a significant connection between them. So too Aeneas is a type of Augustus, while Dido's death on the pyre prefigures the burning of Carthage.

The allegorizing of Virgil's works seems more convincing than in the case of Ovid. The objection to the *Ovide moralisé* (at least as a way of reading Ovid) is not that it attributes meanings to the poems that their author could not have consciously intended, but that the heavy-handed moralizing interpretations were forced on the texts against *any* rational sense of their possible meaning; the myths of the *Metamorphoses* were strained on the exegetical rack. By contrast, the *Aeneid* often seems to have what could be called at any rate a 'sub-allegorical' quality. One could instance the flight through the wood of Nisus and Euryalus after the night raid (IX.381 ff.). At the start of the *Divine Comedy* Dante is lost in a wood, the familiar *selva oscura,* which perhaps recalls Virgil's *tenent media omnia silvae* (*Aeneid* VI.131), if, as seems likely, Dante took these words to refer to the area between the upper and lower worlds. Dante's wood is clearly allegorical, not because its meaning can be precisely fixed, but because it must be to some extent a wood of the mind and part of a spiritual experience. Virgil's wood is hardly of this kind, but it has a rather different quality too from a straight-forwardly 'naturalistic' Homeric landscape. The episode has something of the flavour of a dream, while some of the vocabulary, particularly *perplexum* and *fallacis* (IX. 391-2), might suggest a nightmarish wood of error, not unlike Milton's 'in the blind mazes of this tangled wood' in *Comus* (180) – (Morris' translation makes the connection: 'Where shall I seek thee, gathering up that tangle of the ways/ Through the blind wood?'). Virgil is apparently influenced here, as elsewhere in the *Aeneid*, by his treatment in *Georgics* IV of the Orpheus myth. In both episodes a man 'looks back' (*respexit, Aeneid* IX.389) to find that his loved one is lost. It may be that some basic anxiety presses behind this and the echoes of the Orpheus story when Aeneas loses his wife Creusa, and there is certainly a sense of being in the domain of the mind's terrors. It could also be argued that the wood provides an 'objective correlative' for the feelings of fear of the two men at this juncture. We should not forget the long tradition of allegorical interpretation of Homeric narrative with which Virgil was familiar, and which presumably influenced his own manner of writing.

Finally we may note Virgil's feeling for time, the interlocking of past, present and future. One of the great moments in the *Georgics* is when Virgil looks ahead to the day when the countryman will dig up the rusty weapons and large bones (it was a widespread belief that men were growing smaller) of those killed in the civil wars (I.494 ff.). This passage perhaps inspired some of Pope's finest lines (*Epistle to Burlington* 173-6) which are likewise marked by a sense of the healing changes wrought by time:

> Another age shall see the golden Ear
> Imbrown the Slope, and nod on the Parterre,
> Deep Harvests bury all his pride has plann'd
> And laughing Ceres re-assume the land.

Even if there is no direct influence, the sensibility is Virgilian. The *Aeneid* is full of such moments, some typological (like the pre-echoes of the Punic Wars in book IV), some more freely imaginative like the lines from *Georgics* I. One might instance two passages in *Aeneid* VIII: 347-50, which contrast the golden Capitol of Virgil's day with the wooded spot, already instinct with divinity, visited by Aeneas; and 729-31, in which a wondering but ignorant Aeneas shoulders the weight of the shield, lifting 'the fame and destiny of his descendants.'

K.W. Gransden shows how much Milton learned from Virgil in this respect, and on occasion it may be felt that Milton can surpass his master, if only in so far as the Christian view of eternity transcends Virgil's *imperium sine fine.* (Interestingly in the *Georgics* (II.498) Virgil may have envisaged the possibility of all kingdoms, perhaps including Rome, passing away, though commentators do not interpret his *peritura regna* in this way.) We may take as an example the moment in *Paradise Lost* (VI.880-92) when the Son returns to Heaven after the expulsion of the rebel angels, an event that anticipates the final triumph of the Last Judgement and is couched in the language of Apocalypse:

> Sole victor from the expulsion of his foes
> Messiah his triumphal chariot turned:
> To meet him all his saints, who silent stood
> Eye witnesses of his almighty acts,
> With jubilee advanced; and as they went,
> Shaded with branching palm, each order bright,
> Sung triumph, and him sung victorious king,
> Son, heir, and Lord, to him dominion given,
> Worthiest to reign: he celebrated rode
> Triumphant through mid heaven, into the courts
> And temple of his mighty Father throned
> On high: who into glory him received,
> Where now he sits at the right hand of bliss.

This passage is complexly typological. The palm branches prefigure those of *Revelations* VII.9, which in turn reflect the palms carried by Christ's followers at the entry to Jerusalem. The image of Christ received 'at the right hand of bliss' looks forward to the Ascension; the cosmic time-scale injects a strongly religious intensity. The last line is of especial significance. The present tense ostensibly refers to the time when Raphael is speaking, but, in view of its liturgical overtones, it is easily applied to any present time, whether Milton's or the reader's. Parts of the Mass may be recalled: 'Thou that *sittest* at the right hand of God the Father', 'And ascended into heaven, And *sitteth* on the right hand of the

Father. And he shall come again with glory'. The poet seems to imply familiar Biblical and liturgical phrases almost as an act of prayer; narrative has been tempered by meditation, time takes on the accents of eternity. It is with something of a shock that the reader is then reminded that it is Raphael, not Milton, who speaks. (A rather similar shift of perspective and time, from prayer to narrative, occurs in III.412 ff.)

One aspect of Virgil's use of time is the *post eventum* prophecy. This, it can be felt, on occasion created difficulties for the poet, as Auden saw (*Secondary Epic* 1-5):

> No, Virgil, no:
> Not even the first of the Romans can learn
> His Roman history in the future tense,
> Not even to serve your political turn;
> Hindsight as foresight makes no sense.

It was a commonplace in antiquity that man's ignorance of the future was providential, and Aeneas' status as a moral agent may be felt to be compromised by his knowledge of what is to come: in reality men must take decisions about actions on the basis only of their probable consequences. Auden's complaints thus have some validity (he also mocks Virgil's inability to predict events after the completion of the poem); taking a poet seriously may on occasion mean objecting to aspects of his vision. For example it may be that Virgil's mind moved rather too easily from history to myth. To combat Virgil's view of the significance of the principate Lucan had to 're-historicize' his material, and was thereby able to reveal the evil consequences of the victory of Caesarism, in the loss of liberty both political and spiritual – *cum domino pax ista venit* (*de Bello Civili* I.670).

* * * * *

I conclude with a few words on the character and limitations of this collection. It certainly does not constitute a complete history of Virgil's influence; a great many more pages would be needed for that. The focus is on English literature, and there are in the main only passing references to other European countries. The Middle Ages are not treated in full, partly because this area is well covered in Comparetti's classic study.[27] A piece on Dante is included as a partial exception since he has exerted a greater influence on English writers from Chaucer to T.S. Eliot than any other post-classical poet. The *Georgics*, perhaps Virgil's most fully accomplished work, plays a relatively minor role, since in general its influence has been less than that of the *Eclogues* and *Aeneid* (although a whole book could be devoted to transmutations of Virgil's version of the Orpheus story). There is little about music, although the *Aeneid* supplied the material for many operas; best known are probably Purcell's *Dido and Aeneas* with its eloquent lament (the abandonment of Dido was a popular baroque musical subject), and the massive *Les Troyens* of Berlioz, whose two literary gods were Virgil and Shakespeare.

Different approaches are illustrated: there are straightforward pieces about Virgil's influence on single writers; or on a whole age – for example Norman Vance on the Victorians; L.D. Lerner's essay is on the pastoral genre, about which Curtius commented of *Eclogue* I that 'it is not too much to say that anyone unfamiliar with that short poem lacks one key to the literary tradition of Europe'.[28] A.D. Nuttall's essay exemplifies a different, more comparative approach, in which questions of direct influence are largely set aside, and where the interest lies in exploring differences and similarities in sensibility for their own sake. It seems too early yet to write the history of Virgilianism in this century, and it may be that Virgil's influence on creative artists is to some extent on the wane. (A twentieth-century writer who has responded to Virgil is Auden, one of whose finest poems *Memorial for the City* starts from a suggestive, if wrong-headed comparison of Homer and Virgil, the former seen too much as a camera, objective, valueless, a view more fashionable in 1945 than now.) It seemed more fruitful to seek a contribution from a living writer who has been inspired by Virgil; so in the final essay Gabriel Josipovici, himself very much a modernist, gives an account of Virgil's importance

27. Domenico Comparetti, *Vergil in the Middle Ages*, tr. E.F. Benecke (1895; repr. London 1966).

28. E.R. Curtius, *European Literature and the Latin Middle Ages*, tr. Willard R. Trask (London 1953) 190.

for him personally, which provides insights into the kind of ways influence can operate and into the nature of the creative process itself. Most of the contributors teach at the University of Sussex, but they do not form a school or favour one particular critical approach (the reader will notice some differences of opinion); rather what they do share is a passionate belief in the importance of Virgil's poetry both for its own sake and for what it has meant for others, together with a desire to honour the poet who so richly deserved the words of Gavin Douglas (*Prologue* 3-6):

> Maist reverend Virgill, of Latyn poetis prynce,
> Gem of engyne and flude of eloquens,
> Thow peirles perle, patroun of poetry,
> Roys, regester, palm, lawrer and glory.

Note: I would like to thank Robert Parker and my wife Michelle for their help in the preparation of this introductory essay. C.M.

The Poetic Intention of Virgil's *Aeneid*

R.D. WILLIAMS

Two thousand years ago, in 19 B.C., Virgil began a voyage to Greece in order to visit the parts of the Eastern Mediterranean in which book III of the *Aeneid* is set. He intended to spend a further three years on the revision of his epic poem, but fell ill on the voyage and died shortly after his return to Italy. On his death-bed he left instructions that the *Aeneid* should be burned, but the Emperor Augustus countermanded these instructions, and the poem was published by Varius and Tucca as literary executors. It is true that the poem as we have it lacks some final touches, but in no sense is it an unfinished poem.

Virgil had been preparing all his life to write an epic poem, the literary form which the ancient world regarded as the highest and most important of all. During the course of his preparation for his ultimate task he had written the *Eclogues*, ten pastoral poems, and the *Georgics*, a didactic poem intended to instruct, but principally to inspire, farmers. Both of these exercised a great influence upon subsequent literature, but it is with his epic poem that I shall be here concerned. It is a many-sided poem of exploration of the human condition in which different aspects have particularly appealed to different generations; and before making an assessment of the reasons for which we appreciate the poem I will say something of other attitudes towards it, particularly over the last three centuries or so.

All through the 2000 years since its publication the *Aeneid* has been widely read and greatly influential. It is interesting to see how varied the reasons for this have been. During the Roman Empire it was a staple element in Roman education, being regarded both as a supreme expression of the national character and ideals and as a lesson in how to use language to its uttermost capacity, so that Quintilian found it incomparable for training the would-be orator, and a speaker in Macrobius' *Saturnalia* says that it embraces every sub-division of the use of rhetoric. Towards the end of this period it was also regarded as a repository of wisdom of every kind, a sort of encyclopedia of folk-lore, geography, religion, institutions, philology, philosophy – in fact of all the subjects with which the thinking person would wish to concern himself.

This enthusiasm for the *Aeneid* did not abate during mediaeval times, but it shifted its emphasis. Virgil was now seen as a pagan precursor of Christianity, a kind of prophet like Isaiah of the Christian way of life. This was due partly to the *Fourth Eclogue,* a prophecy of the birth of a child who would inaugurate a new Golden Age, and partly to the moral ideals of the *Aeneid*, particularly the central theme of a man devoted to a divine mission. Allegorical interpretation flourished, and the *Aeneid* was seen as a sort of Pilgrim's Progress as Aeneas made his way through trials and dangers of all kinds towards the divinely-appointed goal. Tales of Virgil the magician gained wide currency, and there was frequent recourse to the *Sortes Vergilianae* (the consultation of the poem opened at random to give its advice).

In the Renaissance emphasis shifted somewhat away from allegory towards an appreciation of the literary and artistic craftsmanship of the poem. Spenser's imagination was captured by Virgil's descriptive power, and Milton used the *Aeneid* as a model very much as Virgil had used Homer, i.e. to use the conventions and techniques of a literary master in order to convey a quite different message. As Virgil had adapted the Homeric poems with their stories of the heroic qualities of great individuals to the Roman ethos of greater social responsibility, so Milton used Virgilian devices of narrative and style to form a framework for his Christian message.

In 1697 Dryden published his translation of the *Aeneid* with a long preface discussing the reasons for the outstanding excellence of Virgil's poem. Two in particular recur again and again. Firstly, he stresses Virgil's pre-eminence in literary skill, in craftsmanship, in the 'rules' of the genre; Virgil is always correct in his use of the techniques of epic poetry, and indeed is sometimes compared favourably even with Homer in this regard. Secondly the *Aeneid* fulfils what Dryden saw as the great aim of epic poetry: 'to form the mind to heroic virtue by example.' He sees in Aeneas an example of the kind of responsible leadership which should be exercised by those in power, thus winning the affection and loyalty of their subjects: he is the 'perfect prince' whose behaviour can teach all of us how to behave better. For Dryden the *Aeneid* is a great ethical sermon. Is that what it is for us?

Reaction against this view – and indeed against the *Aeneid* itself – was often expressed in the Romantic revival which rejected so much that was admired by the English 'Augustan Age.' Of course the hostility towards Virgil was not unanimous, but many of the poets (Coleridge, Shelley, Byron) expressed a view commonly held that the *Aeneid* was a dully didactic poem, lacking the freshness and vigour and sensitivity for which the Romantics looked, that it was prosaic, impersonal, authoritarian. The hero of the poem especially came in for harsh criticism as being insipid, puppet-like, lacking in grandeur and indeed in individuality, the opposite in fact of 'heroic'. These criticisms continued to be voiced off and on for a century or so; would we today make them?

A new emphasis began in the middle of the nineteenth century, set in motion by Sainte-Beuve in his lectures on Virgil. His attitude was that the Romantics were right to look for the qualities in poetry which they did look for, but wrong to think that they were not to be found in Virgil. From this time onwards emphasis was placed on Virgil's sensitivity, on his pathos and sorrow for the unhappy plight of humanity, for the *lacrimae rerum* ('the tears in the world'). This aspect became very dominant in later Victorian criticism, and Tennyson's

> Thou majestic in thy sadness
> At the doubtful doom of human kind

has summarised the attitude of very many critics of the last hundred years. Does it summarise ours?

* * *

Against this background let me try to define a modern attitude to the *Aeneid.* This brief review of other generations' attitudes confirms very strongly that the poem is indeed many-sided, and we today are particularly attuned to the appreciation of the many-sided. The *Aeneid* is essentially a poem of exploration, juxtaposed opposites, dilemmas, disquietingly incongruous elements, seeking to make a unity out of the disparate elements of human life rather than to achieve a facile solution by ignoring what is discordant.

I would like to look at two aspects of this exploration, and I will use the word 'tension' to express the interplay between opposing polarities. The first will be the tension between patriotic optimism and private sorrow; the second between the Homeric hero (which Aeneas is, chronologically) and the Roman leader (of which Aeneas has to become a prototype).

First then the tension between patriotic optimism and private sorrow, between Dryden's view of the poem and the Victorian view. It is easy to select patriotic passages in the poem, and four of them are quite outstanding because of their powerful national enthusiasm and also because of their key positions in the poem. The first of these is Jupiter's speech in book I (257-296) in reply to Venus' complaints that her son Aeneas is trying to fulfil a divine mission and yet is suffering every kind of disaster. Jupiter's speech is serenely consoling as he promises world-wide empire to the Roman people (278-9):

> his ego nec metas rerum nec tempora pono:
> imperium sine fine dedi.
> *To these I set no bounds in space or time:*
> *I have given them rule without end.*

His speech ends with a promise that the harsh generations will become gentle and wars be laid aside, and the trait of mad frenzy (*Furor impius*) in human hearts will be eliminated. It is a fair vision, and one which it is the destiny of Aeneas (and every Roman of a later day) to bring to fulfilment. Two things should be noticed in addition: one that it comes very early in the poem after the initial narrative of the storm which has scattered or sunk Aeneas' ships, and its optimistic message should stay in our minds as tragedy and disaster is heaped upon the Trojans in the events which follow; and the other is that we the readers have been made aware of the glorious future if Aeneas achieves his object, but that Aeneas has not. He does not hear speeches in heaven. He has to grope onwards with only faint ideas of what he is trying to do, and why.

A second great patriotic passage comes in the sixth book at

the end of the first half of the poem, at the turning point of Aeneas' long struggle. It is the vision which he sees in the underworld of the ghosts of future Roman heroes waiting to be born if he achieves his mission. They pass in magnificent array before our eyes – kings of Alba Longa, Romulus the founder of Rome and next to him (out of the chronological order which has so far been followed) Augustus himself who will restore the Golden Age which once existed when Saturnus was king of the gods (VI.791-4):

> hic vir, hic est, tibi quem promitti saepius audis,
> Augustus Caesar, divi genus, aurea condet
> saecula qui rursus Latio regnata per arva
> Saturno quondam . . .

Here is the man, this is he whom you have often heard promised to you, Augustus Caesar, child of the divine [Julius Caesar], who will found again the Golden Age for Latium in the land once ruled by Saturn . . .

Then follow other kings of Rome, and great heroes like Camillus, the Gracchi, the Scipios, Fabius Maximus. The pageant is concluded by the famous words of Anchises (VI. 847-53):

> Excudent alii spirantia mollius aera
> (credo equidem), vivos ducent de marmore vultus,
> orabunt causas melius, caelique meatus
> describent radio et surgentia sidera dicent:
> tu regere imperio populos, Romane, memento
> (hae tibi erunt artes), pacique imponere morem,
> parcere subiectis et debellare superbos.

Others, I doubt not, will fashion bronze statues breathing in softer lines and they will charm living faces out of marble, they will plead law-suits better and chart the movements of heaven with their instruments and tell of the rising of the constellations. But, Roman, remember to rule the peoples with your sway (this shall be your art), to build civilisation upon peace, to spare the conquered and crush the proud.

The contrast is with the Greeks, who are allowed supremacy in visual art, oratory, pure science: the Roman mission is government, civilisation and peace. The idyllic vision did not perhaps come true under the Roman Empire as perfectly as was hoped – but much *was* achieved in civilising the known world and giving it a period of stability. We may be the grandchildren of the ancient Greeks, but we are the children of the Romans.

Space does not permit elaboration on the other two of the four great patriotic passages. The third is the description (VIII.626f.) of the pictures on the new shield made for Aeneas, pictures of great moments in Roman history, with the battle of Actium as the centrepiece, a battle which Virgil presents as an ideological conflict between the ideals and religious beliefs of Rome and those of the East. And he has placed this prophetic vision of a selection of Rome's achievements in the centuries between Aeneas and Augustus at the place where it is most needed – the point at which the war between Trojans and Italians is about to inflict on both sides the most horrible losses. We must be reminded here of the justification – if indeed it is justification – for the deaths of heroic young warriors on both sides. As we read the war-scenes of Books IX-XII we are often made to feel horror and revulsion at human behaviour: if we had not been reminded that it was to achieve the Roman peace that this bloodshed occurred, then it would have seemed altogether senseless. As it is, it still seems senseless; but Virgil has tried to show at the end of the eighth book what it ultimately achieved.

The last patriotic passage occurs during the final scene in Olympus: Juno is ordered by Jupiter to cease her activities against the Trojans, and she agrees on condition that the new people (the Romans) destined to arise from the intermarriage of Trojans and Italians shall keep their old language (Latin), their old name (Latins) and their way of dress (*vestem*). Jupiter agrees, enlarging the third condition from *vestem* to include also *mores* ('way of life'). So this new imperial people will be strong through Italian (not Trojan) qualities – *sit Romana potens Itala virtute propago* (XII.827). And, this of course, was how the Romans thought of themselves in Virgil's day.

These four patriotic passages (and there are many lesser ones scattered through the poem) give the impression that the

Aeneid is a poem of patriotic praise for Augustan Rome, for the happy time when despite all setbacks and failures the Golden Age is to be restored. And indeed, to an extent, it is such a poem. But there is another side to it.

No reader of the *Aeneid* can fail to be moved by the sensitive pathos, the 'touching sadness' with which Virgil records the youthful deaths of which the *Aeneid* is so full. Book II, Aeneas' own description of the fall of Troy, is filled with tragedy, culminating first in the savage murder of Priam and again at the end in the loss of Aeneas' wife Creusa; books IX-XII are laden with death, Nisus and Euryalus, Pallas, Camilla, Turnus himself. Book VI, with the grand patriotic climax referred to above, does not end on the note of triumphant Roman destiny but continues into a mournful pendant about the death of young Marcellus, marked out as Augustus' heir. But the tragedy which involves the deepest and most poignant sorrow is that of Dido, a 'tragic' figure in the fullest Greek sense of the word.

She is portrayed in book I as a wholly admirable queen, a leader of great initiative (*dux femina facti*, I.364), a highly respected queen of her people (I.507 f.), a woman as beautiful as Diana (I.496 f.), a person of deep kindness and sympathy (I.630). Through the intervention of the scheming goddesses she is caused to fall madly in love with Aeneas, and book I ends with an undercurrent of impending disaster beneath the happy banquet scenes.

In the first part of book IV Virgil uses all his skills to arouse our still deeper sympathy for the unhappy queen. The imagery he uses to describe her love is disquieting – wounds, fire, madness and finally plague. Her pleading speech to Aeneas when she learns he is leaving is full of intense pathos as she tells him how she has given up everything for him, and implores him not to leave her. Here Virgil has added an extra dimension to the poignancy of Aeneas' desertion of her by reminiscences of the most personal of all the Roman poets, Catullus. Catullus' sixty-fourth poem, an epyllion, like so many of his lyrics, is concerned primarily with desertion, with the violation of personal relationships by one of the partners, and his Ariadne, deserted by Theseus, is recalled in Dido's first speech to Aeneas. Each woman begins by calling her lover *perfidus*. Each appeals to her one-time hopes of marriage, and Virgil's line is almost identical with that of Catullus, having the same unusual metrical movement.[1] And when Dido refers at the end of her speech to her wish for a child by Aeneas (*parvulus Aeneas*) the diminutive adjective irresistibly takes us into the intimate world of feelings laid bare, so characteristic of Catullus but so alien to the expectations of the epic genre. It is the only instance of a diminutive adjective in the *Aeneid*.

In Dido's final speech we are back with Catullus: she recounts the achievements of her life and adds 'happy would I have been, oh only too happy, if only the Trojan ships had never touched our shores'; Ariadne had said 'almighty Jupiter, if only in the first place the Athenian ships had never touched the Cretan shores.'[2]

After Aeneas and the Trojans had sailed away Dido killed herself as she had planned to do, and we ask ourselves the question with which Greek tragedy so often leaves us – 'Why did so noble a character come to so disastrous an end?' We may say that it was partly Dido's fault (she was untrue to her vow to Sychaeus), partly Aeneas' fault (he should have recognised the situation sooner), partly the scheming goddesses (though we may regard them to some extent as symbolising Dido's own character), but most of all the reason for Dido's death was the Roman mission. That was why Aeneas had to go when he personally did not want to (*Italiam non sponte sequor*, IV.361). Dido is a victim of the foundation of Rome – she is the outsider who does not belong in the great cosmic scheme, and she loses her life (as did many other Carthaginians in the history of Rome's rise to power) so that Rome may prosper. Many readers of the *Aeneid* have been led by Virgil's intensely sympathetic portrayal of Dido's plight to wonder whether such a price should be paid. I think Virgil's answer is that it has to be paid – but why?

1. Compare Catullus LXIV.141 – *sed conubia laeta, sed optatos hymenaeos* – with *Aeneid* IV.315 – *per conubia nostra, per inceptos hymenaeos.*

2. Compare Catullus LXIV.171-2 – *Iuppiter omnipotens, utinam ne tempore primo / Cnosia Cecropiae tetigissent litora puppes* – with *Aeneid* IV.657-8 – *felix, heu nimium felix, si litora tantum / numquam Dardaniae tetigissent nostra carinae.*

tantaene animis caelestibus irae? (I.11).

* * *

The second tension which I want to examine is between the dramatic date of the poem (Aeneas is a Homeric hero, contemporary with Hector, Achilles, Odysseus) and the Augustan value system of which Aeneas is the inaugurator. He has to leave the heroic world of Homer and learn how to become the first Roman. In what ways, if any, must he alter his standards of behaviour?

In book II (the earliest chronologically) Aeneas is still very much the Homeric hero, feeling it his duty when all is lost to make the heroic gesture and seek death. He is visited by a vision of Hector who tells him that the defence of Troy is impossible, and that he must escape and, taking his gods with him, found a great new city. Aeneas' reaction to this message is to ignore it and rush into battle, seeking death among his doomed comrades (III.314 f., 353 f., and 432 f.). It needs a further message from his divine mother to make him think of the safety of his family, and then when he loses Creusa he rushes to try to find her, regardless of his personal safety. He is a very reluctant man with a mission, and all through book III he toils unenthusiastically on his voyage to found his promised city. But slowly, and greatly helped by his father Anchises, he learns more of his destiny, and when the moment of decision comes in book IV between his personal desires and his duty he has changed enough to put his duty first. He has begun to learn that he must sacrifice something of himself because he has, however reluctantly, accepted the responsibility placed upon him by the gods.

The story of Aeneas' wanderings in the first half of the *Aeneid* inevitably points to a comparison with the wanderings of Odysseus, and here Virgil has often deliberately made points of similarity (especially in *Aeneid* I) in order to emphasise the difference. Odysseus was the supreme individualist: he surmounted unbelievable dangers and hardships because of his powers of endurance and his resource when all his companions, lesser men, perished; and he was successful in returning home to resume the kind of life which he had lived twenty years earlier. Aeneas is not resuming the life he had lived before: Troy is destroyed and he must found a new city and a new way of life. To do this he must bring his companions through safely with him: he must often negate his own personal desires for the common good. This is the quality which gives him his epithet *pius*: he is the group hero, feeling all sorts of obligations which prevent him from doing what he personally would like. He does not cut the figure of an Odysseus: he has given too much of himself away.

Similarly in the second half of the poem a comparison of Aeneas with a Homeric warrior of the Trojan War is set up. Again we are led to see Aeneas as differing in many ways. Aeneas is generally portrayed as reluctant to fight: at the beginning of book VIII he lies awake worrying about the outbreak of the war; in book XI when envoys come to seek a truce to bury the dead he says he would have wished to grant one to the living; in book XII, when the arrangements for single combat are broken, he rushes unhelmeted and unarmed into the midst of the fray to try to restrain his men. In the last two hundred lines of the poem we are taken again and again back to the single combat of *Iliad* XXII, and this time we realise that the Achilles figure (Turnus) is in the losing position and that the Trojan will win. Aeneas pursues Turnus as a hound pursues a stag (*Aeneid* XII.749; cf. *Iliad* XXII. 189 f.); they circle the walls (*Aeneid* XII.763; cf. *Iliad* XXII. 158) not for a prize in an athletic contest but 'they fought for the life-blood of Turnus' (*Aeneid* XII.765) as in Homer 'they ran for the life of Hector, tamer of horses' (*Iliad* XXII. 161). As in a dream, the pursued cannot escape nor the pursuer catch his prey (*Aeneid* XII.908; cf. *Iliad* XXII.199). Turnus is wounded and begs for mercy, as Hector had done. Achilles in a cruel and bitter speech had refused all mercy – here, we suddenly realise, is where Aeneas will differ from the Homeric prototype. He has striven, with varying degrees of success, all through the poem to be merciful: he has 'conquered the proud' and now he can 'spare the conquered.' But to our horror he does not: in a fit of violent rage, seeing the sword-belt Turnus had taken as spoils from young Pallas, Aeneas kills him. Virgil leaves us in no doubt about the reason; he kills him for vengeance (XII.948-9):

Pallas te hoc vulnere, Pallas
immolat et poenam scelerato ex sanguine sumit.

*Pallas, Pallas I say, takes your life with this wound,
and exacts vengeance on your cursed blood.*

The reader is shocked at this violent display of fury – yet if he casts his mind back to the episode in book X when Turnus so brutally killed Pallas he will remember that then he could not wait for the moment when Turnus would have to pay for it. Now that he does pay, we are shaken by Aeneas' conduct. Virgil has not commented on the rightness or wrongness of vengeance: what he has done is to end the poem on a sense of deep disquiet over Aeneas' action and of profound sympathy for Turnus, and the last line of the poem dwells not on the final glorious victory for the Roman mission but on the tragedy of Turnus' death (XII.952):

vitaque cum gemitu fugit indignata sub umbras.

His life fled with a groan, complaining, to the shades below.

* * *

The interpretation of the main themes of the *Aeneid* which I have suggested sees the poem as an exploration of contrasting viewpoints of human life, presented so honestly and so vividly that we shift our sympathies, as situation succeeds to situation, from one side to the other. In T.R. Glover's fine phrase: 'There is a wavering about the whole poem'. The poet challenges us all the time to see both sides of the question, and he presents the issues not in moralising or philosophical terms but in a brilliantly woven series of poetically contrived situations.

Virgil in Dante

COLIN HARDIE

All Dante's prose works, with the exception of the *Quaestio de aqua et terra*, (if that is his) quote or adapt Virgil, but there is little or nothing of Virgil in his poetry before the *Divine Comedy*. In it, however, there are many translations, allusions, reminiscences, from single words to whole episodes, even two quotations in Latin: *sanguis meus* from *Aeneid* VI.835 at C 15.28; and *manibus date lilia plenis* from *Aeneid* VI.883 at B 30.21 (both with the addition of *o*). At 20.113-4 Virgil says to Dante that his 'high tragedy', the *Aeneid*, is known to him in its entirety (*tutta quanta*). Dante certainly knew the *Eclogues* and very probably the *Georgics*. But Virgil is also present in person for sixty-four of the one hundred cantos, in his aerial body, an *ombra*, fewer only than in the case of Dante himself, far more than Beatrice's thirty-seven. This extended portrait fully and vividly presents what Virgil might be imagined to be after over thirteen centuries in Limbo in the company of the magnanimous and honoured

1. The *Comedy* is cited in Petrocchi's text (1966-7) as A, B and C for the three *cantiche* on the model of Wilkins and Berger, *Concordance to the Divina Commedia* (Cambridge, Mass. 1965). For Dante's other works the *Testo Critico* (Florence 1921) and *Dante Opere Minori II* (Milan-Naples 1979) have been used, and the following commentaries have been at hand: Giovanni Melodia, *La Vita Nuova* (Milan 1904 and 1925); Tommaso Casini, rev. Luigi Pietrobono, *La Vita Nuova* (Florence 1932); Kenelm Foster and Patrick Boyde, *Dante's Lyric Poetry*, 2 vols (Oxford 1967); Aristide Marigo, reissued with appendix by Pier Giorgio Ricci, *De Vulgari Eloquentia* (Florence 1957); G. Busnelli and G. Vandelli, *Il Convivio*, 2 vols (Florence 1934 and 1937); Gustavo Vinay, *Monarchia* (Florence 1950); Paget Toynbee, *Epistolae* (Oxford 1920; reissued 1966, without the section numbers of the *Testo Critico*, which are used here).

The great *Enciclopedia Dantesca*, edited by Umberto Bosco, 6 vols (Rome 1970-1978) cited as ED has been at hand, in particular, the *voce* 'Virgilio', vol. V (1976) 1030^2-1044^1, by Domenico Consoli and 1044^1-1049^2, 'Echi Virgiliani', by Alessandro Ronconi, and 'Teologia' V (1976), 564^1-568^2 by Kenelm Foster.

The *Lives* of Dante are cited from Angelo Solerti, *Le Vite di Dante, Petrarca e Boccaccio* (Milan 1904) I. Of commentaries on the *Comedy* pagans.[2] The memory, intelligence and will of *ombre* are more acute than in this life (B 25.83-4), and Virgil has learnt much, particularly about the Christian faith and the history of the Church to A.D. 1300. He has even witnessed the Harrowing of Hell, Christ's descent into Limbo to rescue the patriarchs whose names Virgil knows, and the shattering of gate of Hell (A 4.55-63 and 8.124-7). He can quote the Bible (*Luke* 11.27 at A 8.45), and Aristotle, and has clearly read Statius' *Thebaid.*

Virgil's first discourse on Fortune (A 7.70-96) is largely based on Boethius' *Consolation of Philosophy*, not on his own poems, and speaks of angels moving the heavens, a doctrine that in *Convivio* II.4.8 Dante describes as correcting the errors of the pagans due to 'defect of reason' and 'defect of instruction'. The next discourse on the structure of lower Hell is based on Aristotle, but that of B 15.45-84 on the *consorzio dei beni*, partnership in good things, not exclusive possession by a few, is Christian. In B 6.34-48 on the efficacy of prayer Virgil answers Dante's question about *Aeneid* VI.376, but also refers him to Beatrice for further light, as he does also at B 18.46-8, contrasting his reason with Beatrice's faith. We shall see later that his discourse at B 3.28-45 is erroneous, falling below Aristotle's reasoning.

In B 17.91-135 Virgil is given the task of explaining the moral order of Purgatory, the order of the seven deadly or capital sins and the reason for that order. Dante's source was

much use has been made of the excellent recent one of Umberto Bosco and Giovanni Reggio, 3 vols (Florence 1979), cited as Bosco. Also Manfredi Porena, 3 vols (Bologna 1948, 1953 and 1955, rev. 1959); Luigi Pietrobono, 3 vols (Turin 1949, reissued 1956); Hermann Gmelin, 3 vols (Stuttgart 1954, 1955 and 1957); Natalino Sapegno, 3 vols (Florence 1955, 1956 and 1957); Charles S. Singleton, 3 vols (Princeton 1970, 1973 and 1975). Of the many studies of Virgil in Dante, J.H. Whitfield, 'Virgil into Dante' in *Virgil: Studies in Latin Literature and its Influence*, ed. D.R. Dudley and T.A. Dorey (London 1969) 94-118 has been particularly useful. Mario Santoro, 'Virgilio personaggio nella Divina Commedia', *Dante nella critica d'oggi* (=*Cultura e Scuola*, 13 and 14, Florence 1965) 343-55, reviews recent tendencies. Translations are from J.D. Sinclair, *The Divine Comedy of Dante Alighieri*, 3 vols (repr. London 1971).

2. Fiorenzo Forti, *Magnanimitade, studi su un tema dantesco* (Bologna 1977); Giorgio Padoan, 'Il limbo dantesco' in *Il Pio Enea, l'empio Ulisse* (Ravenna 1977) 103-124.

long thought to be St. Gregory, and the presentation of the argument scholastic; but it has now been shown that Dante's source can only be the *Summa de Vitiis et Virtutibus* of the Dominican Guillaume Peyraut (about A.D. 1200-1270), since none of the other numerous schemes put forward in the thirteenth century to relate the seven to a common principle agrees with that of Dante.[3] It must be assumed that Beatrice instructed Virgil about the Mount of Purgatory, and that Virgil had dismissed his adherence to the Stoic doctrine of four evil passions (*hinc metuunt cupiuntque, dolent gaudentque, Aeneid* VI.733). Furthermore Virgil tackles the subject of Love in B 18 with a 'radical critique of the basic concept of love in the poets of the *stil nuovo*, as something irresistible', as Bosco shows (II.287-8). Virgil is presented also in a variety of new experiences and adventures, with changes of mood within a habitual melancholy, from confident to discouraged, from congratulation to rebuke of Dante, and, as I hope to show, more than once in error. The long journey from the savage wood to deepest Hell in the centre of the earth is known to him from his victimization by Lucan's necromantic witch, Erictho (A 9.22-30), but the climb to the Earthly Paradise on top of the antipodean Mountain of Purgatory is new to him as a pilgrim like Dante (B 2.63).

This complex dramatization has of course been endlessly discussed, beginning with the earliest commentators, only a few years after Dante's death. Indispensable though they are, they tend to adopt a simplified and reductive formula, that Virgil is an allegory of Reason, leading to Beatrice, representing Revelation, Theology, the Church, Faith. Also they took too seriously such descriptions of Virgil as *quel savio gentil, che tutto seppe* (A 7.3, 'the gentle sage, who knew all'), and *il mar di tutto 'l senno* (A 8.7, 'the sea of all wisdom'). This has become a tradition, although it has been more recently modified to present a more human and lifelike figure. Likewise, the discourses of Dante's Virgil and others on philosophical issues are not didactic displays of learning for their own sake, but are directed at Dante to correct his errors,

3. Siegfried Wenzel, 'Dante's Rationale for the Seven Deadly Sins', *Modern Language Review* 60.4 (1965) 529-533. The structures of *Inferno* and *Purgatorio* offered by Virgil contrast with his unsystematic *Aeneid* VI, which is not reducible to maps and diagrams.

some of them shared with Virgil, and so are rather parts of the autobiography which the *Comedy* is now recognised much more clearly to be. If the *Comedy* is essentially autobiography concerned with Dante's spiritual history and Virgil's, and with their poetry, and not an encyclopaedia of Christian doctrine, it is not a moral treatise for general edification, but, like St. Augustine's *Confessions*, a justification of speaking about oneself, hero or anti-hero, from beginning to end, the unique experience of a unique man. There has been a strain of hagiography about Dante as well as about his Virgil, and what he says about his nearness to despair and disaster has been neglected (B 1.58-60; cf. A 2.64-66), as has his near self-identification with Pier della Vigna and other major figures, Francesca, Farinata, Brunetto, Ulisse. The idea of Dante's linear development was destroyed by Bruno Nardi,[4] and the discontinuity between the man-centred Aristotelian humanism of the *Convivio* and of the *Monarchy* and the near Thomism (with some eccentricities) of the *Comedy* has been brought out more sharply by Kenelm Foster. Nardi has spoken of a crisis with a profound revision but he has not attempted to date it.

It had better be said at the outset of this essay, which is a brief personal sketch of what Padoan has rightly called *un lavoro ancora tutto da fare,*[5] that it is based on dating the *Comedy's* conception to shortly after April 1311 – i.e. after *Epistle* VII and the actual start on A 1 'before the Gascon deceived the noble Henry' (C 17.82) – about July 1312 (the normal date is 1307-8). I connect Dante's crisis with the strangely neglected *Canzone Montanina* (F and B 89; Barbi, 116) and its accompanying *Epistle* IV. In *Epistle* IV he

4. Bruno Nardi, *Saggi di filosofia dantesca* (Milan 1930; reissued Florence 1967); *Dante e la cultura medievale* (Bari 1942 and 1949); *Nel Mondo di Dante* (Rome 1944); *Dal 'Convivio' alla 'Commedia'* (Rome 1960); *Studi di Filosofia Medievale* (Rome 1960); *Saggi e Note di critica dantesca* (Milan-Naples 1966).

5. There is, so far as I know, no comprehensive and systematic collection and discussion of the evidence. Edward Moore, *Studies in Dante* (Oxford 1896, reissued 1969) I.359-375 lists the reminiscences and references to Virgil in the *Comedy*: 85 + 37 + 13 = 135; compare Ovid 20 + 35 + 17 = 85; Lucan 11 + 10 + 6 = 27; Statius 10 + 9 + 4 = 23. Approximate figures for the Bible are 70 + 160 + 96 = 326; Aristotle 10 + 28 + 36 = 74.

complains that the Lady of his sudden passionate love has forbidden all philosophical and political activity. But his 'praiseworthy resolve' to abstain from womanish poetry, *muliebres cantus*, was shattered, and he wrote his last canzone, *Amor da che convien*, turning back to the style of the *rime dolorose* about Beatrice that he excluded from the *Vita Nuova.*

This may seem to stray far from Virgil. But Virgil is inseparable from virtually all the major problems and controversies in Dante's whole poetic and intellectual development from his eighteenth year when he became Beatrice's poet.[6] The *Comedy* cannot be understood without the earlier stages of Dante's development, since Bosco (II.391-4) rightly shows how much it is the *recupero dello stil nuovo*, a return to Beatrice. However, Dante's art had been enriched by bold experiments in philosophical poetry and in imitation of the Provençal poets and, finally, in the *Comedy*, by his new classicism, incorporating so much from Virgil, vying with the Latin poets (A 4.88-105 and 25.94-97), and putting the vernacular on the level with Latin. The first two quotations from Virgil are concerned with poetic technique, but in *Convivio* IV Dante turns from the manner to the matter of the *Aeneid*, from the allegorical to the literal and historical. The latter is developed in *Monarchy* II and *Epistles* V, VI and VII. Virgil is thus an index of Dante's intellectual development before the *Comedy*, and the question is whether he is the same Virgil there as in the *Convivio* and *Monarchy*, and how much his earlier conceptions continue or are corrected

6. I have discussed several of these problems in various articles, some tentative and now out of date: 'The Epistle to Cangrande again'. *D(eutches) D(ante) J(ahrbuch)* 38 (1960) 51 ff; 'Dante's Canzone Montanina', *Modern Language Review* 55 (1960) 359-370; 'Beatrice's Chariot in Dante's Earthly Paradise', *DDJ* 39 (1961) 137-172; 'Cacciaguida's Prophecy in *Paradiso* 17; *Traditio* 19 (1963) 267-294; 'The "Veltres" in the Chanson de Roland and Dante's Veltro', *DDJ* 41/2 (1964) 158-172; 'Il Canto XIX: The Dream of the Siren' in *Lectura Dantis Internazionale*, ed. Vittorio Vettori, *Purgatorio* (1965) 217-249; 'The Symbol of the Gryphon in *Purgatorio* 29.108' in *Centenary Essays on Dante* (Oxford 1965) 103-131; 'The Date of the *Comedy* and the "Argomento barberiniano" ', *Dante Studies* 86 (1968) 1-16; 'Un cinquencento dieci e cinque, *Purgatorio* 33.43', *DDJ* 51/2 (1976-7) 84-98; 'Dante's "Mirabile Visione" (*Vita Nuova* 42)' in *The World of Dante*, ed. Cecil Grayson (Oxford 1980) 122-145.

or ignored. Here it will be argued that in the *Comedy* a quite new Virgil enters the stage with the second of the 'Two Voices' that some recent work has stressed,[7] the private melancholy and pessimistic, not the public triumphant Imperial voice. The reason for Virgil's pessimism is his exclusion from salvation, if in a Limbo that Dante had assimilated to the Elysium of *Aeneid* VI.

*   *   *

Dante's first quotation from Virgil is in *Vita Nuova* 25, where the personification of *Amor* is defended by the practice of the great Latin poets, afterwards found in Limbo (A 4.88-90), Virgil, Lucan, Horace and Ovid. Dante seems to have got his examples from some handbook, a Mediaeval *Poetria*, since those from Lucan and Horace are, as quoted, not in agreement with their contexts, and the two examples from Virgil are not as relevant as Cupid, twice called *Amor* at *Aeneid* I.663 and 689 (sinisterly substituted for Ascanius by Venus, as described in C 8.1-9) would have been. In the first, according to Dante, Juno, an inanimate thing, that is air,

7. The phrase 'Two Voices' in this connection goes back, not to Wordsworth of J.K. Stephen but to Adam Parry, 'The Two Voices of Virgil's Aeneid', *Arion* 24 (1963) 166-180. This was followed by Wendell Clausen, 'An Interpretation of the Aeneid', *Harvard Studies in Classical Philology* 68 (1964) 139-147; W.R. Johnson, 'Aeneas and the ironies of *pietas*', *Classical Journal* 60 (1965) 360-364, and *Darkness Visible. A Study of Virgil's Aeneid* (Berkeley, California 1976); Kenneth Quinn, *Virgil's Aeneid: A Critical Description* (London 1968), and 'Did Virgil fail?' in *Cicero and Virgil*, ed. J.R.C. Martyn (Amsterdam 1972). See also two reviews of recent work on Virgil: Antonie Wlosok, 'Vergil in der neueren Forschung', *Gymnasium* 80 (1973) 129-143, and Werner Suerbaumm, 'Gedanken zur moderne Aeneis-Forschung', *Der altsprachliche Unterricht* 24 (zu Vergils 2000 Todestag) (1981) 67-103. Most recently R.D. Williams, 'The Aeneid' in *Cambridge History of Latin Literature* (1982) ch. 18.5. For a more balanced view see Jasper Griffin, 'The Creation of Characters in the *Aeneid*' in *Literary and Artistic Patronage in Ancient Rome*, ed. B.K. Gold (Texas 1982) 118-134: 'The Aeneid was to show both the greatness of Rome and also its human cost, not denying or minimizing either of them nor separating them off into compartments in which each one could be developed without mentioning the other, but doing full justice to both and looking both steadily in the eye' (p.130).

speaks to another inanimate thing Aeolus, the keeper of the winds, and asks for the storm. This may pass in the context, but is wholly inadequate for Juno's part in the plot of the *Aeneid* from beginning to end, not only as instigator and director of all the resistance to Aeneas' mission, but also as embodying a spirit of resistance to Rome in the historical wars against the Italians, and, above all, the Carthaginians. Juno hardly figures in the *Comedy* (A 30.1-3 and C 12.10-12); but in C 33.31-2 in the Empyrean Dante had in mind the splendid diabolical scene in *Aeneid* II.601-618, where Venus reveals to her son the real cause of the sack of Troy, not Helen and Paris, not Laomedon, but the hostility of heaven (*divum inclementia, divum*). She removes from Aeneas the cloud (*nubem*), the dim veil of mortality, so that he may see the gods Neptune, Juno *saevissima*, and Minerva at work destroying the city. This is the first and last that Aeneas knows of the bitter enmity of 'the Queen of air and darkness', apart from Helenus' warning at *Aeneid* III.433-439. Dante has transformed, as is his way so often, Virgil's picture. His Latinism *nube*, where *nebbia* would do, points to his source, but the word is now used by St. Bernard praying to Our Lady to clear the cloud from Dante's eyes for the final vision, substituting for Venus' violent *eripiam* ('snatch away') the gentle *disleghi* ('disperse').

The most reductive mode of explaining the pagan gods is as the material elements; less so is the explanation of them as psychological factors in man, and this is what Dante alludes to when in *Convivio* II.4.6 he calls Juno *dea della potenza*, presumably as the goddess whom Paris rejected when he had to choose between power, wisdom and pleasure. Such a treatment would have led up to Dante's *Amor*, an 'accident in substance', a contingent passion in man.

Dante's second example from Virgil is Apollo's oracle at Delos to the Trojans at *Aeneid* III.94: 'an inanimate object speaks to animate', meaning, it would seem, the cauldron from which the voice came (*Aeneid* VI.347). The plot of the *Aeneid* depends on the divine guidance of Apollo, Apollo's priest Helenus, the Penates, Mercury, and so on, just as the plot of the *Vita Nuova* depends on Amor's guidance of Dante. But the final quotation from Ovid's *Remedia Amoris*, is the most apt, since Amor is simply personified by the great authority on love, and the reduction to 'an accident in substance' is not incongruous there, as it is for Virgil and for Dante himself. Dante ends his chapter with a rebuke to any vernacular poet of love who uses a *figura* or *colore retorico* without the ability on demand to strip his words of such a cloak, to reveal their true meaning in prose.

* * *

The enormous expansion, after the *Vita Nuova*, of Dante's experience, poetical, philosophical and political, must here be passed over rapidly. When Dante in 1304, after three years of exile and attempts to re-enter Florence with the coalition of earlier Ghibelline exiles and of his own 'White' Guelphs, abandoned the exiles in disgust and made a party on his own (C 17.61-69), he was thrown back on his resources as poet and philosopher and into a new period of study, so far as an impoverished and wandering life allowed. He wrote the two canzoni on Justice and Liberality because he had so bitterly experienced their opposites, and then expanded *Vita Nuova* 25 into a full-scale treatise in Latin, the *De Vulgari Eloquentia*, in which his next quotation from Virgil occurs, significantly from *Aeneid* VI, but interpreted according to the traditional Mediaeval allegorization that goes back to Fulgentius, developed by Bernardus Sylvestris: *Aeneid* I-VI present the ages of man from infancy to the attainment of maturity, that is philosophical enlightenment. This is alluded to in one word *figurate*. Virgil is thus cited for his philosophical matter as well as for his technical mastery, just as Dante speaks of himself as the poet of *Virtus*, no longer just of *Venus*, the only subject proper to vernacular poets according to *Vita Nuova* 25. But Dante's emphasis is all on technique (*ars, doctrina, scientia*) as shown by the Latin poets, *magni et regulares* with their *doctrinatae poetriae (De Vulgari Eloquentia* II.4.3). Dante ends his section on the weighty themes suitable for treatment in the high tragic style with a warning to those who have composed 'casually' (II.4.1), 'by chance rather than art', and with a passage of high rhetoric and self-confidence:

When anyone purposes to sing of the three great

> subjects in their purity . . . let him first drink of Helicon and then after finely tuning the strings take his bow firmly and begin to play. But to exercise proper caution and discernment is the exacting task, since it can never be attained without mental effort, sedulous practice of the art and habitual mastery of the sciences. It is those whom the poet in the sixth book of the Aeneid, speaking figuratively, calls the beloved of God and raised to heaven by their fiery excellence, sons of the gods. Therefore let those who are innocent of art and science, trusting solely to their native wit, who rush forward to sing of the highest themes in the highest style, stand confuted and cease from such presumption. If they are geese by nature or by indolence, let them abstain from imitating the starward flight of the eagle.

Dante treats his two quotations freely: in the first the Sibyl's words to Aeneas (*Aeneid* VI.126-131), about the easy descent to Avernus and the difficult ascent reserved for few, he puts *amavit Iuppiter* into the Christian words *dilectos Dei*, perhaps because *amavit* would be too erotic, suggesting Ganymede, Semele, Alcmene *et al.* (though Servius glosses *quos diligit Iuppiter*). The last words of the chapter about geese and an eagle are much adapted from Virgil's *Eclogues* IX.35-6, where the aspiring young poet Lycidas modestly says that 'as yet he has produced nothing to the standard of Varius and Cinna', but is 'a goose cackling among swans'. Dante proudly dismisses the geese and elevates the swans into a high-flying eagle; who but himself? Likewise in the last complete chapter of the *De Vulgari Eloquentia* he quotes one of his Pietra poems as something new and never before attempted, comparable to the high enterprise enjoined on a candidate for Knighthood.

In *Convivio* IV Dante discovered the Roman Empire in Virgil's *Aeneid*. He describes his discovery in *Monarchy* II.1, but the nucleus of books I and II is already in *Convivio* IV.45 with Jupiter's words *in persona Dio parlando* from *Aeneid* I. 278-9 (*his ego nec metas rerum nec tempora pono: / imperium sine fine dedi*) to prove Rome's divine right to world government so much needed by mankind. However, Dante completed *Convivio* IV as planned and in IV.26 made use of the traditional Mediaeval allegorization of the *Aeneid*, although his new literal reading of the *Aeneid* as a historical authority is not compatible with the allegory. The allegory may have been already in Dante's mind when he wrote the last stanza of the canzone on nobility about the forms that nobility takes at different ages, but there is nothing of Virgil in it, and only in the much later commentary was Dante glad to adduce the authority of Virgil, to show how the noble 'appetite' of the mind must be ridden like a horse with rein and spur, temperance and courage. 'Our greatest poet' shows this: 'what reining in was that of Aeneas' departure from Dido after such delight from her, to follow an honourable, praiseworthy and fruitful path'; 'what a use of the spur was that when he endured, alone with the Sibyl, to enter into Hell, facing such dangers, to seek out the soul of his father'. It must be said that the Sibyl's words on the easy descent and difficult reascent except for sons of God lend themselves to allegory, because they are so contradicted by what Aeneas experiences in the long descent and easy return, in four words, by the mysterious ivory gate.

This allegorical development of Aeneas in *Aeneid* IV-VI resembles that of Dante himself from the 'fervid and passionate' stage of the *Vita Nuova*, of *Convivio* I.1.16 and 2.15-16 to the 'temperate and mature' love of poetry and philosophy. On a literal reading of the *Aeneid* Aeneas would be about thirty-five, with a nearly grown-up son, when, like Dante, he suffered an exile that was to be permanent and not without warfare. Aeneas is reunited, spiritually, with his father after what Fulgentius calls his 'holiday' (*feriatus*) without him in Carthage. Dante does not speak of his father, but in Brunetto Latini he found that 'dear and kind paternal image' (*cara e buona imagine paterna*) needed by a man under twenty-five, in the dangers of the world (*selva erronea di questa vita, Convivio* IV.24.4 and 12). Brunetto taught him 'to follow his star', i.e. his *ingenium* and thereby 'to make himself eternal' by fame in this world (A 15.55 and 83-5). But the reuniting of Aeneas with Anchises in Elysium is cited (C 15.25-7) for Dante's meeting with his ancestor, the crusader and knight, Cacciaguida, who greets Dante with Anchises' words to

Julius Caesar, *sanguis meus* (without *proice tela manu*), and adds at once *o superinfusa gratia Dei*. What matters now is salvation, as it does for Virgil too in the *Comedy*, and for Dante his vocation as poet, which would, he knew, secure his fame. In the *Comedy* there is no trace of Fulgentius or Bernardus Sylvestris, except perhaps for B 18.136-8, the sloth of some of Aeneas' followers who stayed on in Sicily (V.751).

* * *

The starting-point, 'the decisive illumination', of Dante's 'proof' of the divine providence in the 'birth and process' of Rome is the synchronization of David, ancestor of the Virgin, and Aeneas, ancestor of Julius Caesar at *Convivio* IV.5.5-6, which has recently been shown to come from Brunetto Latini, *Tresor* I.44.[8] From it stems the whole transference of the divine predestination and miracles of the Bible to the Roman Empire, with Virgil as its bible; any doubt about Rome's mission and right to world government is thus 'to speak against our faith' (*Convivio* IV.5.9). Four times Dante rhetorically repeats the phrase, 'did not God set His own hands?' to this or that event. Although Dante cites Livy for the seven kings of Rome, he uses him seldom, as he also does St. Augustine, *Civitas Dei* V.18; his main source for the 'divine process' of Rome is Virgil's 'catalogues' in *Aeneid* VI. 756-833 and the scenes from Aeneas' shield in *Aeneid* VIII. 625-670. Now in *Monarchy* III.4.8 and 11 Dante quotes St. Augustine *de Doctrina Christiana* (I.36) for his condemnation of 'anyone who tries to give the scriptures a sense different from that intended by the writer', who is the Holy Spirit, the *unicus dictator*. But he has no hesitation in ignoring Livy's obvious distaste for his own times (*Preface* 5.9) and even flouts Virgil's authority, when he proves Aeneas' right to rule

8. Giorgio Padoan, ED. II.678 ('un' illuminazione decisiva'); John A. Scott, 'La contemporaneità Enea-Davide', *Studi Danteschi* 49 (1972) 129-134. On Dante's political opinions up to his 'sudden illumination' the best account is that of Ernesto Sestan, 'Il pensiero politico di Dante' in *Scritti su Dante Alighieri* in *Miscellanae storica della Valdelsa* (Castelfiorentino 1965) 9-23.

three continents from his nobility, his ancestry and his three marriages; Africa from his 'marriage' to Dido, on the basis of *Aeneid* IV.171-2 – *coniugium vocat; hoc praetexit nomine culpam* – though Aeneas' words at 338-9 should have more authority – *nec coniugis unquam / praetendi taedas*. Furthermore Dante must have known that Livy has no mention of Aeneas at Carthage or Cumae, and, from the *Confessions* of St. Augustine, which he had read, that Aeneas never went to Carthage, 'according to the opinion of the more learned, whereas the less learned say that they do not know'. Macrobius, whom Dante may not have read, speaks (*Saturnalia* V.16.5) of the *fabula* of Dido, the story everyone knew was false (*quam falsam novit universitas*) – everyone, that is, except Dante!

Though Virgil is not mentioned in the final chapter of the *Monarchy* (III.16), it has often been quoted to illustrate the roles of Dante's two guides in the *Comedy*, Virgil as Reason to the Earthly Paradise and Beatrice as Theology or the Church, Revelation, Faith, thence almost to the end, where St. Bernard as mystic takes her place. On the assumption that the *Monarchy* and the *Comedy* are contemporaneous, Virgil represents human reason enlightened by philosophy, the *philosophica documenta* and *humana ratio quae per philosophos tota nobis innotuit*, by which the happiness of this life can be attained in the exercise of man's own powers, *virtus*. This doctrine of two ultimate goals, reached by different means, is characterized by Kenelm Foster (*ED* s.v. 'Teologia') as 'unacceptable to Christian orthodoxy and to common sense', whereas in the *Comedy* Dante is not far from St. Thomas. There are two guides in the *Comedy*, but only one journey to one goal, not the Earthly Paradise, which is only a temporary halt, and Virgil does not know the way to it in Purgatory, where he is as much a pilgrim as Dante, and has none of the 'indisputable authority' there that Consoli (*ED* s.v. 'Virgilio') attributes to him.

It is in his quotation from Virgil in *Monarchy* I.11.1 (*iam redit et virgo, redeunt Saturnia regna*, *Eclogue* IV.6) that Dante anticipates the next phase of his imperialist doctrine, because he seems there to attribute to Virgil a view of manifest destiny to be seen in contemporary events. Dante was soon to see in the Emperor Henry VII's coming into Italy the very 'hand of God' at work. It is one thing to see a providence in the distant past, quite another in the turmoil of the present; it is a Utopian delusion, predestined only to disappointment, especially if it leads to rash prophecy, the claim to know the divine will.

* * *

When Dante quotes *Eclogue* IV and says that the Virgin is Justice, he does not take it out of context, as his mention of her alternative name, Astraea, shows. He explains *Saturnia* as also called *aurea*, and he no doubt had in mind the passage in the *Aeneid*, where the Golden Age in Latium is celebrated under Saturn himself and his great-grandson, King Latinus (*Aeneid* VII.45-9). *Aeneid* VII.202-4 and VIII.319-325 give different accounts, since in VIII Saturn civilizes a savage people and gives them laws. The most important passage is *Aeneid* VI.791-4 on Augustus' restoration of the Golden Age, and Latinus' continuation of Saturn's age into the Iron Age of warfare that now threatens it is linked to Augustus by the description of Latinus' palace, a replica of the temple of Jupiter Capitolinus in Virgil's day, as *augustum* (*Aeneid* VII. 153.170), a word not otherwise used by Virgil. *Eclogue* IV is read without reference to the prophetic Christian interpretation of the Virgin as the Virgin Mary, and even in B 22. 70-73 Statius, who aided by grace owed his conversion to the *Eclogue*, still translates *torna giustizia.* (But is it likely that Statius at the end of so many years in Purgatory should think of political justice in a state and not of righteousness as it is discussed by St. Paul?) Dante's interpretation, in the *Monarchy*, less Mediaeval than we might expect, depends on his new historical reading of Virgil as a whole. His claim (*Monarchy* I.1.3-5) that he was 'attempting new and hidden truths' is not unfounded as a reading of Virgil. Even the pagan commentators on Virgil had little more to say about the Empire than that restoring the Golden Age is part of the regular praise of the Emperor.

Dante says of *Eclogue* IV that in it Virgil 'wished to commend the age that seemed to emerge in his time'. 'Seemed' suggests a doubt that Dante otherwise does not attribute to his imperial Virgil, nor feel himself. Did he perhaps write 'saw' (*videbat*)? Dante was perhaps prone to see a providence in Henry VII's election as Emperor, because, just as he was ready with his theory, the means to its realization seemed to appear, just as his discovery of philosophy seemed sanctioned by God (*non forse sanza divino imperio, Convivio* II.12.5). But it is one thing to see something of this kind in one's own life, quite another to see it in contemporary events.

Henry was elected in November 1308, and decided in August 1309 to come to Italy. In September / October 1310 or so Dante addressed a letter (*Epistle* V) to the Princes and Peoples of Italy full of high-flown rhetoric, mixing quotations and reminiscences of the Bible and Virgil. Most alarming is the prophetic afflatus, what Longinus (3.5) called 'the Bacchic thyrsus in the wrong place', here in politics not poetry, re-phrasing arguments from the *Monarchy*, but applying them explicitly to Henry VII. Six months later from the Casentino, the upper Arno, Dante wrote *Epistle* VI to the Florentines, 'the undeserved exile to the criminals within the city', threatening them with destruction for their madness and arrogance, 'inevitable shipwreck' for resistance to the 'most manifest will of God'. For so his 'prophetic mind', quoted from *Aeneid* X.843 (*praesaga mali mens* without *mali*), reads 'the unmistakable signs', which are probably astrological.

On April 17 1311 Dante addressed a third Letter (VII) to the Emperor himself, addressing him as *tu*, not *vos*, with three explicit quotations from Virgil: 'then most of us, forestalling our longings in our joy, chanted with Virgil of the Golden Age and the return of the Virgin; then *Aeneid* I.286-7 and IV.272-6, Mercury's message to Aeneas in Carthage 'think of Ascanius', by whom Dante means Henry's son John, 'who shall wreak his wrath like a lion on any new Turnus'. Dante uses the contemptuous plural *in Turnos* i.e. all Henry's opponents, especially King Robert of Naples. Florence is compared to Amata, who hanged herself (*Aeneid* XII.603) but Dante uses the words that describe the suicide of Judas. In sections 9-10 he describes his feelings when doing homage to Henry after his coronation in Milan on January 6 1311, kissing his feet: 'then my spirit rejoiced within me, when I said to myself in silence, "behold the Lamb of God, behold him who taketh away the sins of the world" *John* I.29'. Whitfield argues that this is not blasphemy but that, in Mediaeval fashion, the Emperor has assumed the typology of the Saviour. If it is not blasphemy, it offers Henry more than Virgil offered to Augustus, and is the high point of Dante's parallelism of Church and Empire; in the *Comedy* he restores the quotation to its owner (B 16.19; C 17.33 and 24.2). But, underlying *Epistle* VII's triumphalism, there is an acute anxiety that Henry's delay in Lombardy would give his chief enemy, Florence, time to strengthen its position. *Eia, rumpe moras*, 'away with delay', Dante says to Henry, quoting *Aeneid* IV.569, Mercury's second order to Aeneas to leave Carthage. In fact Henry appeared before Florence only a year and a half later to lay ineffective siege and retire after a month.

* * *

Nardi has argued that between *Convivio* and the *Comedy* Dante thoroughly revised his philosophy. Some of the six recognized changes are fundamental, on the origin of the soul, on prime matter, and on the spots in the moon, provided they are seen as showing that souls differ in quality and not just quantity of the same substance. More recently Kenelm Foster has shown that the revision was not piecemeal of this or that doctrine, but a comprehensive change of attitude, especially about grace. The revolt of Dante's sensuous nature described in the *Canzone Montanina* (which I date 1311-2) had led him back to Beatrice, and helps to account for the genesis of the *Comedy*: Dante had recognized again the marks of the ancient flame (B 30.48).

A very different Virgil appears in A 1 – *quantum mutatus ab illo* – not a triumphal poet (*victor et Tyrio conspectus in ostro*) on a four-horse chariot, returning to Mantua with the Muses (*Georgics* III.10-21 – lines surely remembered in C 25.1-9 *se mai continga, modo vita supersit*), if life allowed, as it did not for either.

Since Dante had ceased to allegorize Virgil's poems, why should he allegorize Virgil himself? If he wanted a figure of Reason, Aristotle was the obvious choice, as well up to date in Limbo, as Virgil now is, in the Christian faith. The essential question is whether Dante still allegorized Aeneas' descent into the Underworld, or treated it as a historical fact, a physical reality, or regarded it as a visionary imagination, a *fictio* but not *rhetorica*, not willed, but given by grace through the *imaginativa* (B 17.13), in 'sensible form' (C 10.54; A 2.15). He knew that Virgil had not descended in the same sense as Aeneas, since he says (*Aeneid* VI.266) *sit mihi fas audita loqui*, 'may I be allowed to speak what I have heard', and the necromantic descent engineered by Lucan's witch Erictho had to be invented so that Virgil should be the experienced guide to deepest Hell, but not beyond in Purgatory. Dante's *altro viaggio* under Virgil's guidance (A 1.91) is based on Aeneas'. Just as Aeneas has encounters with his recently dead friends, Palinurus, Dido, now an enemy, Deiphobus, the group of warriors, in addition to permanent officers like Charon, so has Dante. But Dante not only enters the City of Dis, merely seen in the distance by Aeneas and reported by the Sibyl, but goes on in the same direction, making one journey to the Earthly Paradise, whereas Virgil's Elysium is a spiritual paradise from which Aeneas comes back to where he started. If reunion with Anchises means knowledge of God, Dante certainly acquires such wisdom and more, vision of His Essence. Dante says (A 2.26-7) that Aeneas understood things that were the cause of his victory. Aeneas is said to be a new man, reborn after his experience, as many critics maintain, although there is no allusion to *Aeneid* VI in the subsequent books, and no sign in Aeneas of desire for his future fame (*Aeneid* VI.889).

Dante may also have imitated from Virgil the pattern, which he had cited in *Convivio* IV.26.9 allegorically of Aeneas, the Sibyl and Anchises, of the man, the superhuman female intermediary, and the almost divine figure. This is the pattern which Jung has proposed for the psyche: consciousness, meeting positive and negative 'shadows', and so, by 'integrating' them, makes contact with the deeper layer, the *anima*, and, with its guidance, meets the archetypes of the Wise Old Man, who has the answers. This may have come spontaneously to Dante. In the *Comedy* he mentions the Sibyl only in passing, and then as giving oracles written on leaves, not as guide (C 33.66). But when in 1320 he re-read the *Eclogues* in order to write his own, he could well have noticed that the pattern occurs in *Eclogue* VI, where two shepherds (i.e. poets) in search of a song, with the help of a nymph, Aegle, 'gleam of light', capture Silenus, the repository of Dionysiac wisdom. His inspired song, worthy of Apollo and of Orpheus, passing from the creation to the reign of Saturn, and the theft of Prometheus, culminates in Gallus, Virgil's contemporary, who is given the pipe of Hesiod for a Callimachean poem, not an ambitious epic of war. The pattern is repeated in *Georgics* IV with the shepherd Aristaeus, helped by his mother, the nymph Cyrene, in her underwater cavern, to catch the Old Man of the Sea, Proteus, who provides the clue that Cyrene can interpret to restore the hive of bees. In the *Comedy* Beatrice commissions the poem and Cacciaguida, compared to Anchises, specifies it more precisely. St. Bernard is the last and greatest of the series of wise old men.

Dante may well, when he began the *Comedy*, have been out of humour with allegory, almost as much as Croce (*La Poesia di Dante*, Bari, 1920), and for similar reasons. If made obvious, as in Prudentius' *Psychomachia*, it is boringly abstract; if not explained, an enigma open to much dispute and confusion. Dante was annoyed that his two Canzoni on the Lady Philosophy were taken, probably rightly, as celebrating a sensuous, not a rational, love; when years later he returned to allegory in *Tre Donne* he made it clear that he was discussing Justice, *Drittura*. The *tre donne benedette* of A 2.124 are all real women by contrast, and intended as such. In *Convivio* II.1.4 he says that allegory is a means of concealment invented by the wise, with which his remark in *Vita Nuova* 19.22 may be compared: 'I am afraid that I may have revealed my meaning to too many people'. The *Convivio* and of course the Latin treatises were addressed to an elite, but not the *Comedy*, despite the difficulties of the philosophical discourses; it was intended *in pro del mondo che mal vive* ('for the world's good which lives ill' B 32.103), and it was both widely popular with Venetian gondoliers and attracted learned commentators. In the *Monarchy* Dante had to deal with his opponent's biblical allegories and argues against them (*Monarchy* III.4-13), beginning with sun and moon as the two institutions, Church and State. Particularly effective is the attack on St. Peter's 'two swords' (*Luke*, 22.38), where the literal sense is supported by a description of St. Peter's direct and impulsive character. In the *Comedy* we are in the other world, where the literal sense is already 'anagogical'. Only public historical events, such as the Exodus, can have three further senses over and above the literal, and even in the *Convivio* (II.1.9-12) Dante firmly says that the literal sense must come first. There are of course a number of incidental allegories in the *Comedy*, but these are either clear or obviously not literal.

* * *

Dante's uncertainty about the figure whom he sees in the dim light, *dove il sol tace* (60), arises because it *per lungo silenzio parea fioco*, a much tormented line. The metaphor in *tace* has been applied to *silenzio*, as dimness, and *fioco,* normally 'enfeebled' more often in voice then sight, but here 'dim to sight'. *Silenzio* has been taken allegorically to mean the voice of reason, long silenced by Dante, or of the imperialist, long neglected until Dante's *Monarchy*. A literal sense seems better, that, as Dante rushes down crying out for help, the figure, without response until Dante is near, seems almost dumb because of his long silence. Virgil's reply as it proceeds is no less puzzling: his reference to Lombard is a deliberate anachronism, hinting that Virgil knows the history of Italy after his time; he was not born 'under' Julius, though of course in his lifetime; and *ancor che fosse tardi* is usually taken as 'too late to be known and honoured as a poet by Julius, as later by Augustus', because in 44 BC he was scarcely yet a poet. But in *Georgics* I.466-514 Virgil was to mourn Julius' death. Augustus is called *il buono*, 'the good'; probably his title 'Emperor' is deliberately suppressed. As Virgil's great preoccupation will prove to be his exclusion from salvation, 'late' could well mean 'late in the pagan era', as he died only nineteen years before the Nativity. But anyhow, the next line admits of no dispute: *al tempo de li dei falsi e bugiardi* ('in the time of the false and lying gods'). This can mean only that Virgil's prophecies are now known by him to be false. (It is worth noticing too that Virgil is represented in

A 20 as so hostile to diviners and magicians that he corrects his own account of the origins of Mantua in *Aeneid* X.198-200 and clears Mantua of any connection with magic, despite the interest that he shows in *Eclogue* VIII.65-109 and *Aeneid* IV.493 and 504-521.) A 19.123 shows Virgil's knowledge of Papacy; he presumably knows that the Empire is in abeyance. Then he characterizes his *alta tragedia* by reference to the burning of proud Troy (compare B 12.61-3, *Troia in cenere, Ilion basso e vile*) not to Aeneas' victory in *Aeneid* XII. This tragic elegiac note of the *Aeneid* is soon amply confirmed. Finally Virgil puts a question to Dante, which must be ironical, since A 2 will show how well he knows the answer: 'Why do you not climb the delightful mountain that is the cause and principle of all joy?' This and the earlier description of 'the hill lit by the Sun which leads men straight on every path', must refer to Dante's mistaken belief in *Monarchy* III.16 and in the *Convivio* that philosophy 'wholly known', and *virtus* 'in our power', can lead to happiness in this world, 'symbolized by the Earthly Paradise'. The mountain is not, as is often said, an anticipation of the Mount of Purgatory, but its antithesis, polar or rather antipodean opposite.

Dante pays no attention to Virgil's disillusionment about the *Aeneid*; he is thrilled to meet the great poetic artist and to claim him as his model of the grandest 'tragic' style. But to this gushing tribute to him as master and authority Virgil pays no attention; what is at stake is not Dante's style, but his salvation, and Virgil's own. So he curtly and drily says: *A te convien tenere altro viaggio* ('Thou must take another road'), and enlarges on the deadly danger of the she-wolf, until the greyhound comes to put her to death after driving her down into Hell. Likewise Virgil will guide Dante down into Hell and through Purgatory, but not to the blessed, a task reserved for one of them, *anima più degna*, since 'the Emperor who reigns above' so ordains 'since I rebelled against His law'. Here then is the only Emperor, who *imperium sine fine dabit*. This is the first of Virgil's complaints about his relegation to Limbo; how could he rebel against a Law that he did not know?

* * *

In Virgil's prophecy of the Veltro, a tercet (106-8) returns to the *Aeneid*, as though Dante had not fully understood the implications of 'proud Troy' with which 'humble Italy' is contrasted. At *Aeneid* III.522-4 Italia is thrice triumphantly saluted by the Aeneadae, and *humilis* means 'low-lying'. But now it means 'humbled' politically, the *serva Italia* of B 6.76 or *Italia morta* of B 7.95. Then Virgil mentions four who died in Aeneas' war in Latium, two on each side, so interlaced as to separate the inseparable Euryalus and Nisus. Camilla is mentioned as in Limbo at A 4.124, and Turnus, in contrast to the contemptuous plural of *Epistle* VII.18, 'died for Italy'. The abrupt end of the *Aeneid* has been much debated. Turnus' death is described in the same line as Camilla's at *Aeneid* XI.831, an echo of Homer's line, repeated twice for the deaths of Patroclus and Hector (*Iliad* XVI.856 and XXII.362). But the *Iliad* has two further books of reconciliation, the Games and Priam's coming to Achilles' tent for Hector's body, whereas we are left in the *Aeneid* with Dido's curse. No wonder Maffeo Veggio added a thirteenth book and Gavin Douglas translated it. Was Turnus guilty, deserving of death, and Aeneas still *pius* in not sparing his life, as a victorious wolf does when its rival offers its throat? Dante seems to have come round to something like the voice of the recent critics. When at B 6.75 Virgil and Sordello embrace because both came from Mantua, although separated by nearly thirteen centuries, Dante breaks out into an apostrophe, *Ahi serva Italia*, in which he also strangely interpolates (118-124) a direct address to God, as

O sommo Giove
che fosti in terra per noi crucifisso,
Son li giusti occhi tuoi rivolti altrove?
O è preparazion che ne i'abisso
del tuo consiglio fai per alcun bene
in tutto de l'accorger nostro scisso?

O Jove supreme who wast crucified on earth for us, are Thy just eyes turned elsewhere, or is it preparation Thou makest in the abyss of Thy counsel for some good quite cut off from our perception?

He may have had in mind Virgil's unique direct invocation of Jupiter when he approaches the last battle of the war, and the slaughter by both Turnus and Aeneas (*Aeneid* XII. 503-4).

tanton placuit concurrere motu
Iuppiter, aeterna gentis in pace futuras?

Jupiter, was it your will that nations,
Destined to live at peace for ever, should clash so bitterly?

(tr. C. Day Lewis)

Sommo comes from *Aeneid* I.380 and VI.123. The *aeterna pax* was long in coming, only after the many wars of Rome to conquer Italy. By Dante's time Italy was again as much divided as in prehistoric times. If, then, Virgil is disillusioned and no longer interested in the Roman Empire, was Dante also in the *Comedy* disillusioned after Henry VII's failure, or does he still echo the imperial voice? His position was now very different from Virgil's, certain as he was of salvation and assured of his absorbing vocation as poet, which made his exile tolerable.

The answer to this question begins with Dante's doubts about the journey, though he has accepted Virgil as guide. He begins and ends his speech to Virgil (A 2.10-36) questioning his fitness for the 'war', but in between he cites the two examples of St Paul and Aeneas, called the father of Silvius (*Albanum nomen, tua postuma proles, Aeneid* VI.763), an element of hope, not of melancholy, in the *Aeneid*. Dante now understands that he is to follow their example, and, like Aeneas, he will be in the body, *sensibilmente*; only when he enters the first heaven (C 2.36-9) does he share St Paul's doubt whether he was in the body or not (*Corinthians* II. 12.2-4). In four tercets Dante considers Aeneas' descent, in emphatic and scholastic language (*il chi e 'l quale*), and Aeneas' nobility and character (*la quale e 'l quale, a voler dir lo vero*). Rome and its Empire were established by their predestined father, as the sacred site, the see of St Peter's successor; and the final 'high effect' of Aeneas' victory is 'the Papal mantle'. Dante seems to console Virgil for the failure of his prophecy since the Empire is vacant, by assuring him that Aeneas' descent was not in vain but had an even higher purpose. Dante does not yet know how much Virgil knows about the Church, and that knowledge turns out to be surprisingly extensive. In particular he knows that all is not well with the Papal mantle when he congratulates Dante on his denunciation in A 19.21-6. The clear subordination of the Empire to the Church is no surprise if the *Comedy* is after Dante's crisis about Henry VII. In C 6 in Justinian's great speech about the Empire the same subordination is no less emphatically repeated: all that the Roman Eagle had done or still was to do is scanty and insignificant (*poco e scuro*, 85) compared to what Tiberius and Titus contributed to the Church. Justinian had begun by saying that he had been a monophysite until directed to the true faith by the Pope, and only then, when in step with the Church, was he inspired by God's grace to his great task, reform of the Law. He briefly condemns both the appropriation of the sacred standard and opposition to it (33), and enlarges on it (100-111), condemning Guelphs and Ghibellines alike. This forbids us to call Dante's subordination of Empire to Church in A 2 *il guelfismo de Dante*. Like Henry VII, Dante did not want the name of either faction attached to his conception of the Empire. This conception he maintains in the *Comedy*, but, I would argue, only in theory, as a distant ideal, now that Henry VII has come too late (B 6.96), or too early (C 30. 137-8).

Aeneid VI, the reason for Virgil's selection as guide, is the basis on which Dante has built two-thirds of the *Comedy*, by drastic rearrangement and systematisation so as to lead to the Pauline *Paradiso*. Aeneas sees the City of Dis on his left but does not enter it, as Dante does; the Sibyl describes it (*Aeneid* VI.548-627). But Dante has kept and developed an essential element in *Aeneid* VI, the encounters with those whom Aeneas had known personally, into an unchronological autobiography, including many whom he had not known, but who were significant to him.

No feature of Virgil's Underworld has been more discussed than the mysterious golden bough (*Aeneid* VI.136-155). Servius suggests that it is *quiddam mysticum* in the rites of Proserpina, and that to descend into the Underworld is to celebrate her rites, possibly such as are implied in the Orphic-Pythagorean tablets from South Italy and practised in the

Antrum at Baiae, perhaps known to Virgil. On to such a ritual anticipation of the experience to be expected after death Virgil has grafted the Sibyl, priestess of Apollo and of Hecate, the underworld form of Diana. The bough is effective in overcoming Charon's resistance (406), silenced at A 3.94-6 by Virgil's formula. The 'gift of Proserpina' (*Aeneid* VI.142 and 637), now in Aeneas' hands, is finally fixed by him to the threshold of the confronting gate in the walls, and thereupon the Sibyl and Aeneas are in Elysium. Dante has characteristically changed this reminiscence of the golden bough (B 1.134-6):

> qual elli scelse
> l'umile pianta, cotal si rinacque
> subitamente là onde l'avelse.

> *as was the lowly plant he chose such did it spring up again immediately in the place where he had plucked it.*

Avelse is a latinism for Italian *svelse* echoing *avulso* at *Aeneid* VI.143. The bough of real gold is now a smooth rush, the only plant that can grow where the waves break on the mud of the island's beach, and Virgil uses it to provide a girdle for Dante and to bathe Dante's face which was tear-stained and blackened by the mists and smoke of Hell. Only so can he properly be presented to the guardian angel of the gate of Purgatory who engraves seven Ps, *Peccata*, on Dante's brow with the point of his sword. This is a transformation of Virgil's mysterious self-renewing precious metal into the simplest of plants as a symbol of nature's inexhaustible production. The setting is new. Virgil's sedge (*ulva, Aeneid* VI. 416) grows on nasty mud like that of A 8, but in B 1 it is soft and fertile, lit by the much-quoted *tremolar della marina* in the light of dawn. (B 1.117).

* * *

Dante has been thought severe and lacking in humour, but he provides amusing comments on his gushing address to Virgil in A 1.79-87 as the master of the style whose beauty brought him honour, *bello stilo che m'ha fatto onore*. This honour is confirmed by Lucia's words to Beatrice (A 2.105), and Beatrice knows that Dante will listen to such a stylist as Virgil when she tells him to help Dante *con la tua parola ornata* (67) and again refers (113) to his *parlar onesto*. But the *Comedy* is so called (A 16.128 and 21.2) just after Virgil's reference to his *alta mia tragedia* (A 20.113) because it is not in the high tragic style, and this contrast is dramatized in A 30, in the *tenzone, contentio*, a rapid exchange of insulting repartee in verse between opponents, who are here the forger of gold florins, maestro Adamo, and Virgil's Sinon, *il falso greco di Troia* (98). The scene begins with Adamo's nostalgia for the idyllic landscape of the Casentino, but when he points to Sinon and names him, fisticuffs and insults fly, as Sinon reacts with a blow on Adamo's inflated dropsical stomach. The exchange lasts from 102-129, and Dante listens enrapt *del tutto fisso*, until Virgil intervenes and scolds him: 'Go on gazing; in a moment I shall really quarrel with you!' Dante is so ashamed (132-141) that Virgil declares his shame to be excessive, but reminds Dante of his constant presence on the watch for such exhibitions of 'low taste' (*bassa voglia* 148). The whole scene is in comic realistic vulgar language, far from the choice tragic style praised in the *De Vulgari Eloquentia*. When Dante meets his friend Forese Donati, he seems to remember Virgil's watchful company, in expressing regret for 'what you were with me and I with you' (*qual fosti meco e qual io teco fui* B 23.116), the only independent evidence of which is their *tenzone*, Dante's three abusive sonnets and Forese's three replies (F and B 72-74; Barbi, 73-78). He says to Forese that Virgil drew him from that life; this seems to imply more than a literary fault. In fact Dante's experiment in the comic style is an important antecedent of the comic elements in the *Comedy*, a departure from literary orthodoxy in the mixing of styles. But already in B 9.70, Dante tells the reader to note how he raises his style to suit his new matter; he does so even more in *Paradiso*, now *poema sacro*, not comedy. As a sign of this in *Inferno* there are seven uses of Latin, in *Purgatorio* thirty-eight and in *Paradiso* forty-one, only two Virgilian, the rest from the Bible and hymns. But even in *Paradiso* the word *mamma*, deprecated in *De Vulgari Eloquentia* II.7.4, appears touchingly at C 14.64 and again at 23.121. When Virgil rebuked Dante's *bassa voglia*, had he forgotten his own *tenzone* in *Eclogue* III.1-27, admittedly a youthful poem, where the coarse word is omitted (8-9)? Dante assuredly had not.

Virgil's association with Dante begins with his rather dry remarks at A 1.91; and again at A 2.43-45, after Dante's speech about not being Aeneas or Paul, he goes at once to the point: 'you are afraid' and need not be. He can be *più che padre*, tender and protective, but also severe in his rebukes as at A 7.70-71, 20.27 and 30.148, or strangely congratulatory, as with Filippo Argenti in A 8. But Virgil himself is also rebuked, by Cato (B 2.120 and 3.79), and by the lady at B 19.28, *fieramente*. He is also deceived by Malacoda (A 21. 109-111), earning a wry comment from Fra Catalano (A 23. 142-4), at which he strides off, in a huff (*turbato un poco d'ira*). He can also be astonished, as at A 23.124, when he sees Caiphas crucified (*crucifisso in terra con tre pali* 111), and is told that he gave the advice 'it is expedient that one man should die for the people' (*John*, XI.50). The reasons for this horror and dismay are much discussed, but without reference to *A.* V.815: *unum pro multis dabitur caput* ('one life shall be given for many'). Virgil cannot be surprised by all the too familiar Roman punishment, but he may be at his own anticipation of the gospel. There is humour too in the scene in B 21.100-136, when Statius says that he would accept another year of Purgatory to have lived when Virgil lived. Virgil gives Dante a look as if to say 'be quiet', but Dante smiles, as if winking, and Statius notices this.

Whitfield rightly draws attention to Virgil's surprisingly complete knowledge of the Christian faith in the *Comedy*. Certainly Dante brings his Virgil as close to Christianity as he can, and so this Virgil is nearer to Dante than the historical Virgil, poet of the *Aeneid*. But it is going too far to say that Dante speaks through Virgil 'with no regard for what Virgil had been', as Whitfield suggests. He does give him a 'reality separate from himself', when he loses him at B 30.45-51 so pathetically like Orpheus losing his Eurydice in *Georgics* IV. Virgil is aware that he cannot avail himself of his knowledge of God whom he did not know in his lifetime (A 1.131) but does, within the limits of Reason, as he says B 18.46-48, contrasting his reason with Beatrice's faith (the overinterpretation of this passage is one cause of the traditional allegorizing of Virgil and Beatrice). The recognition of Virgil as a rounded if inconsistent person is a quite recent advance in understanding, and goes back to de Sanctis (quoted by Consoli, *ED* V.1042):

> He, Dante, means to construct an allegory, and look, out comes poetry; he has personification in mind and from his pen emerges a person. Theology becomes Beatrice, Reason becomes Virgil; Man, in general, as it were Everyman, becomes Dante Alighieri, complete live beings with infinite aspects of their own that are independent of the concept of which they ought to be symbols.

Is it likely that so reflective and self-conscious an artist as Dante was unaware of what he was doing?

* * *

There are two passages of the *Aeneid* which Dante has dramatized. Before the appearance of the angel (A 9.64-106), Virgil has been thoroughly discomfited by the resistance of the devil at the gate of the City of Dis. He tries to reassure Dante (A 8.104-5) but, after his vain colloquy, he comes back downcast and sighing, with 'brow shorn of all confidence'. Virgil seems baffled by his repulse, not remembering what Dante remembers from *Aeneid* VI.553-6:

> porta adversa ingens solidoque adamante columnae,
> vis ut nulla virum, non ipsi exscindere bello
> caelicolae valeant: stat ferrea turris ad auras,
> Tisiphoneque . . .
>
> *In front, an enormous portal, the door-posts columns of adamant,*
> *So strong that no mortal violence nor even the heaven-dwellers*
> *Can broach it: an iron tower stands sheer and soaring above it,*
> *Whereupon Tisiphone sits . . .*

The gate of Hades and the attack of Titans and Giants on Heaven are familiar, but who besides Virgil imagined the gods attacking the City of Dis? I know of no other, nor it seems did Padoan, when he suggests (*Il pio Enea, l'empio Ulisse* 150) that the lines are the source of Dante's episode, 'a tacit polemic against the pagan master'. It is strange, however, that Virgil himself cites the victory of Heaven in the harrowing of Hell, and refers back to the inscription at the outer gate (A 3. 1-9) which he declines to explain to Dante, and at A 1.127 had expressly said that God rules everywhere (*In tutte parti impera e quivi regge*). Dante himself had come close to the dualism of an impregnable Hell when he doubted whether 'prime matter' was created by God (*Convivio* IV.1.8), and regarded the matter as the cause of individuality (*Convivio* III.6.6).

The second passage is Anchises' philosophical discourse at *Aeneid* VI.724-730, expressing the same neoplatonic dualism of spirit and matter, soul and body. The body, the prison of the soul, cause of all passions, fears, desires, griefs and pleasures, infects and dulls the fiery spirit. This passage is in the background of Virgil's two attempts to explain the nature of his 'aereal body'.

When the sun comes up at B 3.16 it reveals what the 'darkness visible' of Hell had concealed, that Dante casts a shadow but not Virgil. In alarm at being abandoned, Dante turns and 'his comfort', Virgil, reads his thought and explains, quoting his epitaph and his death at Brindisi from Donatus-Suetonius' *Life* (35-6) with apparent confidence: God provides 'similar bodies', capable of suffering pain, heat and cold, but does not wish to unveil to us *how* he does so (*come fa*, 33); but the 'how' of it is as far beyond our Reason as the infinite mystery of the Trinity; 'be content, mankind, with the fact' (*il quia*, 37); if complete knowledge had been permitted the Incarnation would not have been necessary. The fruitless desire to know is now an eternal grief to Aristotle and Plato and many others, and 'here he bowed his head, said no more, and remained in distress'. The use of Aristotelian scholastic language in *il quia* is to be noted. Dante tactfully makes no comment, but the question comes up again in B 25 when Dante sees aereal bodies emaciated by hunger. He hesitates, like a young stork trying to fly for the first time, but Virgil reads his mind: 'you have drawn your bow; shoot!' Dante begins with the forbidden word, 'how?', when no food is needed (20-21). Again Virgil begins confidently: 'your problem will be easy, if you recall *how* Meleager wasted away' and died when the firebrand, snatched from a fire at his birth, was burnt by his mother, Althaea, in revenge, causing his death 'at a distance'; and again, 'if you think *how*, when you start, your image starts in a mirror'. These are two examples of external causes 'not a rational argument', as Reggio notes; and the first, the external soul, is worse, being just magic.

But Virgil's confidence evaporates: *ecco qui Stazio*, 'to heal your wound'. To Virgil Statius excuses his presumption in explaining *la veduta etterna*, in Virgil's presence, and to Dante, 'his son', throws light precisely on the 'how' (*il come*, 36). This play on *come* is often missed by the commentators. Statius provides a basically Aristotelian account of human generation, from blood to plant to animal and the rational soul, carrying it, however, beyond Aristotle to the other world, but stopping short of the resurrection of the body. There can be no doubt that Statius rejects Anchises' dualism and Aeneas' comment on re-embodiment, (*quae lucis miseris tam dira cupido? Aeneid* VI.719-721). That Dante had shared Virgil's error can be shown by a single phrase in the *Comedy* when compared to one in the *Convivio*, namely A 10.58: *se per questo cieco / carcere vai per altezza d'ingegno* ('if you goest through this blind prison by height of genius'), the very words used by Virgil (*carcere caeco, Aeneid* VI.734), to describe the body, though Cavalcante is referring to Hell and is disembodied. In *Convivio* II.4.17 Dante says 'the eyes of the mind are closed so long as the soul is bound and imprisoned, *incarcerata*, by the organs of our body'; eternity and body are contraries.

Virgil also knows about the brighter bodies of the blessed, when he congratulates Cato, with a touch of envy as well as flattery, on *la vesta ch' al gran di sara si chiara* (B 1.75). But he seems unaware of the causes in the *Aeneid* of his failure in the *Comedy*; he is bewildered by the repressed impediment to his ability to avail himself of his Christian knowledge for salvation. This can help to explain his inconsistency when he complains of his relegation to Limbo, from A 1.125 onwards; 2.52, *sospesi* ('suspended'); 4.45 *sospesi* again; 4.31-42 Virgil's companions in Limbo 'did not sin', but they did not 'truly worship God' and 'for no other fault' 'they live in longing without hope'. In B 7 Virgil explains himself to Sordello at some length: he is damned only for lack of faith *per null' altro rio / lo ciel perdei che per non aver fé* (7-8) and again, *Non per far ma per non far ho perduto* (25) – but he then shows that he knows of the Fall and original sin, since he is with the innocent babes, dead before they were exempted by baptism from sin (*l'umana colpa*) and with those who, without the theological virtues followed the cardinal virtues (*sanza vizio / connobber l'altre e seguir tutte quante*). Thus Virgil is made to contradict himself within four lines.

Dante's plan demanded that his Virgil should reach the Earthly Paradise and no further, so that Beatrice could take over without leaving Dante unguided, and Virgil's two connected dualisms were sufficient excuse for not 'saving' him. The whole question of the salvation of pagans has been thoroughly and expertly discussed by Kenelm Foster, *The Two Dantes* (London 1977); in his earlier book, *God's Tree* (London 1967) 54, he had said that 'we may not on principle presume to know what Dante thought about the *real* Virgil's real fate'. Just so Dante is careful to see that his vision gave no information about anyone's destiny (C 13.130-142, 20. 133-135 and 21.97-99). He says this only in *Paradiso* in order not to undermine the impact of what he 'saw' in Hell and Purgatory, inexorable condemnations of aspects of his own past, shown to him for his salvation.

Dante did his best for Virgil and the others in Limbo, not within the limits of orthodoxy, but beyond them, by his bold liberal innovation of adding to the *Limbus Patrum* and *Limbus Puerorum* the *Limbus* of the magnanimous pagans. This got him into trouble: Guido da Pisa says 'here and in some other places he speaks poetically, not theologically' (Cioffari, 71); Boccaccio was troubled;[9] the Dominicans of

9. Boccaccio, *Sonnets*, 122-126, in *Tutte le Opere*, ed. Vittore Branca, discussed by Giorgio Padoan, *L'Ultima Opera di Giovanni Boccaccio*, 'Le esposizioni sopra il Dante' (Padua 1959) 10 and 59-60, and in his excellent edition of the *Esposizioni, Tutte le opere* VI (Verona 1965) xxi-xxii. Boccaccio at first thought he was doing a useful work in giving public lectures in Florence, but the strictures of a friend, probably a prelate, accused him of 'prostituting the Muse' by revealing poetry to the vulgar, and Boccaccio as a 'pre-humanist'

Florence in 1333 forbade the reading of *il Dante*, and a century later St Antonino, archbishop of Florence, roundly condemned Dante's conception (Solerti, 152-3). Dante even holds out hope of something better. Beatrice's praise of Virgil to God, promised at A 2.74, should not lack effect. His and the others' fame on earth acquires *grace* for them in Heaven (A 4.76-78). Virgil's Rhipeus, whose name suggests the blameless Hyperboreans (*Aeneid* II.339, 394 and 426-428), is found in Heaven, along with Trajan (C 20), and *grace* is mentioned three times (71, 118 and 122). *Deo aliter visum* indeed! Aeneas' bitter complaint is turned into wonder, *chi crederebbe?* (67), at God's grace in response to 'lively hope' (95, 108 and 109).

Dante makes the problem of the just pagans his own in his 'profound grief' (*gran duol me prese al cor*, A 4.42), and 'the insistent question' (C 19.69) is given an answer (*soave medicina*, C 20.41), that predestination is a mystery; and so Dante leaves Virgil to God's mercy. In *Monarchy* II.7.4-5 he had dismissed the question in his brisk way. Perhaps it arose insistently only when he planned to make Virgil, now *non omo, omo già fui*, so important in the *Comedy*.

* * *

The last scene in the long drama of Dante's encounters with Virgil came about outside the *Comedy* but in connection with it, in the last years of its composition. In 1319/20 Dante was in Ravenna, under the patronage of its *signore*, Guido Novello da Polenta, and received a letter from Guelph Bologna, the great international university city, written by Giovanni del Virgilio. The letter is in fifty-one Latin hexameters, more Horatian than Virgilian, though Giovanni calls himself a follower of Virgil (*vocalis verna Maronis*); it alludes to *Eclogues* VIII.55-6 and IX.36, and speaks of Virgil as Dante's guide in the *Comedy* inviting Dante to a sort of *tenzone* about Latin and Italian. He speaks admiringly of the *Comedy* and had read it at least to the end of *Purgatorio*.

confessed to the fault and folly, felt justly punished by his illness, and promised not to commit it again.

But he at once complains that Dante is throwing pearls before swine, writing in the vulgar tongue above the heads of the vulgar and providing nothing for the 'clerics' who despised the vernacular. He suggests themes for a traditional epic on a contemporary war, and promises Dante a wreath and a grand reception in the *gymnasia* of Bologna, and fame in all four regions of the world. He pretends already to hear Dante's *maius opus*, the Latin '*clangor* of Mars', and asks, as the goose to the swan, 'the Master' to reply.

Dante, who had referred to Virgil as the poet of the *Eclogues* (*cantor de li bucolici carmi*, B 22.57) to introduce Statius' tribute to *Eclogue* IV, now replied in a Virgilian pastoral, assuming rather ironically the mask of Tityrus and giving Meliboeus' mask to his friend, like him in exile from Florence, Dino Perini.[10] It is a lively narrative of his dialogue with Perini. When Perini asks about Mopsus' letter, Dante simply laughs and then, *posito vix denique risu*, explains in terms flattering to Mopsus as the devoted lover of poetry. But 'indignation' (38) from Juvenal, *Satires* 1.79, breaks out: he will wait until the *Comedy* is completed before assuming the crown of ivy and laurel, and then only in Florence, in lines equivalent to C 25.1-9. To convert Mopsus he suggests sending to him ten vessels of milk from his beloved ewe, probably ten cantos of *Paradiso* rather than ten *Eclogues* like Virgil's. On the whole Dante is not unkind in his lesson to del Virgilio on how to write a Virgilian poem, but he is ironical and gives no ground whatsoever on the main issue. It was no new issue but had been decided by Dante in *Convivio* I, despite his later writings in Latin, in his impassioned defence of Italian against Latin. The *Convivio* was to do for Italian what Cicero had done in his philosophical works for Latin against Greek (*Conv.* I.11.14, citing Cicero,

10. See G. Martellotti, 'La riscoperta dello stile bucolico (da Dante a Boccaccio)' in *Dante e la cultura Veneta* (Florence 1966) 335-346; Giorgio Padoan, 'Sulla presunta falsificazione della Egloghe Dantesche da parte del Boccaccio' in *Studi sul Boccaccio* (1964) II. 475-507, now also in *Il pio Enea, l'empio Ulisse* (Ravenna 1977) 223-251, with ample bibliographical references; Enzio Cecchini, 'Le egloghe' in *Dante: Opere Minori* (Milan-Naples 1979) 647-689; Giorgio Brugnoli and Riccardo Scardia, *Dante Alighieri: Le egloghe* (Milan-Naples 1980) introduction, bibliography, text, translation, and excellent notes.

de Finibus I.1). Now in the *Comedy*, with an even acuter sense of Italy's need of a common language as a step to unification, he would do for Italian poetry what Virgil had done for Latin, establish its language and style, not just the high tragic style, but mixing all three styles which Virgil had, in Mediaeval theory, exemplified separately as he advanced with apparent inevitability (*pascua rura duces*) from the *humilis stylus* of the *Eclogues* to the *mediocris* of *Georgics* and the *gravis* of the *Aeneid*, as shown in the diagrammatic form of the wheel (*Rota Virgilii*).

Giovanni, the 'pre-humanist', in touch with the Paduan circle of Lovato and Albertino Mussato, whose coronation as poet in 1315 for his Senecan tragedy *Ecerinis* is in the background of all talk of the poetic crown, was delighted with Dante's humanistic reply, and his answer in ninety-seven verses, carefully counted and reduplicated by Dante in his second *Eclogue*, contains only one or two pinpricks. He sets aside his 'greater pipes' and takes up 'the slimmer' (*tenues*, 31-2) to reply to Dante in kind, in the pastoral convention as Mopsus to Tityrus, but without any dialogue. 'If you despise me, I shall quench my thirst in the Phrygian Musone', a small stream near Padua, he says, almost certainly hinting at *Mussato*, to whom he later in 1325 wrote a Virgilian eclogue of two hundred and eighty lines.

Ironically Dante's Latin pastorals set off an immense effusion of them, especially in Italy, with Petrarch's twelve *Eclogues*, Boccaccio's sixteen, and their many followers in Italy and the European Renaissance. Petrarch got his crown on the Capitol in Rome for his Latin epic on Scipio, the *Africa*, unfinished though it was, and little read. Dante died too soon to receive his crown in Florence and how long, if he had lived, would Florence have taken before offering it? Why crown him again for whom St Peter himself had made a crown (C 25.12)? He was assured of his fame, and, as he says to his friend, Forese Donati (B 24.76-78):

> non so . . . quant' io mi viva;
> ma già non fia 'l tornar mio tantosto
> ch'io non sia col voler prima a la riva.

I know not how long I shall live; but truly my

return will not be so soon that in desire I shall not be sooner at the shore.

Note: This essay is an excerpt, made by the editor of this volume, with some adjustments, from a much longer study.

Virgil and Shakespeare*

A.D. NUTTALL

Most scholars now think that Shakespeare had read at least the earlier books of Virgil's *Aeneid* in Latin.[1] It is, to be sure, a field in which certainty is elusive. In 1767 Upton, Whalley, Dodd, Grey and others were trounced for believing in Shakespeare's classical learning by the formidable Richard Farmer, in his *Essay on the Learning of Shakespeare*. But Farmer's richly informed scepticism was largely founded on a negative dogma, namely that the availability of a translation precludes reference to the original. Edmond Malone, despite an almost abject deference to Farmer,[2] argued persuasively for Shakespeare's basic competence in Latin.[3] In our own century J.A.K. Thomson in his *Shakespeare and the Classics* (London 1952) is a sort of surviving Farmerian, obstinately unimpressed by T.W. Baldwin's elaborate defence of Shakespeare's 'small Latine'. Indeed, proof in such matters may be impossible. Shakespeare actually quotes Virgil in the original language at *2 Henry VI,* II. 1.24, but the quotation could easily have been supplied by a friend. In *Titus Andronicus*, V.3, Marcus tells the story of Sinon and the Wooden Horse from *Aeneid* II, and at line 86 speaks of 'the fatal engine'. The echo of Virgil's *fatalis machina* (*Aeneid* II.237) seems inescapable, but in Peele's *Tale of Troy* (1589) we find a

* References to Shakespeare are to Peter Alexander's edition of *The Complete Works* (London 1951).

1. See especially T.W. Baldwin, *William Shakspere's Small Latine and Lesse Greeke*, 2 vols (Urbana, Illinois 1944); Virgil K. Whitaker, *Shakespeare's Use of Learning: An Inquiry into the Growth of his Mind and Art* (San Marino, California 1953); Percy Simpson, 'Shakespeare's Use of Latin Authors' in *Studies in Elizabethan Drama* (Oxford 1955) 1-63; Glynne Wickham, General Introduction to *The London Shakespeare*, ed. John Monro, 6 vols (London 1955) I xvi-xvii; John W. Velz, *Shakespeare and the Classical Tradition: a Critical Guide to Commentary, 1660-1960* (Minneapolis 1968).

2. Letter to R. Farmer (London 1792) 7; this is available in facsimile, bound in one vol. with J. Ritson, *Cursory Criticisms on the Edition of Shakespeare published by Edmond Malone* (London 1969).

3. See his *Life of William Shakspeare,* in *The Plays and Poems of William Shakspeare*, 21 vols (London 1821) II esp. 103-5.

string of parallels, including the word 'fatal'.[4] Even Baldwin can find himself pulled up from behind, so to speak, by Farmer. Commenting on *The Tempest*, IV.1.102, 'Great Juno comes; I know her by her gait', Baldwin invokes the classical sources, including *Aeneid* I.405 (*et vera incessu patuit dea*) and then remembers Farmer's demonstration (*op.cit.* 19 f.) that the idea was commonplace.[5]

But the cumulative case for real acquaintance with Virgil's Latin is strong. The Principal *loci* are the Trojan painting in *Lucrece*, 1366-1526 (cf. *Aeneid* I.455-93 and II.13-267),[6] the account of Aegeon's travels in *The Comedy of Errors*, I.1 especially 28-32 (cf. *Aeneid* II.3), the player's speech about Priam in *Hamlet*, II.2.446-513 (cf. *Aeneid* II.506 ff.) and Hamlet's mistake over the 'Hyrcanian beast' at II.2.444 (*Aeneid* IV.367 mingles for a moment with his memory of *Aeneid* II),[7] the references in *The Tempest* to the storm, the supernatural preservation of the mariners and the ship, harpies, Dido and Iris, together with Ferdinand's greeting of Miranda (in order, I.1; V.1.221-5; III.3.52; II.1.73-95; IV.1. 75-83; I.2.421-7, to be compared, respectively, with *Aeneid* I.89-91; I.390-1 and 399-400; III.225-8; I.343-52; IV.700-2; I.327-34).[8] Beyond these lie dozens of more or less possible references. Between the lists compiled by R.K. Root in his *Classical Mythology in Shakespeare* (New York 1903) and Baldwin's demonstration that Shakespeare's phrasing in Virgilian passages is sometimes closer to the glosses provided in Cooper's *Thesaurus* (the standard Latin dictionary of the time) than to Phaer's translation, a credible case has certainly been made.

4. See note *ad loc.* in the New Arden ed. of *Titus Andronicus* by J.C. Maxwell (London 1953).

5. *William Shakspere's Small Latine and Lesse Greeke*, vol. II 481.

6. See note *ad loc.* in the New Arden ed. of the *Poems* of Shakespeare by F.T. Prince (London 1960).

7. See Sir John Sheppard (J.T. Sheppard). 'Shakespeare's Small Latin', *The Rice Institute Pamphlet* (Houston, Texas) 44.3 (1957) 70-86, esp. 85.

8. See J.M. Nosworthy, 'The Narrative Sources of *The Tempest*', *Review of English Studies* 24 (1948) 281-94. R.S. Conway gives a list of possible echoes of Virgil in 'The Classical Elements in Shakespeare's *Tempest*', in *New Studies of a Great Inheritance* (London 1921) 165-89.

But none of this is the real business of the present essay, which is with resemblance, not influence. In Castiglione's *Book of the Courtier* the Count says 'yf we wyll folow them of olde tyme, we shall not folowe them'.[9] The mere fact of close imitation differentiates imitator and model for the simple reason that the model was not, in that way at least, imitative. We see the *distinctiveness* of Virgil most vividly when we watch him treading in the steps of Homer. With Shakespeare's allusions to Virgil the point is stronger still, since they are far less integral to the fabric of his work than Homer is to Virgil's. These passages, above all, are of their time: mannered, ornamental, clever – manifestly poetry of the English Renaissance. Shakespeare is seldom less Virgilian than when he is citing him. The question posed in this essay is thus a very different one: where is Shakespeare really most like Virgil? In each poet we find an immense act of historical imagination; Virgil's is his *Aeneid*, Shakespeare's his English Histories. Let us begin with a place in the *Aeneid* which Shakespeare the schoolboy probably never reached (for the stream of allusions dries up at Book VI).

In the eighth book of Virgil's *Aeneid* Aeneas comes to the site of Rome. The city in which he was born and grew up, Troy, was burned by the Greeks. Ever since, Aeneas has been sailing the seas with his beaten, dispossessed company, following a tenuous skein of ambiguous hints and beckonings from the gods, until he comes at last to Italy, the land anciently his yet unfamiliar, unrecognised. The ships move up a green, silent river, which, as Virgil's original audience must have realised with growing excitement, is the Tiber (Aeneas is approaching closer and closer to the place where they now sit, listening to the greatest Roman poet) and comes to a sort of village in the forest, ruled by the Arcadian King, Evander. Everything is very quiet. And then Evander and Aeneas do something which does not happen very often in ancient literature: they go for a walk, at the precise latitude and longitude where, in Virgil's own time, so many hundreds of years later, vast amphitheatres will stand, and baths, paved squares and streets. But the two strollers see only hills, trees and

9. Sir Thomas Hoby's translation (1561), ed. Walter Raleigh, (London 1900) 69.

cattle. The vast urban shapes of imperial Rome exist only in the more immediate memory of the listener and, as Virgil lets fall the familiar names, the later Capitol and Tarpeian House are superimposed on the pastoral scene before us like a sort of ghostly filter. But then something strange happens. Aeneas himself actually sees, rising from the foliage, huge, shattered buildings, great arches and walls. What he is in fact looking at is the ruins of the ancient Saturnian city. And so the ghosts of past and future momentarily coalesce, so to speak, and an effect of uncanny reverberation is produced.

Perhaps the strangest thing of all about this reverberation is the way it will not be silenced; its echoes continue, beyond the world of the poem, to Virgil's own world and then most strangely, even beyond that. Virgil's poem is a celebration of the rise of the Roman Empire, of the rule of law, peace and civility. Many hundreds of years later, in the eighteenth century, the English historian Gibbon wrote his great work on the decline and fall of that same Empire, on the terrible paradox of history whereby the rational, the just and the strong were defeated by ignorance and darkness. Gibbon tells us in his *Memoirs* how the idea of writing this story 'started to his mind'.[10] He was, he says, sitting in the ruins of the Capitol as the bare-foot friars were singing Vespers in the Temple of Jupiter Capitoline (thus Gibbon; the friars themselves would have called it the Church of Araceli) when the thought came. One can picture the scene (memories of the etchings of Piranesi may help). The eighteenth century Capitol, cattle wandering, grass and trees growing everywhere among and over the gigantic ruins of a former age, vast arches shattered and curtailed, which only a learned imagination could now complete in the air, the deep radiance of the Italian autumnal sun and – and here a gust of indignation must have passed through Gibbon – the friars creeping insect-like among the ruins, symbols of what Gibbon himself called 'the triumph of barbarism and religion'.[11] But – all around – vast crumbling images of a lost architectural splendour. What Gibbon was looking at, so long after, and what Aeneas

10. *The Memoirs of the Life of Edward Gibbon . . . by Himself*, ed. G. Birkbeck Hill (London 1900) 167.

11. *The History of the Decline and Fall of the Roman Empire*, ed. J.B. Bury, 7 vols (London 1896-1900) vol. VII.308.

gazed on, so long before, are the same.

Thus a system of echoes set up within the poem extends itself far beyond the poem and far beyond the poet himself – not, of course, foreseen by Virgil yet essentially a product of the thing he made. Aeneas at the site of Rome is not the only example of this kind of reverberation. Virgil's Dido, the Carthaginian Queen, who keeps Aeneas from his mission, prefigures the historical Cleopatra, who in turn appears in Shakespeare's *Antony and Cleopatra*. Aeneas, while he lingers, strangely paralysed and un-manned by his love, dressed by her in oriental garments, recalls the figure of Hercules in womanish attire in the house of Omphale, and then (beyond the poem) Antony in Shakespeare's Egyptian court – we may remember Cleopatra's words (*Antony and Cleopatra*, II.5.22-3):

> Then put my tires and mantles on him, whilst
> I wore his sword Philippan.

And further off still is the figure of another hero subdued by a woman, Samson. The whole is summed up in the older meaning of the word 'effeminate', that is 'overcome by a woman, or women'. Thus Samson was called the most effeminate of men, and in Caxton's translation of the *Aeneid* the word 'effeminate' is used of Aeneas himself, to translate Virgil's *uxorius*, transmitted through the French of the *livre des eneydes*, at IV.266.[12]

This reverberation, begun by Virgil and extended by the history of Western culture, is constantly present as we read the *Aeneid*. We may account for it in part by explaining that Virgil is the first great poet of what has been called the typological imagination. That is, like the mediaeval interpreters of the Bible (though of course with much less ostentation of system) he habitually saw things as analogous to one another, all things implicit in all other things: Aeneas was a kind of Augustus, Augustus a second Aeneas, Troy a pre-echoing of Rome, Rome a second Troy. Notice, further, that the discernment of analogies is not, in Virgil, an idle or an arbitrary exercise. There are central points, or nodes, which

12. *Caxton's Eneydos*, 1409, ed. W. (or rather M.) T. Culley and F.J. Furnivall (London 1890) ch. XVI 63.

are seen as being objectively of immense historical importance. And Virgil's power of identifying these points was very sure. If there are turning points in history, the principate of Augustus is surely such a turning point. Rome really is the city of which all other cities are in some sense imitations. In this the *Aeneid* differs fundamentally from the epics of archaic Greece, the *Iliad* and the *Odyssey*. There the narrative is utterly stark: Achilles is himself alone, and the death of Hector is only a dreadful fact in an unsympathising world. But Virgil's task was to celebrate the Empire, while, *at the same time* working from the Homeric legend, the matter of Troy. From this dilemma, perhaps, the Virgilian method sprang: *idem in alio*, the poem of individual heroic achievement in which all future history is *implicit*. In this way (and this is the point to which I have been working) Virgil became the great poet of *Time*. But can we also say that he is the first poet of *history*?

History, it is often said, is not history unless it rises above mere chronicle. The book which merely recounts series of events, 'and then and then' and so on, is not yet history though it may well provide the material of history. For, it is said, the historian is interested not so much in the mere succession of events as in their significance. Virgil, as we have seen, found significances everywhere, and so, if history is chronicle plus significance, Virgil must be called the historian poet.

Yet something is wrong. I can sum up what is wrong by saying that the typological imagination is interested in sameness while the historical imagination is interested in difference. To see Aeneas as a kind of forerunner of Augustus – that certainly will immediately attract the attention of the historian; but to see him as a cosmic pre-echoing, so that the reader experiences a *frisson* at the work of fate – this, surely, is antipathetic to the historian, who must always swiftly follow up his intuitions of similarity with a demonstration of the differences. I am not saying that the historian has no need of those fundamental intuitions of identity; to put the matter at its lowest, deprive the historian of analogy and you cut off his right arm. But the unifying impulse must be held in check by an unsleeping vigilance, a critical interest in *differentiae*; and this, it might be said, is missing from the endlessly rich Virgilian world of images, types and anologues.

And so we revise our description of the historian: he is a man who is interested in the way things change, in radical transformation. It is surely a consequence of this drive to find always the most fundamental *locus* of change that has in recent years drawn the best efforts of historians away from the outer world and towards the inner world, or, to put it simply, from battles to minds. More and more historians have come to be absorbed by ways in which the human heart is transformed. Indeed things have now come to the point where the man who affirms that the human heart at all times and in all places is the same brands himself as unhistorical. The conventional wisdom which tells us that, say, falling in love in thirteenth century Paris and falling in love in nineteenth century London are exactly the same then comes under heavy attack. Men do not just fight fresh battles, enact fresh laws; they become different in themselves.

C.S. Lewis explained the matter as it appears to the historian of literature thus:

> How are these gulfs between the ages to be dealt with by the student of poetry? A method often recommended may be called the method of the Unchanging Human Heart. According to this method the things which separate one age from another are superficial. Just as, if we stripped the armour off a medieval knight or the lace off a Caroline courtier, we should find beneath them an anatomy identical with our own, so, it is held, if we strip off from Virgil his Roman imperialism, from Sidney his code of honour, from Lucretius his Epicurean philosophy, and from all who have it their religion, we shall find the Unchanging Human Heart, and on this we are to concentrate. I held this theory myself for many years, but I have now abandoned it. I continue, of course, to admit that if you remove from people the things that make them different, what is left must be the same, and that the Human Heart will certainly appear as Unchanging if you ignore its changes. But I have come to doubt whether this study of this mere L.C.M. is the best end the

student of old poetry can set before himself.[13]

Lewis thinks of the poets as *exemplifying* change, not as fellow analysts of change, fellow historians. And this surely is reasonable. Yet I, a moment ago, seemed to be requiring exactly that sophistication from Virgil, asking that he, in the 1st century B.C., should know the historical changes of the human heart.

But what has happened to my argument? I have tried to show that the sort of significance Virgil uses has an anti-historical bias, a mystical tendency to assert identity at the expense of difference. And yet at the same time I assert that Virgil had this supposedly modern intuition that consciousness itself can be transformed. The answer is that this special intuition exists in the poem quite independently of the system of typological correspondences, as a sort of ground-swell, working from below. It is often said, I know, that the idea of an historically evolving consciousness is not found before Scott. He, surely, was the great originator, with his ageing Jacobites, pressing their obsolete codes of honour, adrift in an alien age. Yet I say again, Virgil knew. And, I add, Shakespeare knew as well. I do not say that either poet was *accurate* in his psychological history, only that both have some conception of what psychological history might be; neither could say, I suppose, what precise change in human consciousness was going forward at a given date, but both knew (and this is sufficiently remarkable) that such changes do occur.

* * *

Virgil's Aeneas is a post-heroic man. The earlier heroes of Homer are men of superlative energy and splendour. The world in which they kill and are killed is without meaning – or to turn the coin over – they themselves are without conscience. Long term responsibility, commitment, contrition do not figure in their lives. In the whole of the *Iliad* no military leader ever pauses to consider the responsibility he carries

13. *A Preface to Paradise Lost* (London 1942) 61-2.

prospectively, as a burden of office. One cannot imagine a Homeric hero with a *mission*. We know that when Odysseus regains his home his rule will be prosperous, magnanimous and peaceful (*Odyssey* XXIV.482-6) and the suitors, if they are not punished for their sins, are at least taught that they should not wrong an *agathos*, one better (greater) than they (*Odyssey* XXIV.455-60). But no one could say that Odysseus's mission is to bring justice, peace and civility to Ithaca. He just wants to get home. But for Aeneas home-coming itself assumes the partly mystical character of a mission. The world of Homer is certainly not destitute of personal affection or social obligation. Husbands and wives, parents and children, comrades in arms love one another and the laws of hospitality are respected. But the reference of all this is curiously immediate and limited.

But Virgil's Aeneas is gradually educated in all the remoter obligations. At first, in burning Troy, he is Homeric man, fighting mindlessly. But the gods teach him to turn from the battle, to take his aged father Anchises on his shoulders, his little son Iulus following, to look for a new city. As we read on, the image of the hero, mysteriously deflected from the fighting, burdened, assumes a symbolic importance. Aeneas is burdened with a past and a future, with such strange novelties as moral responsibility. And for all this there is, we find, a terrible price to pay – hardly less in fact than the extinction of his spontaneous human energies. The crucial relationships for him now are the linear ones – ancestors, father, son, descendants – the lateral relation of erotic love can only be a threat to his mission. Dido, like war, is a distraction.

Such a man can easily appear contemptible. Aeneas struggling to explain his departure to Dido, hanging back and dithering on the edge of combat, will always affront our more superficial sympathies. Achilles in his cruelty somehow leaves a cleaner taste. Yet the pain surrounding the strangely impeded figure of Aeneas, physically experienced by this reader as a kind of thick sensation in the throat, implies nothing less than the creation by Virgil of a truly moral world. The old world and the new have not the same consciousness. The tragic significance of the *Aeneid* is that innocence and virtue find themselves opposed.

* * *

I mentioned just now a certain sensation in the throat. Only one character in the *Aeneid* produces this in me, and only one in Shakespeare. The Shakespearean character is Prince Hal in the *Henry IV* plays and *Henry V*. But first let us recall Hal's situation. Like Aeneas, he is a late-born man, delivered over to a world which has lost its freshness. Hal's father, Henry IV, obtained his crown by deposing Richard II. Richard, though in many ways fairly repellent, was the true anointed king, God's regent on Earth. This fact alone has power to irradiate the England of the play *Richard II*. The dying Gaunt rebukes the king for his betrayal of the realm, yet throughout the speech (save for a single phrase) the praise of England remains in the present tense. The England of the usurper Henry, lacking its point of intersection with the divine order, is greyer, less definite, less heraldic. War is seen less in terms of its high intelligible crises and more in terms of sheer mess – 'bloody noses and cracked crowns . . . I never did see such pitiful rascals . . . tut, tut, good enough to toss, food for powder, food for powder, they'll fill a pit as well as better. Tush, man, mortal men, mortal men . . . There's not three of my hundred and fifty left alive, and they are for the town's end to beg during life' (in order, II.3.93, IV.2.66 f, V.3.37 f).

Like the *Aeneid* with its *tot labores, tantae molis* (I.10, 33), the first part of *Henry IV* opens with an overwhelming impression of weariness, of more to do than can be done – 'so shaken as we are, so wan with care . . .' *Richard II* was about the fall of a king, but it was a true king that fell, and this gives the drama a unified spectacular tragic structure. With the two loosely joined parts of *Henry IV* we get a cooler dramatic technique, inclining more to piecemeal explanation and an agnostic pluralism. In both *Richard II* and *Henry IV* we find scenes of meditation on the idea of England, but how different! In *Richard II*, we have a tiny jewelled allegory, in which two unnamed gardeners, in measured verse, liken the conduct of a kingdom to their own simple art. All is structured, everywhere is correspondence and analogy, all thoughts begun are concluded. But in *Henry IV* we have instead the Gloucestershire scenes, where Falstaff, Shallow and – name of names – Master Silence ramble on together in the orchard of Shallow's ramshackle farm. These scenes are naturalistic, full of inconsequential remarks, of voices tailing away into nothingness, of memories, of mundane queries about such things as the present price of bullocks, of a sense of imminent death. In the absence of conclusive structures we are given instead an atmosphere compounded of last year's apples, the grey heads of old men, of sweetness and barrenness, and of futility.

This is the non-kingdom which Hal is to inherit from his father, the non-king Henry. Somehow he must unify the kingdom, make the crown real again. This I think is the key to Hal's character. He has a mission (and there can be no doubt that it is a fully moral mission – unless the country is unified the blood and suffering will be endless). He dedicates himself utterly to the mission, and, in its service, to a strange plan. He needs, on his inheritance, to seize the initiative, and for this he needs an element of spectacular surprise. In fact, the people must be surprised (I use the word in its etymological sense – 'taken unawares') by majesty. But if majesty is to surprise it must be preceded by its opposite – ignominy, irresponsibility. And so the bizarre logic of the situation tells Hal that he must humiliate himself in preparation for his sudden blaze. He must appear to neglect his royal responsibilities, must fritter his time away in vicious idleness, with criminals and drunks, until the moment comes. Like Kim Philby in our own time he has proposed to himself a life of systematic duplicity; a life of endless conviviality in which he is to have no friend, no possibility of ordinary candour.

I have said that the mission of Aeneas involved the extinction of his humanity. The process there is relatively slow. He fights in burning Troy, he falls fully in love with Dido. But he is plucked from her by the gods and must visit his dead father Anchises in the Underworld, the figure of authority, of Time Past pointing to Time Future, before he can return to his mission, now unhesitating, unswerving, almost inhuman. We can see at once why Virgil sent his hero back to his father, but why to the world of the dead? – unless Aeneas must in a manner die himself for Roman life. With Hal too the mission involves the extinction of personal humanity. Hal, likewise, is brought back – not indeed to a dead but to a dying father. But now the Shakespearean twist: Hal's chosen life is partly for his father's sake but it cuts him off from his father at the most important time.

I propose to go over this episode in some detail. I will give a warning before I start. A certain thing happens in the scene, and then, a little later a character under enormous emotional pressure gives an account of what happened.

In *2 Henry IV*, Act 4, Scene 4, the King lies in the palace of Westminster. There is talk of Prince Hal, his way of life, of the fact that at this of all times no one knows where he is. Then Westmoreland enters with good news, the rebellion is over. The king cries out (91-3):

> O Westmoreland, thou art a summer bird,
> Which ever in the haunch of winter sings
> The lifting up of day

But the shock of the good news is too much and the king faints. Then, on reviving a little, he asks to be conveyed to an inner part of the room and that the crown be put beside him. Here, in Peter Alexander's text, we move to Scene 5. And now, out of step and out of time, Prince Hal suddenly enters, talking in too loud a voice, for which he is politely rebuked by Warwick. The Prince moderates his voice and says that he will sit beside the now sleeping king. The rest all withdraw. Then the Prince's eyes fall on the crown, and he speaks (IV.5.21-47):

> Why doth the crown lie there upon his pillow,
> Being so troublesome a bedfellow?
> O polish'd perturbation! golden care!
> That keep'st the ports of slumber open wide
> To many a watchful night! Sleep with it now!
> Yet not so sound and half so deeply sweet
> As he whose brow with homely biggen bound
> Snores out the watch of night. O majesty!
> When thou dost pinch thy bearer, thou dost sit
> Like a rich armour worn in heat of day
> That scald'st with safety. By his gates of breath

There lies a downy feather which stirs not.
Did he suspire, that light and weightless down
Perforce must move. My gracious lord! my father!
This sleep is sound indeed; this is a sleep
That from this golden rigol hath divorc'd
So many English kings. Thy due from me
Is tears and heavy sorrows of the blood
Which nature, love, and filial tenderness,
Shall, O dear father, pay thee plenteously.
My due from thee is this imperial crown,
Which, as immediate from thy place and blood,
Derives itself to me.
(Putting on crown)
Lo where it sits –
Which God shall guard; and put the world's whole strength
Into one giant arm, it shall not force
This lineal honour from me. This from thee
Will I to mine leave as 'tis left to me.
(Exit)

But the king is not dead. Again he revives, to find himself alone. He calls for Warwick and the rest. Where is the Prince? and then, a moment later *Where is the crown?* (60-62):

The Prince hath ta'en it hence. Go seek him out.
Is he so hasty that he doth suppose
My sleep my death?

Then Warwick returns to say that he found the Prince weeping in the next room and that he is coming at once. The Prince enters and the king orders all the rest to leave. Hal speaks first (92-94):

Hal: I never thought to hear you speak again.
King: Thy wish was father, Harry, to that thought.
I stay too long by thee, I weary thee.

Then follows the great speech of censure, every line of which falls like a blow. And then the Prince must answer (139-169):

O pardon me, my liege! . . .
God witness with me, when I here came in . . .
Coming to look on you, thinking you dead –

And dead almost, my liege, to think you were –
I spake unto this crown as having sense,
And thus upbraided it: 'The care on thee depending
Hath fed upon the body of my father;
Therefore thou best of gold art worst of gold.
Other, less fine in carat, is more precious,
Preserving life in med'cine potable;
But thou, most fine, most honour'd, most renown'd,
Hast eat thy bearer up'. Thus, my most royal liege,
Accusing it, I put it on my head,
To try with it – as with an enemy
That had before my face murd'red my father –
The quarrel of a true inheritor.

Here if you like comes the thick feeling in the throat of which I spoke. For the most terrible thing about that scene is that Hal – in the most venial way – lies. He did *not* address the crown as an enemy, nor was it in that spirit that he took up the crown in his hands. Shakespeare, I think, does not want us to make any mistake about this, for he shows us the two things in succession, first the taking up of the crown, and then the Prince's account of it under pressure. We know that when the Prince found his father dead he experienced two great emotions one after the other; first real (and immense) grief for his father, and then a quite different feeling: 'Now it has come. Now I am the king'. In the story he tells his father he changes things, so that his thoughts are of Henry throughout.

Yet we can hardly say that we have 'seen through' Hal, discovered the cold ambition that lies beneath. Shakespeare refuses to make it so easy for us. What we have seen, and what the Prince has dissembled is, precisely, *not* ambition but dedication. This is merely the worst of his ordeals. There is a fierce irony in the fact that this was the prince with the common touch, the easy manner with all sorts and conditions, for no character in Shakespeare is so utterly alone.

* * *

But now I have assembled my material and must return to

my original question: is there, then, in *Henry IV* that pitch of historical genius which sees not only the changing fortune of war and constitutions but the subtler transformations of culture and consciousness? I have noted, at the level of dramatic technique, the contrast between the England of *Richard II* and the England of *Henry IV*. While the anointed king was still on the throne, the country itself seemed still partly taken up with the supernatural. Parables, allegories, Eden, Paradise naturally express the character of this island in the older play. But the England of the Usurper has been abandoned to the bleak natural order.

In all this the notion of a possible historical change of consciousness is, I confess, at best only implicit. However, Shakespeare sets his Hal against Hotspur; Virgil sets his Aeneas against Turnus, and in these figures both poets make the notion fully explicit. Hotspur is certainly more culturally primitive than Hal. His energy is half-divine, and his language breathes a freshness which no one else in the play can match. Hal looks at him with a kind of envy – the moral world in which he moves is so simple. Sir Francis Bacon once wrote *antiquitas saeculi iuventus mundi.*[14] He was arguing (as it happens) for the moderns against the ancients, and brilliantly turned the tables by saying 'If it is age you like, then you should read the moderns, so much has happened, so much has been learned, that we are far older then they, who lived in the world's infancy'. So Hotspur, who is the old order, is above all young. When he receives his death wound from Hal he cries (*1 Henry IV*, V.4.36)

> O Harry, thou hast robb'd me of my youth!

Responsibility, prudence, caution, strategy, these at first mean nothing to him. Honour is his watch-word. The king wishes his son were like this, but if he had been it would have been disastrous. Only at the end, when his last battle is impending, does Hotspur begin to think (the measured, bitter reply to Blunt in IV.3 brings the change of style which marks the change of heart). Shakespeare brilliantly makes him wish (V.2.48) that only he and Hal might fight that day. Here

14. *Of the Advancement of Learning*, Book I, in *The Philosophical Works of Francis Bacon*, ed. J.M. Robertson (London 1905) 58.

Hotspur's impetuosity is fused for a moment with pity for the other victims of war. But impetuous he remains. At the end of V.2 he will not stay to read the letters brought by the messenger.

Turnus runs closely parallel to this. He is the dazzling opponent of Aeneas in the Latin Wars which occupy the closing section of the *Aeneid* and is killed by Aeneas in the last book. He belongs to the green world to be remolded by Aeneas to a civic, legal ideal, and at the same time he is an archaic Homeric warrior. As with Homer's heroes, long term policy or the future of the race plays no part in his thoughts; in the end he asks only to be allowed to barter death for glory (*letumque sinas pro laude pacisci, Aeneid* XII.49). The very language of Turnus resembles Hotspur's in its helter-skelter impulsiveness (so far, that is, as the decorum of the Latin hexameter permits). At one point in the battle Juno makes a phantom Aeneas, and Turnus is drawn in pursuit of the taunting, jeering shadow away from the fighting; at last he realises he has been tricked and bursts out in a sort of frenzy of wounded honour (*Aeneid* X.675-678):

> . . . quid ago? aut quae iam satis ima dehiscat
> terra mihi? vos o potius miserescite, venti;
> in rupes, in saxa (volens vos Turnus adoro)
> ferte ratem saevisque vadis immittite syrtis . . .
>
> *What am I doing?*
> *What gulf, what chasm, is deep enough to hide me?*
> *Pity me, winds; dash this accursed vessel*
> *On rocks, on reefs, on any savage quicksands.*
> (tr. Rolfe Humphries)

Somehow, though the mood is different, this extremism is akin to Hotspur's when he speaks of honour (*1 Henry IV*, I.3.201-205):

> By heaven, methinks it were an easy leap,
> To pluck bright honour from the pale-fac'd moon;
> Or dive into the bottom of the deep,
> Where fathom-line could never touch the ground,
> And pluck up drowned honour by the locks . . .

I have observed that with both Aeneas and Hal the most

important relationships are the lineal ones – in Hal's case, that with his father, and in Aeneas's with both father (Anchises) and son (Iulus). But of course Aeneas's pursuit of flying Italy is crucially interrupted by Dido, queen of Carthage. Brooks Otis in his admirable book has noticed how subtly the poet manages this great movement of distraction from the main impulse of the poem. Aeneas is lost and baffled, looking for Rome yet with the image of lost Troy still dominant in his consciousness. Anchises, his father, who constantly held him to his course, has died. Then after shipwreck, he meets Dido, whose situation strangely mirrors his own. She too has lost the person who guided her, in her case her husband Sychaeus; she too has had to flee and is now founding a great city. Again we have a strange Virgilian coalescence of images of the city and Aeneas can forget his destiny in present happiness. Meanwhile Cupid, to forge the love between them, assumes the infinitely ironic form of the lineal son, Iulus. But Aeneas must kill Dido just as, later, he must kill Turnus. The image of the stricken deer is applied, in simile, to Dido and when the Latin wars begin they stem from another stricken deer, killed this time by Iulus.

But here, it will be said, my analogy breaks down. Hal has no Dido, no mirror-love to tear him from his purpose; in the sequence from the first part of *Henry IV* to *Henry V* we have no tragic queen who dies of a broken heart.

Yet someone (if we can believe Pistol in *Henry V* – and I think we can) lay dying with a heart 'fracted and corroborate' (II.1.121). We have come to the place where my analogy with Virgil is indeed broken by an explosion of genius, yet at the same time in a manner sustained. We have come to Falstaff. For Shakespeare has chosen to give us something hilarious, a Dido in the form of an Anchises. The great distracting love of *Henry V* is an old man – and he drinks. Moreover there is in Falstaff a kind of mirroring, but this time, as I have implied, it is the father who is mirrored, the figure of authority in the figure of misrule.

Auden has remarked that if you look at Hal's associates in his wild first career, it is all very *odd.*[15] What sort of person would you expect to find in company with a young prince

15. *The Dyer's Hand and Other Essays* (London 1963) 183.

out on the tiles? Presumably every generation has its own term for the answer to this question: young blades, mashers, Bright Young Things, the Beautiful People, Jet-setters. But what do we find? Well, admittedly there is one who may be young, Poins – but then the stage is filled by the most extraordinary bunch of seedy old has-beens, in chief an aging, obese alcoholic, and with him various strutting scare-crows from that strange Shakespearean underworld of discharged officers and decayed soldiers, and various superannuated prostitutes. Why?

The answer is not I think to be given in terms of psychological probability. It is thematic. It is Falstaff that Shakespeare needs and he needs him first of all as a kind of parody father-figure. The thing first hits one visually – the grey-haired physically disgraced old man and the superb youngster. Then the point is brought home by a brilliant comedy routine in which Falstaff plays the part of Henry admonishing his errant son.

In this tableau the stereotype of the generation gap is reversed. Instead of the drop-out son and the stern father figure, it is Falstaff who is a sort of aged hippy – fundamentally uncontrolled, given over to the pleasure principle – certainly a drop-out from practical society, with his particular drug (alcohol), contempt for legal and other conventions, with his own lyrical mode of speech. And meanwhile Hal's, we gradually learn, is a rigidly controlled psychology, dedicated to effective government and the subordination of personal pleasure to political ends.

When Falstaff plays Henry the fun is uproarious but by the end (we may be only half aware of this) Falstaff finds himself pleading for the love of Hal (*1 Henry IV*, II.4.456-63):

> but, for sweet Jack Falstaff, kind Jack Falstaff, true Jack Falstaff, valiant Jack Falstaff – and therefore more valiant, being, as he is, old Jack Falstaff – banish not him thy Harry's company, banish not him thy Harry's company. Banish plump Jack, and banish all the world.

The laugh is killed – 'valiant Jack Falstaff' raises a smile but 'more valiant, being, as he is old Jack Falstaff' silences us with truth.

And the Prince answers, from a mask-like face: 'I do, I

will'. It is all out, Falstaff has been told that he has not, can never have the Prince's love. Hal is inside out. Instead of concealing his human features beneath a stiff impersonal mask, he wears the golden mask of kingship beneath an ordinary smiling human face.

With Falstaff Shakespeare's history indeed begins to break free of the comparison with Virgil's. I think the basic reason is that the effect of Falstaff is to make our vision of historical process at once larger and more sceptical than anything to be found in the *Aeneid*. Virgil's account of the divine mission of Aeneas is not of course univocal. Some scepticism there is. Yet it remains essentially inarticulate, a sort of remote singing of the imagery – green places defiled with blood, the man from the world of the dead against the living and the young, wild creatures maimed, pastoral wrecked. But in Shakespeare the political scepticism is intense and fully present to consciousness. Falstaff teaches us the way.

I have said that in the exchanges of Falstaff and Hal the stereotype of wild son and authoritarian father is reversed. Falstaff is that other kind of archetypal old man which derives, by a kind of creative mis-reading, from Paul's *vetus homo*, the old man we must put off in order to put on the new, the old Adam, the unregenerate, the happy inhabitant of Arcadia but excluded from the New Jerusalem.[16] But what now of Hal's own father? Surely there the stereotype is straightforwardly maintained.

Actually it cannot be, and this we learn largely from the insistent parody of the Falstaff figure. Falstaff cannot be a figure of authority because he is a criminal. But what if the king himself is a criminal? This is a subversive idea, and there is no doubt that it is present in the play. The dubiousness of the king's right to rule is morally fundamental. Hal knows that it is dubious, and that all his dedication hinges on the

16. See *Romans* VI.6; *Ephesians* IV.22; *Colossians* III.9. Robert P. Miller gives examples of 'the creative misreading' from Alanus and Rabanus Maurus in his 'Chaucer's Pardoner, The Spiritual Eunuch and The Pardoner's Tale', *Speculum* 30 (1955) 180-99. Compare *1 Henry IV*, III.3.164f. (Falstaff speaking): 'Dost thou hear Hal? Thou knowest in the state of innocency Adam fell; and what should poor Jack Falstaff do in the days of villainy? Thou seest I have more flesh than another man, and therefore more frailty'.

decision that it is better to maintain a usurpation than to let the realm slip into anarchy. Hal has decided, but the issue is not closed.

There is a certain sort of learned critic who loves to point out that Falstaff must be classified as an evil force, since he stands for drink, conviviality and pleasure and has no sense of his responsibility to the great cause, the putting down of rebellion. But perhaps all this depends on the authenticity and rightness of the order which is being maintained. But these same learned critics come at length in their dogged progress upon the fact that the king's rule is inauthentic. The rebels are not more rebellious than the king himself. And the effect of this is to re-open the ethical debate about Falstaff. Dr Johnson was right when he reminded the reader – who, be it noted, he assumed all those years ago would be distressed at the departure of Falstaff – that Falstaff utters no single 'sentiment of generosity' in the course of the plays. And yet Auden can see Falstaff as a parabolic figure of Charity.[17] How is this?

It is partly, I think, an effect of style. Falstaff speaks a golden Shakespearean English which makes him the centre of a small world of joy wherever he goes. Above all, in the very jaws of senility and death, he is life, and whenever he comes near there is a real danger that the great war-lords will be seen for what they perhaps are – mere bloody men, agents of death.

What Ruskin called 'the Pathetic Fallacy' is very near the centre of Virgil's literary art – the notion that nature is in sympathy with human emotion. In Homer when the hero falls wounded to the death, the ground that receives him is called, still, the life-giving earth. But in Virgil, when the lover weeps the sky weeps also. 'Pathetic Fallacy' is an odd name for this trope, since, surely, no one was ever deceived by it. But in its larger manifestations I think perhaps people have been to some extent bemused by it. The notion, fundamental to the *Aeneid*, that history is in some sympathetic relation with the journey of a simple man, who carries divine authority for his subjection of those he meets – this has really fooled people. But in Shakespeare there is Falstaff, and,

17. *op.cit.* fn. 15, 198.

in the face of that luminous cynicism, all mystiques of authority falter and turn pale. Not the specific moral anguish of Hal – that is a true counterpoise to what Falstaff stands for – but the *mystique* fails. When Aeneas comes to Latium the first thing he does, before he has talked to anyone, is to mark out the plan on the ground of his settlement (*Aeneid* VII. 157-9). Such is the awful confidence of the god-directed. And this shows us the terrible thing about a mystique like this, namely that it has such concrete and practical effects. Would that Falstaff had been by when he did it.

Yet (with Falstaff one has to go on and on saying 'yet' since he is 'poem unlimited') even while Falstaff impugns the practical mystique of the ruler, he is made the great expression in the play of what we might call the impractical mystique. Falstaff, who cannot get on with live King Henry, is on the best of terms with Dead King Arthur. If a sense of England as a sort of ruined Arcadia or Eden survives at all in *Henry IV* it is because of Falstaff and his circle. This comes partly from the language of the Falstaff scenes with its preference for immemorial, rustic ways of measuring time – 'I have known thee these twenty-nine years *come peascod time*' (*2 Henry IV*, II.4.368-71). There is a speech in *As You Like It* which always calls Falstaff to mind, and I think I can piece together why. This is the passage (I.1.105-9):

> They say he is already in the Forest of Arden and many merry men with him; and there they live like the Old Robin Hood of England. They say many young gentlemen flock to him every day, and fleet the time carelessly, as they did in the golden world.

Falstaff himself in his first scene says, 'Let us be Diana's foresters, gentlemen of the shade, minions of the moon' (*1 Henry IV*, I.2.25-6). There you have the forest, and the gentlemen – surely merry ones too. Then in V.3 of the second part Pistol speaks of 'golden times' (95) and Silence sings in a quavering voice of 'Robin Hood' (102). And so the elements of the *As You Like It* speech are reassembled.

Moreover, there is a trail of references to King Arthur (king over the lost England). These are of rising power. In *2 Henry IV*, II.4.33 Falstaff enters singing 'When Arther first in court' and then breaks off with a request to Francis to empty the jordan. Then in the great pastoral/comical/elegiacal scene, III.2, Shallow says that long ago he was Sir Dagonet in Arthur's show (273). Since, according to Malory, Dagonet was Arthur's fool and Shallow here plays fool to Falstaff the effect of the allusion is to turn Falstaff for a second into a sort of grey echo of Arthur himself. But the most powerful reference of all comes in *Henry V*. There Pistol, Hostess, Nym, Bardolph and the Boy are talking about how Falstaff died, and whether his soul is in Hell or in Heaven. Bardolph cries (II.3.7-15):

> Would I were with him, wheresome'er he is, either in heaven or in hell!

But then Hostess answers:

> Nay, sure he's not in hell: he's in Arthur's bosom, if ever man went to Arthur's bosom. 'A made a finer end, and went away an it had been any christom child; 'a parted ev'n just between twelve and one, ev'n at the turning o' th'tide.

Comic malapropism can be strangely powerful. The hostess has confused the story in Luke about Dives and Lazarus (that is, the story of the poor leper who was shut out from the rich man's gate, even as Falstaff was shut out from the presence of Hal, and how the poor man was after death raised up to Abraham's bosom while the rich man was left in Hell – is there anybody left who can believe that Shakespeare was unequivocally against Falstaff when the imagery can do things like that?). To that most potent story she has joined the story of the old king who still lies sleeping under Snowdon or perhaps Glastonbury Tor till we need him again.

Falstaff is not like Hotspur a specimen of an earlier culture. Rather he spans and sums in his own person all change, all shocks. Introduced in Part One as irrelevant to clocks and watches – 'What the devil hast thou to do with the time of the day?' says the Prince (*1 Henry IV*, 1.2.7), he is, as we learn in Part Two, soon to die. He is an old man but he is also a kind of timeless baby. We may notice how the hostess's account of the death of Falstaff in *Henry V* is a wonderful description of a baby – 'I saw him fumble with the sheets, and play with flowers and smile upon his fingers' end' (II.3.15-7).

* * *

I began my comparison of two great poets with a Virgilian coalescence of images of the city. I will end with a Shakespearean coalescence of images – not of the city, but of the human form in time. I have said that Falstaff is a sort of aged baby. There is a point where the two images are made to glimmer and join. Falstaff says, 'I was born about three of the clock in the afternoon, with a white head and something a round belly' (*2 Henry IV*, I.2.176 f.). We hear the words and, as we listen, what do we see? A white head and a round belly.

* The author is grateful to Michelle Martindale for criticisms and suggestions.

Parts of this essay first appeared in the author's *A New Mimesis* (London, Methuen 1983) ch.3. We are grateful to the author and publishers for their permission to reprint this material.

The *Aeneid* and *Paradise Lost*

K.W. GRANSDEN

In a recent book on the Classics and English Renaissance poetry[1] Gordon Braden (discussing Ben Jonson's 'Drink to me only', and its obscure, and long undetected, source in Philostratos) suggests that the point of this kind of allusion lies precisely in its undetectability, 'its total effacement into the present situation'. He remarks *en passant* that the epic style of allusion is quite different: here 'a perspective on the past' is exactly what is sought. One can read Jonson's song (or, one might add, sing it) without knowing Philostratos, but 'there is an important sense in which one cannot read *Paradise Lost* without knowing the *Aeneid*'.

Milton proclaims to the informed reader the classical references in *Paradise Lost*: far from trying to conceal his indebtedness, he expects it to be appreciated, so that it becomes part of every proper reading of the poem.[2] Yet it is also true that, once the informed reader has observed the signal of a classical parallel in a passage of Milton, the context of the original line, phrase or motif is to be subordinated. The reader himself has subsumed it into the new structure. The omnipresent (though to the uninstructed reader invisible) transformations in the Christian vernacular of material from pagan epic are not merely there for adornment and enrichment. They constitute a palimpsest in which the teleological epic of Christian heroism transcends, while leaving deliberate evidence of, the epics of pagan heroism. To take an example (*Paradise Lost* XII.369-371):

he shall ascend
The throne hereditary, and bound his reign
With earth's wide bounds, his glory with the heavens.

This is the conclusion of Michael's prophecy of the royal

1. Gordon Braden, *The Classics and English Renaissance Poetry*, (New Haven and London 1978) 170.

2. A useful bibliography of works dealing with Milton's use of classical epic is in the Introduction to Francis C. Blessington, *Paradise Lost and the Classical Epic* (London 1979) xi-xii and 104 f.

line of Israel, which is to culminate in the advent of Christ. Fowler[3] observes that 'the diction recalls Virgil's prophecy with respect to Augustus in *Aeneid* I.287 (*imperium Oceano, famam qui terminet astris*)'. But one must go further. The entire prophecy of Jupiter in *Aeneid* I is structurally relevant. We may add that the prophecy which Virgil placed in his first book Milton places in his last, thus creating out of the *Aeneid* and *Paradise Lost* a kind of vast double epic constructed in a symbolism of returning symmetry: the prophecy of Jupiter is renewed and transformed into Judaeo-Christian teleology.

Moreover, Jupiter's prophecy in *Aeneid* I is reinforced by that of Anchises in book VI. This is structurally closer in some ways to Michael's, since the addressee is Aeneas who, like Adam, has the burden and responsibility of inaugurating the destined sequence of history. And if we turn to Anchises' speech, we find diction no less relevant to Michael's words than the words of Jupiter (*Aeneid* VI.781 f.):

> . . . illa incluta Roma
> imperium terris, animos aequabit Olympo.

> . . . *that famous Rome will make her empire equal to the earth, her spirit to heaven.*

Here the antithesis 'earth / heaven' corresponds exactly to Milton's, whereas in Jupiter's words the antithesis was 'Ocean / heavens'. The point, of course, is that both allusions are needed so that we recall at this crucial and climactic moment of Milton's poem the whole Roman infrastructure of the *Aeneid*, and can make as we read the great 'leap' from the Roman empire to the city of God. Fowler likewise observes that there are parallels also in Old Testament prophets to Michael's words: but it is Virgil who has given the lines their shape and rhythm, not Isaiah or Daniel.

We may perhaps think of the stained glass windows of Chartres cathedral, in which a series of types and antitypes are arranged in correspondence to offer instruction to the 'fit' viewer. Thus the story of Eve's journey into experience can appropriately be illustrated by Milton with typological

3. *The Poems of John Milton*, ed. John Carey and Alastair Fowler, (London 1968) 1045. This is the best available edition of the poem; all quotations from *Paradise Lost* are taken from it.

allusions to Narcissus, Pomona, Pandora, Venus, Juno, Dido, Proserpina, and these excursions into the world of Renaissance humanism make legitimate appeals to the senses as well as contributing to the complex and often ambivalent character of Eve. The various word-pictures of Eve naked in a classical landscape as in some Renaissance painting help to place her as both goddess and mortal, natural and sensual.

Typological correspondence is, of course, not the same as co-identity. Eve transcends her models. In the famous lines (*Paradise Lost* IV.269-272) about Proserpine, who

> gathering flowers
> Her self a fairer flower by gloomy Dis
> Was gathered, which cost Ceres all that pain
> To seek her through the world,

the phrase 'all that pain' is often said to be moving because it makes us think of the pain that followed the Fall and perhaps of Christ's suffering. This underlying sadness is certainly there for us: it is part of our feeling about Milton's ambivalence towards the classics. But this passage is an example of one of Milton's favourite figures: it begins 'Not that fair field of Enna . . .' so that the *locus amoenus* of the earthly paradise is specifically dissociated from the Sicilian landscape of pagan pastoral, while at the same time the reader is asked to hold in his mind briefly, before dismissing it, all that 'fabled' pain of the pagan goddess which takes up so many hundreds of lines of Ovid's *Metamorphoses* V, so that the phrase becomes ironical as well as sad (*Metamorphoses* V.462-3):

> quas dea per terras et quas erraverit undas,
> dicere longa mora est.

It would take long to tell through what lands and what seas the goddess wandered.

The plot of *Paradise Lost* tells how evil, instigated by Satan, is turned to good, by God. Reverting to the palimpsest, we can see that this is also the plot of the *Aeneid*, with Juno as the type of Satan, at least until *Aeneid* XII, when, in a conclusion which shows to the highest degree the nobility of which paganism was capable, Juno's opposition to destiny ceases and she 'becomes' a Roman deity. No such transformation is possible for the arch-fiend – or perhaps we should say that his transformation from a parody of the old epic hero in books I and II to a serpent works the other way: its implacable reductiveness is the antithesis of the divine reconciliation scene of *Aeneid* XII. Nevertheless, Satan's psychological motivation is adapted by Milton from the Juno of the *Aeneid*: his 'sense of injured merit' (*Paradise Lost* I.98) is Virgil's *spretae . . . iniuria formae* (*Aeneid* I.27). Both phrases are introduced in the first books of the epics, establishing a strong thematic parallel. Juno is tormented by the *aeternum . . . sub pectore vulnus* (*Aeneid* I.36) which followed the judgement of Paris; Satan is tormented by the 'thought of . . . lasting pain' (*Paradise Lost* I.55), which followed his inability to accept another 'judgement' which had exalted a rival (Christ) over him. Both Juno and Satan stir up war. The release of the monster Sin by Satan in *Paradise Lost* II corresponds to the release of the Fury Allecto by Juno in *Aeneid* VII. Juno's famous verse (VII.312)

> flectere si nequeo superos Acheronta movebo
> *If I cannot bend the gods above I will move Hell*

is structurally imitated by Milton in 'Better to reign in hell than serve in heaven' (*Paradise Lost* I.263). Juno's fresh onslaught against the Trojans in the second half of the *Aeneid* is a model for Satan's onslaught against Eve in the second half of *Paradise Lost*, when he reappears in the narrative (after the long central passage of Raphael's story of the holy war and the Creation, 'improved / In meditated fraud and malice' (*Paradise Lost* IX.54 f.).

The theological complexities of Milton's God lie beyond the scope of this essay. Nevertheless, we may say that he contains not only Jehovah but also the supreme deity of Homer, Virgil and Ovid in *Metamorphoses* I, and that the unstable and varying tone of his utterances must in part at least be traced to his ambiguous origins. As Christ he is a transfigured Apollo – that Apollo who interceded with the gods on behalf of Hector in *Iliad* XXIV. In Milton's hierarchy Christ, always speaking second, expresses and enacts the providence of the Father. When God 'begot' Christ (as Augustus had begotten, that is adopted as his heir, Marcellus), this was not only a political transaction but the inauguration of a new moral order. And it was this innovation which Satan (no romantic revolutionary he, but an arch-reactionary) objected to: the phrase 'this new world' is repeated indignantly through the Niphates top soliloquy, while in book IX he expresses his resentment of the earthly paradise and his jealousy of divine innovation because it implies improvement ('For what god after better worse would build?' *Paradise Lost* IX.102). The new Troy which Aeneas will found is destined to transcend the old Troy, destroyed by the trick of the wooden horse and the malice of Hera-Juno.

When we first meet God the father, 'high throned above all highth' (*Paradise Lost* III.58) Milton is alluding, not to Jupiter's first appearance in the *Aeneid* but to *Metamorphoses* I.178, where Jupiter sits in council *celsior ipse loco*. It may also be the Jupiter of this council who is recalled when God, hearing of Satan's rebellion, says (*Paradise Lost* V.721-4):

> Nearly it now concerns us to be sure
> Of our omnipotence, and with what arms
> We mean to hold what anciently we claim
> Of deity or empire . . .

Jupiter calls the council in *Metamorphoses* I to discuss the punishment of Lycaon who has tried to 'put to proof his high supremacy'. Lycaon had actually said (*Metamorphoses* I.222 f.):

> experiar deus hic discrimine aperto
> an sit mortalis . . .

I will try by open experiment whether he is god or mortal.

The parallel with Satan is clear. Lycaon is turned into a wolf for his rash experiment; Satan too is transformed and debased. Jupiter has already decided the punishment, and the council is summoned to give public and formal notice of a decision already made. Jupiter begins with a show of concern: *Non ego pro mundi regno magis anxius . . . / . . . fui* (I was never more troubled about the world than now, i.e. not even during the rebellion of the giants, *Metamorphoses* I.182). In *Paradise Lost* V Christ dismissed God's show of concern ('Mighty father, thou thy foes / justly hast in derision', 735 f.). Zeus in *Iliad* XX had put up a show of concern lest Achilles storm the walls of Troy beyond what is fated (*hypermoron*).

Zeus's concern is not exactly a joke, nor is that of God the father. The confrontation of god and hero, or of greater hero and lesser, is a common epic motif. There is a ritual of challenge and response in which the challenger may lose, or there may be a temporary stalemate (e.g. at the end of *Paradise Lost* IV when Satan challenges Gabriel). Satan, Lycaon, Achilles, are beings great enough to elicit a concerned response from the deity.

God's smile when he utters his show of concern ('and smiling to his only Son thus said', 719) is the smile of Virgil's all-wise Jupiter at *Aeneid* I.254 when he confronts the troubled Venus (*olli subridens*) and also at *Aeneid* XII.829 when he pretends to be overruled by Juno (*olli subridens*) and her demand that the name of Troy should vanish from history and that of Rome take its place. When Milton's God says 'what I will is fate' (*Paradise Lost* VII.173) he formulates, perhaps more clearly than Virgil's Jupiter ever does, a concept that is nevertheless central to the moral structure of the *Aeneid*: the will of Jupiter is co-ordinate with destiny. So too in *Aeneid* X Jupiter comes near to formulating another doctrine central to *Paradise Lost*: that of free will (*Aeneid* X.112 f.):

rex Iuppiter omnibus idem
fata viam invenient.

King Jupiter is the same to all men; fate will find the way.

The richness and complexity of Milton's classicism is the culmination of English Renaissance humanism. That tradition had produced in Spenser's *The Faerie Queene* an epic which was also a thesaurus of classical images and allusions, a tapestry shot through with glittering motifs from the pagan past, used quite unselfconsciously, and with a sensuous appreciation of their colours and resonances, to adorn a pageant of Christian virtues. *Paradise Lost* is a darker and less innocent work, as befits its 'great' yet also 'sad' argument. Indeed, it might be said that the paradise lost in the poem is, on one level, that innocent love of classical literature which could allow it to enjoy uncensored commerce with revealed truth.

When Milton came to the Creation and the Flood in his universal poem, he could hardly have stuck to Genesis alone. In turning the events there briefly and starkly narrated into full-scale epic episodes, he had before him the monumental though unfinished *Devine Weekes and Works* of Du Bartas, translated into English by Joshua Sylvester in 1605,[4] which aimed to set forth in a single poem the 'days' of man from his creation to the last judgement, an epic on an awe-inspiring scale whose only true model would be the Bible itself. He also used Ovid's *Metamorphoses* and the mediaeval tradition of Ovid 'moralised',[5] whereby the pagan poet was seen as shadowing, though incorrectly, the truths of divine revelation. For Milton, as for Dante, Ovid was second only to Virgil among the Latin poets. He delved into Ovid as into the archaeology of fable and used correspondences to adorn and elaborate the texture of biblical truth. He even found occasion to correct earlier mistranslations. In his description of Eve as Narcissus the phrase 'with thee it came and goes' (*Paradise Lost* IV.469) correctly renders Ovid's tenses, for the metre shows that *venit* in *tecum venitque manetque* (*Metamorphoses* III.435) is past, though Sandys and most other versions read 'comes'.

In contrast to Sylvester/Du Bartas, who accused the pagan poets of fighting against divine truth, Milton makes specific allowance in *Paradise Regained* (IV.351) for those in whom

> moral virtue is expressed
> By light of nature not in all quite lost.

If it was Ovid who provided for the Renaissance the principal thesaurus of pagan mythology, it was Virgil who, in his 'Messianic' Eclogue (IV) and in the Stoic *pietas* of his Aeneas, seemed most poignantly to shadow forth, as he had for Dante, the universal moral order of revealed truth. It was from Virgil that Milton took the twelve-book structure of the second and subsequent editions of *Paradise Lost* (were the ten books of the first edition due to Lucan's *Pharsalia?*), from Virgil that he took the high style to which Dante's humility did not aspire, from Virgil that he took his grandest and most central typological correspondence: Aeneas is to Augustus as Adam is to Christ. The more 'occasional' mythological allusions, often to

4. *Bartas, His Devine Weekes and Works* (1605), tr. Joshua Sylvester. Facsimile reproduction with introduction by Francis C. Haber (Gainesville, Florida 1965).

5. See L.P. Wilkinson, *Ovid Recalled* (London 1955) chs. xi-xii.

Homer or Ovid, are richly decorative but sometimes more critical: it is here that the 'not' and 'more' which signal the tradition of 'overgoing' the classics recur, that tradition which asserts that some fabled event has been surpassed in divine revelation. But even here Milton's treatment is far from invariably reductive, and often deeply ambivalent. Most striking is the long description of Adam and Eve in book IV while they still enjoy prelapsarian sexual happiness, without guilt, as the Homeric gods did ('he in delight . . . / . . . Smiled with superior love, as Jupiter / On Juno smiles . . .', 497-500). And later, Adam and Eve retire to a 'blissful bower' (*Paradise Lost* IV.690; the echo of Spenser's Bower of Bliss is perhaps ominous), whose flowers specifically recall the flowers in *Iliad* XIV.347-9, when Hera beguiled Zeus to her bed: indeed, Eve's beautiful speech to Adam at *Paradise Lost* IV.635-59 does constitute a kind of beguilement.

Virgil himself uses the 'overgoing' figure in *Aeneid* VI when he compares Augustus to Hercules and Bacchus, but says that Augustus's achievements surpass those of his mythological types, both of whom were deified 'culture-heroes' who civilised the world from west to east (*Aeneid* VI.801 ff.):

> nec vero Alcides tantum telluris obivit,
> fixerit aeripedem cervam licet . . .
> nec qui pampineis victor iuga flectit habenis
> Liber . . .

> *Neither indeed did Hercules traverse so much space of earth although he shot the bronze-footed deer, nor Bacchus who in triumph controls his chariot with reins of vine shoots.*

Dryden's version employs the formula perfectly ('Not Hercules more lands and labours knew . . .').

Many of the 'not' and 'more' formulas in *Paradise Lost* are associated with Eve and the Garden of Eden, and as such are central to the moral structure of the epic. It is as though Milton had embedded into the 'Virgilian' form of his poem, – with its proclaimed hero (Aeneas) and its real hero (Augustus) together forming a teleological pattern – a second, Ovidian, epic, with its chief character a metamorphosed Eve. By confrontations with Ovidian romantic epic Milton is able to isolate the sensuality of Eve and place her outside the world of moral insights and intellectual instruction which Adam inhabits. None of the classical parallels to Pomona, or Pandora, can do justice to Eve as she really was: the unfeigned Venus. The ambivalence which surrounds her is central to the poem and to the tensions between pagan and Christian material which pervade it. When Eve eats the apple all nature groans; like Proserpina she has married death, and we recall also Dido in the cave (*Aeneid* IV.169 f.):

> ille dies primus leti primusque malorum
> causa fuit . . .
>
> *That day was first the cause of death and first the cause of woe . . .*

But Eve, unlike Dido, is a survivor, and her suggestion of a suicide pact is rejected by Adam, who proclaims (*Paradise Lost* IX.913-914 and 955-959) his indissoluble bonds with her as a marriage, in thematic antithesis to Aeneas. Only for Dido had that other love been consummated in marriage, and that dubiously: *coniugium vocat, hoc praetexit nomine culpam* ('she called it marriage, under this name she cloaked her infidelity', *Aeneid* IV.172). Eve's *culpa* becomes *felix* as Milton works out the doctrine of the 'fortunate Fall'.

It is not merely that Milton overgoes his classical models in the similes, both fondly lavish and morally reductive, with which he adorns and illustrates his poem. He uses the tradition exemplified by Sylvester/Du Bartas in the formula which bids the pagan poets be silent in the face of Christian truth (*The Second Week*: 'Eden' 79-86):

> Ye pagan poets that audaciously
> Have fought to dark the ever memory
> Of God's great works; from henceforth still be dumb
> Your fabled praises of Elysium . . .
> For the Almighty made his blissful bowers
> Better indeed than you have feigned yours . . .

But he is far too sophisticated and too much in love with classical poetry to be so naively dismissive. In *Paradise Regained*, however, he does assert the moral and temporal priority of biblical over pagan deities and culture. In *Paradise Regained* IV.196 ff. Satan tempts Christ with the poetry and philosophy of Greece. Christ rejects these pleasures as 'false, or little else but dreams' (291). The Old Testament, says Christ, shows (*Paradise Regained* IV.338-342)

> That rather Greece from us these arts derived;
> Ill imitated, while they loudest sing
> The vices of their deities, and their own
> In fable, hymn, or song, so personating
> Their gods ridiculous, and themselves past shame.

So in *Paradise Lost*, in one of the most famous examples of a classical fable 'corrected', Homer's 'erring' version of the fall of Hephaestus-Mulciber ('For he with this rebellious rout / Fell long before . . .'). Milton alludes to the tradition that the pagan gods were fallen angels. But he lingers over Homer's account, serene, light hearted almost, from the youth of the world (*Paradise Lost* I.740-748):

> and how he fell
> From heaven, they fabled, thrown by angry Jove
> Sheer o'er the crystal battlements: from morn
> To noon he fell, from noon to dewy eve,
> A summer's day; and with the setting sun
> Dropped from the zenith like a falling star,
> On Lemnos the Aegean isle; thus they relate,
> Erring; for he with this rebellious rout
> Fell long before;

The first two uses of 'fell' refer simply to the law of gravity. Hephaestus fell because Zeus pushed him. But at 'fell long before' the Christian significance of 'fell' comes fully back into our reading, so that we register a kind of enormous thematic pun. By putting the false and true versions of the 'fall' together, Milton manages to be simultaneously both diachronic and synchronic. The poem is a vast manipulation of time, making the whole of human history available to the reader, as Anchises unfolded it to Aeneas, diachronically, *in ordine*. But just as in the ecphrasis of the shield, and in Anchises' presentation of the *heldenschau* in *Aeneid* VIII and VI, events can be presented synchronically (the shield with its pictures, the procession of heroes, passing before Aeneas's eyes), so in *Paradise Lost* every classical allusion passes through the reader's mind at the same time as it is being corrected. The process is itself part of the meaning of the poem. The reader is beguiled and seduced by the beauties of the past as Christ was beguiled by Satan, but he is also given the means of distinguishing truth from fable and, while placing and enjoying the allusions, is also in a position to, and expected to, make a correct revaluation.

An interesting instance of a classical image 'corrected' by means of cross-reference to Judaeo-Christian truth occurs at the end of book IV when God puts out golden scales to judge between Satan and Gabriel – 'The fiend looked up and knew / His mounted scale aloft' (*Paradise Lost* IV.1013 f.) – a translation of Homer's γνῶ γὰρ Διὸς ἱρὰ τάλαντα (*Iliad* XVI.658; Hector recognised the sacred scales). Why did Satan recognise a pagan symbol? Milton is appealing to the learned reader's conspectus of the past (so, too, he says at *Paradise Lost* II.613 f. that the water of Lethe flies 'as once it fled / The lip of Tantalus'; 'as once' means in the pagan myth). But when Zeus and Jupiter used the scales, the pan carrying the doomed one's fate *sank*. Satan's scale rises, for 'rather Greece from us these arts derived'. The operation of the scales is corrected in accordance with scripture (*Daniel* V.27) – 'thou art weighed in the balances, and art found wanting'. Addison noted this double borrowing but did not observe the difference between the pagan and the Christian image.[6]

It is here that we reach the heart of Milton's indebtedness to the *Aeneid*. For the Augustan reader of the *Aeneid*, there had to be a synchronisation of two time scales: the narrative 'past' of the Aeneas story, itself made vividly present to the reader through the Latin use of the historic present, and the future revealed to Aeneas through prophecy and culminating in the reader's 'now'. But for Milton, and for us, any reading of the *Aeneid* will involve degrees or gradations of pastness, from the remotest Mycenean legend to the culminating return of the Golden Age under Augustus. What Milton's God prophecies as the destiny of the human race recalls Jupiter's promise to the war-weary Romans (*Paradise Lost* III.336 ff. and *Aeneid* I.291):

6. Joseph Addison, *A Criticism and Notes upon the twelve books of Paradise Lost* (*Spectator*, 321). This collection of suggestive and forward-looking essays on the poem remains essential reading.

And after all their tribulations long
See golden days, fruitful of golden deeds,
With joy and love triumphing, and fair truth.

aspera tum positis mitescent saecula bellis

Then war will be abandoned and the rough ages will grow soft.

In the structure and symmetries of his verses and paragraphs, Milton is a Virgilian. Fowler pointed out that Milton's style is not neo-classical, in that it is co-ordinate and paratactic. Virgil's style is highly co-ordinate and characteristically paratactic, with frequent use of epexegesis and of the figure labelled by Henry 'theme and variation' (otherwise *amplificatio* and *variatio*). (The style of the earlier *Eclogues* is simpler and more end-stopped; the *Georgics* is transitional; but in the *Aeneid* enjambement and paragraphic writing, in which, as Prince said about Milton, 'the sense is diffused through a larger block of words',[7] is normal). It is here that Milton is most profoundly classical, and, in particular, most profoundly indebted to the *Aeneid*. When we look at the actual construction and diction of his verses, we realise that the debt to the *Metamorphoses*, in contrast, is of a different and more occasional order – the striking and eye-catching detail, the parallel myth. Only the *Aeneid* offered the proper blue-print for *Paradise Lost*.

* * *

F.T. Prince, in *The Italian Element in Milton's Verse*, cites a passage from Annibal Caro's translation of *Aeneid* VI (273 ff.). The Latin begins with a typically Virgilian verse, symmetrically disposed in two parts about the third-foot caesura, the second phrase a *variatio* or *amplificatio* of the first ('theme and variation'). This type of verse is sometimes found with asyndeton, and here Manuscript P reads *primis*, but I follow the Oxford text:

vestibulum ante ipsum primisque in faucibus Orci

Caro produces a line more Dantesque in structure than

7. F.T. Prince, *The Italian Element in Milton's Verse* (Oxford 1954 122, quoted by Fowler 431.

Virgilian just by removing the parallelism:

nel primo entrar del doloroso regno.

Verses constructed on this pattern are numerous in the *Aeneid* and are too familiar to need much illustration.

luctantis ventos tempestatesque sonoras (I.53)

occasum Troiae tristisque ruinas (I.238)

Milton imitates the figure frequently:

That with sad overthrow and foul defeat (I.135)

Of nuptial sanctity and marriage rites (VIII.487)

Strongly to suffer and support our pains (I.147)

Of stunning sounds and voices all confused (II.952)

Equally common is the linking of two clauses; examples from the *Aeneid*:

mobilitate viget virisque adquirit eundo (IV.175)

tempestas sine more furit tonitruque tremescunt
ardua terrarum et campi (V.694)

nunc sinite et placitum laeti conponite foedus (X.15)

abstulit atra dies et funere mersit acerbo (XI.28)

but all the heavenly choir stood mute,
And silence was in heaven; (III.217)

Confusion heard his voice, and wild uproar
Stood ruled (III.710)

Now came still evening on, and twilight grey
Had in her sober livery all things clad (IV.598)

Repetition of a single word, or of the same word in another form (*figura etymologica*), or of a group of words, in the same or the following line, is extremely common in Virgil and indeed in all Latin poets; examples from the *Aeneid*:

divum inclementia, divum (II.602)

si pereo, hominum manibus periisse iuvabit (III.606)

vincant, quos vincere mavis (X.43)

and from *Paradise Lost*:

> Happy, but for so happy ill secured (IV.370)
>
> Forbids us then to taste, but his forbidding (IX.753)

Some of Virgil's repetitions carry a heightened emotional pathos and intensity; examples from the *Aeneid*:

> diu, res si qua diu mortalibus ulla est,
> viximus (X.861)
>
> inde domum, si forte pedem, si forte tulisset,
> me refero (II.756)
>
> hic tibi mortis erant metae, domus alta sub Ida,
> Lyrnesi domus alta (XII.546)
>
> vel pater omnipotens adigat me fulmine ad umbras,
> pallentis umbras (IV.25)

Milton in *Paradise Lost* offers parallels to this usage, the first very close to that from *Aeneid* IV quoted immediately above:

> on the ground
> Outstretched he lay, on the cold ground (X.860)
>
> Then thou thy regal sceptre shalt lay by,
> For regal sceptre then no more shall need (III.339)
>
> if ever, then,
> Then had the sons of God excuse (V.446)

Milton employs the *figura etymologica* in what seems a clear imitation of Virgil:

> adnuit et totum nutu tremefecit Olympum
> (*Aeneid* X.115)
>
> So frowned the mighty combatants, that hell
> Grew darker at their frown (*Paradise Lost* II.719)

Word-play is common in Latin poetry. Virgil is especially fond of it; from the *Aeneid*:

> arma amens capio; nec sat rationis in armis (II.314)
>
> mortaline manu factae immortale carinae (IX.95)

And from *Paradise Lost*:

> And to repair his numbers thus impaired (IX.144)

whole legions armed,
Their armour helped their harm (VI.655)

Virgil's noun-adjective phrase patterns are frequently imitated by Milton. A common structure in the *Aeneid* is one in which a noun is qualified first by a simple adjective and then by an adjectival (usually participial) phrase:

gens dura atque aspera cultu
debellanda tibi Latio est (V.730)

sancta ad vos anima atque istius nescia culpae (XII.648)

pii vates et Phoebo digna locuti (VI.662)

inlustris animas nostrumque in nomen ituras (IV.758)

Examples from *Paradise Lost* are:

Though huge, and in a rock of diamond armed (VI.364)

Wild work in heaven, and dangerous to the main (VI.698)

Faithful hath been your warfare, and of God
Accepted (VI.803)

Great things, and full of wonder in our ears,
Far differing from this world (VII.70)

Or with asyndeton: from the *Aeneid*:

urbs antiqua ruit multos dominata per annos (II.363)

antiqua cupressus
religione patrum multos servata per annos (II.714)

moenia lata videt triplici circumdata muro (VI.549)

And from *Paradise Lost*:

Bind their resplendent locks inwreathed with beams,
Now in loose garlands thick thrown off (III.361)

Of glimmering air less vexed with tempest loud (III.429)

Of goodliest trees loaden with fairest fruit (IV.147)

Perhaps the most characteristic single feature of the *Aeneid* is the way in which sense units are built up against the metrical pattern by enjambement and the delaying of some key word. This structure is hardly used at all in the *Eclogues*, where there is far more endstopping and correspondence beween the verse unit and the sense unit, nor is it typical of the style of the *Metamorphoses*. Compare the following from the *Aeneid, Paradise Lost* and Dryden's translation of the former, respectively:

> et iam prima novo spargebat lumine terras
> Tithoni croceum linquens Aurora cubile (IV.584)
>
> Now Morn her rosy steps in the eastern clime
> Advancing, sowed the earth with orient pearl (V.1)
>
> Aurora now had left her saffron bed
> And beams of early light the heavens o'erspread

Only Dryden offers a complete sense unit in the first line.

Perhaps the commonest use of enjambement in the *Aeneid* occurs when there is a major sense break after the first foot or foot and a half of the line. This sense break does not correspond to the metrical caesura which will occur either in the second or third foot (again a pattern much less often employed by Ovid); from the *Aeneid*:

> haec fessos tuto placidissima portu
> accipit; (III.78)
>
> vittis et sacra redimitus tempora lauro
> occurrit; (III.81)
>
> non potui abreptum divellere corpus et undis
> spargere? (IV.600)
>
> ast alios secum includit recipitque ruentis,
> demens (IX.727)

This pattern is so common in *Paradise Lost* as to constitute a hallmark of its style. To take a single passage at random, we find in the fifty lines on the Flood (*Paradise Lost* XI.712-62) sense-breaks at the beginnings of lines as follows:

Allured them;	And stabled;
Contending,	Their order;
Contrived;	Sent up amain;
Wide hovering;	Uplifted;
Impetuous;	

Adjectives and participles are probably the parts of speech most frequently carried over by enjambement in this way (e.g. 'Thus they relate, / Erring').

Milton's 'Latinate' inversions have received much attention. They should be seen as an imitation of Virgil's epic style. A common function of inversion in the *Aeneid* is to direct the reader's attention to shifts in the narrative and to elicit from him a corresponding shift of attention, as in *Aeneid* IV.260 f.:

> Aenean fundantem arces ac tecta novantem
> conspicit
>
> *Aeneas building battlements and making new houses he (Mercury) sees,*

where the reader's attention is focused first on Aeneas, the beheld, then on Mercury, the beholder. So also in *Aeneid* IV.219 ff.:

> talibus orantem dictis arasque tenentem
> audiit Omnipotens, oculosque ad moenia torsit
> regia et oblitos famae melioris amantis.
>
> *Him as he prayed in such words, and grasped the altar, heard the Omnipotent, and turned his gaze to the royal city and the lovers forgetful of their better fame.*

We focus on Iarbas, who has been praying to Jupiter. We then shift our attention through the linking inversion ('Him heard the Omnipotent') to Jupiter; after this our attention is turned, like Jupiter's, to Dido and Aeneas. The reader is manipulated by the syntax. So, too, in *Paradise Lost* V.219 ff.:

> Them thus employed beheld
> With pity heaven's high king, and to him called
> Raphael.

Dryden's translation of the *Aeneid* often removes the inversions and loosens the manipulative hold which Virgil's syntax retains on the reader:

> the mighty Thunderer heard
> Then cast his eyes on Carthage where he found
> The lustful pair.

*   *   *

Epic narrative is both diachronic and synchronic. It is first of all diachronic: the poet tells events in order. But the *Iliad* often looks back on events before 'the wrath of Achilles' and its terrible consequences, and forward to the fall of Troy, not itself part of the poem. Nor does Achilles die in the *Iliad*, yet the reader's awareness of his early doom, conveyed by the story teller through Achilles's own mouth and that of his mother, in the very first book, is inseparable from any reading of this tragic epic. The *Odyssey* offers a more complex structure, for Odysseus himself tells, at greater length than Nestor had in the *Iliad*, of his earlier experiences, to an audience consisting both of Alcinous and his court, and the reader, for whom, in consequence, the events of the *nostos* and earlier events exist synchronically in the totality of the narrative structure.

This 'double' time-scale was elaborated by Virgil and, following him, by Milton. In the *Aeneid*, Virgil needed to involve all readers, so that in the 'teaching' of Anchises and the 'prophetic' pictures on the Shield Aeneas becomes a figure of the reader, as in *Aeneid* VI.756-759:

> Nunc age, Dardaniam prolem quae deinde sequatur
> gloria, qui maneant Itala de gente nepotes,
> inlustris animas nostrumque in nomen ituras,
> expediam dictis, et te tua fata docebo.
>
> *Come now, I shall set forth in words what glory shall attend the Dardan race, what descendants are in store from Italian stock, famous souls and heirs of our name, and I will teach you your destiny.*

Milton followed Virgil in transposing classical (i.e. for Virgil, chiefly Homeric) formulae and responses into nobler models, superior moral structures, argument 'Not less but more heroic . . .' (*Paradise Lost* IX.14). Compare, for instance, Jupiter's speech to his daughter in *Aeneid* I.257-296, in which he unrolls the book of destiny and reveals the future of Roman civilisation, with God's speeches to his son in *Paradise Lost* III about the future of mankind. Virgil employs a series of resounding future tenses which are really 'future in the past' – *geret, ponet, explebit, transferet, condet, veniet, nascetur* – tenses which render authoritative, by synchronic narrative, events which have already been diachronically confirmed in historical time. Jupiter can thus switch tenses freely from future to present and past (*Aeneid* I.278 f.):

> his ego nec metas rerum nec tempora pono;
> imperium sine fine dedi
>
> *For them I set no bounds of place or time:*
> *I have given them empire without end.*

So God the father 'past, present, future . . . beholds' (*Paradise Lost* III.78). He too uses a series of future tenses and also modulates into present and past (*Paradise Lost* III. 172. ff.):

> As my eternal purpose hath decreed.
> Man shall not quite be lost, but saved who will . . .
> once more I will renew
> His lapsed powers . . .
> yet once more he shall stand . . .
> Some I have chosen of peculiar grace,
> Elect above the rest; so is my will.

In both poems history is unfolded as moral process, co-ordinate with the will of the supreme deity, which the forces of evil can thwart in the short run but cannot ultimately alter.

Books V-VIII and XI, XII of *Paradise Lost* are not part of the diachronic narrative 'of man's first disobedience', the theme announced by Milton in his proemium. They are 'digressions', 'flashbacks' and 'prophecies', yet the diachronic narrative is subsumed in their larger teleological structure. In narrative time, books I-II follow V and VI, so there is an intricate spiral structure. The diachronic narrative actually begins at V.577, so that the 'first' lines of the whole concept are, significantly, about time itself.

> As yet this world was not, and Chaos wild
> Reigned where these heavens now roll,
> where earth now rests
> Upon her centre poised, when on a day
> (For time, though in eternity, applied
> To motion, measures all things durable
> By present, past, and future) . . .

In a less complex but analogous way we can work out a diachronic sequence for the *Aeneid* in which the 'first' line is spoken by Aeneas (II.13)

> fracti bello fatisque repulsi
> ductores Danaum tot iam labentibus annis . . .
>
> *Broken by war and driven back by fate the leaders*
> *of the Greeks so many years now slipping by . . .*

Here the concepts of time, fate and war are echoed from the actual opening of the epic. God's 'opening' speech to the angels in *Paradise Lost* V emphasises the theme of disobedience stated in the first line of the poem and reinforced by Milton in his proemium to book IX.[8]

When Raphael assumes the role of divine instructor, Adam becomes the Christian reader, 'fit audience'. Later, Adam himself takes over the role of narrator-instructor. The roles of learner and teacher are interchangeable; the reader learns that Adam is Raphael's equal in eloquence and in access to divine knowledge. Neither is complete alone. And there are some things the reader cannot know; for these he must (like Aeneas when he looks at the shield), accept figures, *rerumque ignarus imagine gaudet* ('not knowing the events he rejoices in their representation', *Aeneid* VIII.730). Adam, like Aeneas in book VI, is centrally placed in the dialogue with Raphael to receive and transmit true knowledge. Milton invents a pretext for Adam to take over the narrator's role: 'My story, which perhaps thou hast not heard' (*Paradise Lost* VIII.205). So in Ovid Jupiter tells the other gods the story of Lycaon, 'which, being recent, is not well known' (*Metamorphoses* I. 164). The mediating audience within the poem allows the reader to come in on the story, to respond to diachronically articulated experience. The great dialogues of secondary epic are both entertaining and instructive: the encounter of Aeneas and Evander in *Aeneid* VIII, a 'theoxeny' in which a greater being (angel, hero soon to be deified) is received into the house of a lesser being, provides a model, as does the story of how Baucis and Philemon entertained the gods in *Metamorphoses* VIII. In Virgil's episode, the 'god' is the learner, the

8. So far as I know, Addison (*Spectator*, 327) was the first critic to make this point about the time scale of the two epics.

poor host the teacher. So too when Aeneas is received in the gorgeous court of Dido, he comes, as did Odysseus, out of the sea, in poverty (*omnium egenos, Aeneid* I.599). There it is he who is the story-teller, Dido the listener and giver of aid. The roles of learner and teacher are complementary and interchangeable.

For Milton as for Virgil the didactic element is crucial. Aeneas learns to accept his destiny; Adam says to Michael at the close of the poem 'Greatly instructed, I shall hence depart' (*Paradise Lost* XII.557). 'Hence': out of the poem, into our own lives; out of innocence through correct instruction into experience and history. Through Adam, as through Aeneas, the reader himself becomes fully armed; destiny has taken him into her confidence. In *Paradise Lost* the revelation of Michael continues and completes the revelation of Raphael.[9]

Dante claimed authenticity for the Divine Comedy by vouching for a personal vision: the words 'I saw' recur through the poem, words first used by Odysseus in his personal account of his meetings with the dead. Milton in his blindness chose another way, to 'tell of things invisible to mortal sight' (*Paradise Lost* III.55), basing himself on *Aeneid* VI.266 f.:

> sit mihi fas audita loqui, sit numine vestro
> pandere res alta terra et caligine mersas.

> *May it be allowed me to tell what I have heard, and with your assent to reveal things hidden deep in earth and darkness.*

Milton wants to know, not to see. Voices recur through his epic: the great central drama of the holy war and the Creation are narrated by Raphael in flashback; we hear the voice of God (as we never do in Dante), the voice of the Muse dictating nightly to the poet's ear, the voice of Raphael which so charmed Adam that when it stopped he 'thought him still speaking' and responded with words which are also the required response of the reader (*Paradise Lost* VIII.5 ff.):

> What thanks sufficient, or what recompense

9. 'The principal actors in this poem are not only our progenitors but our representatives' (Addison, *Spectator*, 273).

Equal have I to render thee, divine
Historian, who thus largely hast allayed
The thirst I had of knowledge.

Throughout the *Aeneid*, too, oracles and divine messages (including the speaking statues of the Trojan gods) reveal to Aeneas the *iussa deum* on which the poem's structure is built. Virgil even splits the role of divine interpreter as Milton does: first the Sibyl, whom Aeneas begs not to write her prophecies on leaves as she usually does (*ipsa canas oro, Aeneid* VI.76); then Anchises. Words are the beginning of all epic: 'tell, O Muse, sing', said Homer, and for Virgil the *vates* is still the inspired bard through whom truth may be authentically reaffirmed.

When Michael uses of Christ a formula used by Virgil about Augustus

He shall ascend
The throne hereditary, and bound his reign
With earth's wide bounds, his glory with the heavens,

the concept of *imperium sine fine* is reaffirmed in a wider area of meaning, until in the total Christian context of Milton's epic of revealed truth a meaning becomes available of which earlier 'meanings' were paradigms, and the process of 'overgoing' can be taken no further.

* Some of the material in this chapter first appeared in *Essays in Criticism* 17 (1967) 281-303, and is reproduced with permission of the editor.

Virgil and the Visual Arts

NIGEL LLEWELLYN

The poetry of Virgil is a major source of subject matter for visual artists, and his works have been subjected to a wide range of interpretations.[1] If we take the story-line of the *Aeneid* as an example it is clear that some painters have felt obliged to limit themselves quite strictly to what amounts to as literal a translation of the epic as is possible into a visual language. In their purest form we can group such representations under the heading of 'illustration'. Other artists are more generally 'inspired' by the text and are concerned to evoke the mood of the poetry rather than limit themselves to narrative accuracy. Of course many if not most paintings which take their subject matter from Virgil are both illustrative of passages in the text and inspired by the poetic atmosphere of the complete work. Visual artists are forced to confront the fact that theoretically they can only show the viewer one moment at a time. Even when an artist has the opportunity to present a series of pictures in a narrative sequence any plot on the scale of the *Aeneid* which has to be translated into a visual language poses enormous problems of organization.[2] Any picture which included only those motifs found in a few lines of the poem might be described as theoretically faithful but would appear virtually incomprehensible to the viewer.

To overcome this and complete what is not only a more satisfactory picture – but perhaps paradoxically one which is in practice more faithful to the text – the artist casts around for material preferably from within the poem but if not from his imagination or from wider research. To give some examples of this process at work I shall take a small group of pictures dating from the seventeenth and eighteenth centuries, and

1. For a full bibliography, see *Virgilio nell'arte e nella cultura europea*, Exhibition Catalogue (Rome 1981).

2. For a detailed consideration of the problems of narration in *Aeneid* cycles, see E. Langmuir, '*Arma Virumque*: Nicolò dell'Abate's *Aeneid Gabinetto* for Scandiano', *Journal of the Warburg and Courtauld Institutes* 39 (1976) 151-170.

also explore some of the arguments presented in this same period about the famous Hellenistic sculpted group, the Laocoon (plate 8).

The points made so far refer only to one aspect of the complete Virgilian iconography: those pictures showing scenes from the *Aeneid*, the *Georgics* and the *Eclogues*. In addition, there are two other important areas for consideration under our title. In both cases a lack of space prevents anything but a summary treatment here. The first topic is the iconographic tradition for depicting Virgil himself (i.e. the portrait tradition), and the second is the illustration of the popular Medieval legends about the poet's life and exploits.

In both cases the character and image of the poet underwent a major change as a consequence of his Medieval reputation as a wizard and a fallible human being. The classical portrait tradition, whose very existence is much disputed, shows the poet as one might expect moving in the cultivated circles of early Imperial Rome.[3] This was the intellectual Virgil whose moral promptings reputedly encouraged Augustus to renounce his cruel methods and whose integrity led Dante to choose him as an exemplary virtuous ancient. During the Middle Ages a new image of Virgil became popular and formed the basis of another portrait tradition, that of Virgil the Magician. The poet dressed in wizard's cloak and hat appears in a well defined iconographic type in northern Europe until well into the seventeenth century.[4]

The legends concerning Virgil *Magus*, often illustrated throughout this period, originated mostly in Naples, the site of the poet's tomb, and present him as lustful, vindictive and corruptible. His exploits, presented as fables, were clearly designed both to entertain and act as moral *exempla*, functions which parallel the intentions of the real Virgil's own epic poetry. A later tradition of scenes from Virgil's life draw their subject-matter from material which is more supportable historically.[5]

3. See the so-called Virgil, a copy after Praxiteles, in the Capitoline Museum, Rome.

4. See e.g. the portrait by Ludger tom Ring (1496-1547) in the Münster Museum.

5. E.g. Angelica Kauffmann's picture of Virgil composing his own

A review of the conventional iconography shows that the pictures in what we might call the heroic tradition were also intended not only to instruct through illustrations of the lives of men and women of exemplary character, but also to entertain and, even more importantly, to be more instructive through being entertaining. The idea, as old as antiquity and given renewed significance during the Renaissance and the Enlightenment, that art could perform its didactic functions more successfully when it was able to attract and engage the attention of the viewer, is well illustrated in the large-scale decorative scenes from the *Aeneid*, a tradition established in Italy and found throughout Europe since the early sixteenth century.[6] These mural and ceiling paintings also remind us that artists or their patrons have had to make careful decisions about exactly what to select from the mass of available material in a work as long and complex as the twelve books of Virgil's epic. It has rarely been thought necessary in larger scale works to use the divisions of the text to establish limits for decoration, to employ twelve spaces or scenes to represent the twelve books of the epic.[7] The selections of particular scenes were sometimes traditional, often very personal but almost never random. The rule of decorum, or suitability, was frequently applied to help those responsible for the choice. Thus scenes from the *Aeneid* intended to decorate a boudoir might be those which included in their programme the beautiful goddess Venus; a Council chamber might show Aeneas founding the State or making a wise or difficult decision; alternatively, a soldier might require scenes showing suitable feats of arms for the decoration of his palace.[8]

epitaph at Brindisi (Christies' Sale 22 November 1974, lot 163); or Ingres' painting, now in Brussels, of Augustus and his family listening to Virgil reading the *Aeneid* (1812), a subject drawn from the *Life of Virgil* by Donatus. The latter subject also appears in a painting of 1787 by J.J. Taillasson recently acquired by the National Gallery, London.

6. Tapestry is related to mural painting in this respect; see R. Rubenstein, 'G.F. Romanelli's Dido and Aeneas Tapestry Cartoons', *Art at Auction* (London 1968-9).

7. See E. Langmuir, *op. cit.* fn. 2 above.

8. For the role of decorum as part of the theory of iconography, see E.H. Gombrich, 'Introduction: Aims and Limits of Iconography' in *Symbolic Images* (London 1975) 1-25.

Such was the range of experience offered by Virgil's text that the *Aeneid* took its place amongst the great source books of iconographic vocabulary along with Homer, Ovid, the Bible and the modern epics of Tasso and Ariosto.[9] Indeed, as a standard source, Virgil was frequently called upon to supply subject-matter for students in academies of art. In 1812 the French Academy set as a theme for young artists wishing to be considered for the *Prix de Rome* an episode from *Georgics* IV: *Aristaeus mourning the death of his bees,* which had been killed by the nymphs who were angry with him for chasing Eurydice on her wedding day. François Rude's bronze *Aristaeus* is more an exercise in the canon of human proportion handed down from Praxiteles than a careful illustration or an inspired evocation of the poem.[10] The young artists' subject follows the convention of the period that painters and sculptors had to follow poetry and drama in order to elevate their own practice.

Because the educated classes knew the tale so well, the *Aeneid* offered a wealth of allusive and symbolic material which could be interpreted with great subtlety and flexibility, and this fact was clearly recognised by both patrons and artists. The choice of a scene from the *Aeneid* as subject-matter for a painting did not necessarily reflect great learning. Many such subjects formed part of an artist's stock vocabulary. To paint Dido it was not always necessary to consult Virgil. In scenes of the apotheosis of Aeneas (a Virgilian subject but not one for which Virgil supplied a text) the hero in his traditional costume is presented to the gods, also traditionally identified, and the iconography could therefore provide an illustration of any one of a number of similar subjects.[11] It does not have a specific text, although it does have an iconographic programme.

*   *   *

9. For a parallel to illustrations of Virgil, see E.K. Waterhouse, 'Tasso and the Visual Arts' *Italian Studies* 3 (1946-8) 162 ff.

10. *The Age of Neoclassicism,* Exhibition Catalogue (London 1974) 274, pl.65.

11. E.g. that by the Sicilian Neoclassical painter Guiseppe Velasco in the Villa Belmonte, Palermo; A. Ottimo della Chiesa, *Il Neoclassicismo nella pittura italiana* (Milan 1967) pl.51.

The decorative scheme for the armour store on the first floor of the Royal Palace at Turin, undertaken ca. 1740 by Claudio Francesco Beaumont (1694-1766), demonstrates that, although iconographic choice might initially be controlled by decorum, composition places an additional set of potentially conflicting pressures on artists and patrons. The central scene of this cycle shows the gods on Olympus who look down on episodes from Virgil's epic drama.[12] In one corner Venus seeks arms for her son Aeneas from her husband Vulcan (*Aeneid* VIII.383) – a suitable enough subject for an Armoury. But next to this Aeneas prays to Juno (*Aeneid* VIII.85), a scene included to balance the episode of her inviting Aeolus guardian of the Winds to disperse the Trojan fleet (*Aeneid* I.52) which appears opposite. The ceiling also shows the Triumph of Love and even Psyche, neither of which has much to do with the Trojan legend. A preliminary sketch for Dido's suicide by Beaumont's assistant Milocco[13] shows how Beaumont had to sort out those scenes which were suitable for the physical spaces available. Virgil's text describes the funeral pyre upon which Dido dies as 'built up to a great height' (*pyra . . . sub auras / erecta ingenti, Aeneid* IV.504 f.), but such an image would clearly not have been possible given the spaces with which Beaumont was working, in this case a roughly rectangular area largest in its width within an elaborately curvilinear frame.

The fresco cycle undertaken by the great Venetian decorative painter Giovanni Battista Tiepolo (1696-1770) in the Villa Valmarana in suburban Vicenza in 1757 shows a set of intentions very different from those of Beaumont at Turin.[14] Tiepolo was praised by his contemporaries for his learning and his imaginative inventiveness, both essential qualities for an artist concerned with history paintings on a grand scale. His scheme of decoration uses several of the stock secular

12. V. Viale (ed.), *Mostra del Barocco Piemontese* (Turin 1963) vol. II 83-84.

13. Torino Museo Civico inv. nos. 33-34 (= V. Viale (ed.), Catalogue II pl.218a).

14. M. Levey, 'Tiepolo's Treatment of Classical Story at Villa Valmarana: A Study of Eighteenth Century Iconography and Aesthetics', *Journal of the Warburg and Courtauld Institutes* 20 (1957) 298-317.

sources I mentioned earlier (see groundplan): specifically, the two ancients, Virgil and Homer *versus* the two moderns, Tasso and Ariosto. Homer did not figure very much as a source for artists until the eighteenth century (Italian translations of his epics started to appear in the late 1720s), so at the Villa Valmarana Tiepolo was engaged in something quite new.[15] The common theme for his selections from all four poets was love. In his decoration of the ground floor of the villa (or as it was then known the *palazzina*) Tiepolo had five spaces to consider: a hallway along the central axis surrounded by four rectangular living rooms. The hallway is decorated along both flanking walls and on the ceiling with a scene from Homer: *The Sacrifice of Iphigenia*. The first room to the right with scenes from the *Iliad*, shows how Tiepolo selected his subjects to fit his overall programme. Here a story with an amorous theme, albeit a very bitter one, has been rather artificially manufactured from Homer's text. The walls show the quarrel between Agamemnon and Achilles over the slave-girl Briseis; how she is pulled forth for Agamemnon to take his pleasure with her, while Athena restrains the jealous Achilles from killing Agamemnon. The goddess Thetis comforts Achilles in his loss and, to symbolise the whole tone of the room, there is a Cupid with arrows. Athena sits above on a cloud.

The scenes from the *Aeneid* are located in a room diagonally across the hallway. Here Tiepolo seems to be more at home with his subject-matter; and he places his actors not within *proscenia*, as with the Homer scenes, but within flat frames with grisaille decorations (plates 1-3). On the ceiling above, presiding and controlling where she can, is Venus the protagonist of the plot. Over the door are personifications of Peace and War representing in visual terms one of the most important polarities in the text. On one side, in a smaller space, Tiepolo painted in grisaille a popular episode from the eighth book in quite an unremarkable way (*Aeneid* VIII.383). The other three walls show larger scenes and they have in common an emphasis upon the magical or supernatural side of Virgil's epic. All three are concerned with the tragic love of Dido for Aeneas, but the points stressed are the divine

15. *Ibid* 303.

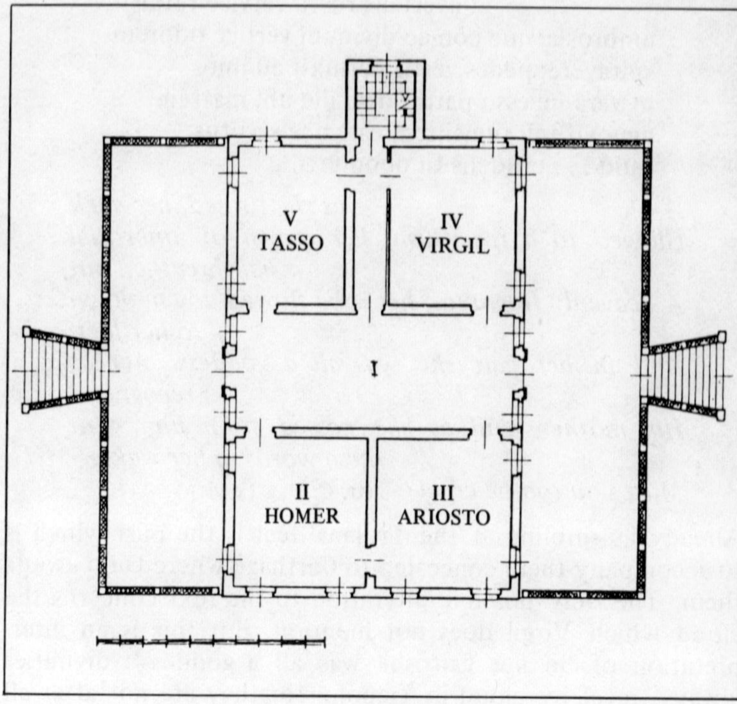

Plan of the Palazzina Valmarana. I Hallway; II Room of the *Iliad*; II Room of the *Orlando Furioso*; IV Room of the *Aeneid*; V Room of the *Jerusalam Liberated.*

protection which the hero is given and his sense of duty.

The first subject (plate 1) is taken from Book I where Venus has appeared to Aeneas and his faithful friend Achates on the coast of Libya in disguise as a huntress and (*Aeneid* I.402 ff.):

et avertens rosea cervice refulsit,
ambrosiaeque comae divinum vertice odorem
spiravere; pedes vestis defluxit ad imos;
et vera incessu patuit dea. ille ubi matrem
agnovit tali fugientem est voce secutus:
quid . . . crudelis tu quoque . . .

as she turned, her neck
Glowed to a rose-flush, her crown of ambrosial hair breathed out
A heavenly fragrance, her robe flowed down, down to her feet,
And in her gait she was all a goddess. Aeneas recognised
His mother, and as she passed from him, sent these words in her wake:–
Must you too be cruel? (tr. C. Day Lewis)

Already assembling at the Trojans' feet is the mist which is to accompany them concealed to Carthage where Dido awaits them. The only possible alteration to the text concerns the cloud which Virgil does not mention. But this is an interpretation of 'in her gait she was all a goddess': divinities always travel by cloud in Tiepolo, for they are not after all human and have to be seen to act like gods.

In the next scene (plate 2) Mercury also appears to Aeneas on a cloud in just this same way. Here Tiepolo conflates two incidents from Book IV where the god is sent to earth to order Aeneas to leave for Italy. The first of these episodes takes place when Mercury appears to Aeneas who is 'superintending the work on towers and new buildings' (*fundantem arces ac tecta novantem, Aeneid* IV.260). Later the god appears to the Trojan in a dream 'just as he'd looked before' (*vultu redeuntis eodem,* IV.556), 'high up on the poop of his ship' (*celsa in puppi*, IV.554). Tiepolo shows Aeneas dressed as he is described in the earlier passage but sleeping on dry land with his fleet in the distance. Here again pictorial conventions present special difficulties to the artist; for gods only appear in visions, in dreams, in heaven or in disguise. Aeneas is conveniently shown deep in slumber. Tiepolo is thus interpreting rather than simply illustrating Virgil's text for, having delivered his first rebuke to the love-lost Aeneas, Mercury 'vanished into thin air, far beyond human ken' (*procul in tenuem ex oculis evanuit auram*, IV.278). For the painter the clouds become symbols of the supernatural, and he uses them in exactly the same way in religious painting to support the Virgin when she appears to groups of Saints.

In the last of these three scenes (plate 3) the gods are once again at play, and Tiepolo joins with them and the viewer in poking fun at Aeneas' merely mortal attempts at controlling his destiny. Cupid adopts a disguise as Aeneas' son Ascanius and is presented to Dido. He promptly sows the seeds of passion in both their hearts. The Queen fondles him, unaware of 'the strength of him who was settling insidiously there' (*insidat quantus miserae deus, Aeneid* I.719). Earlier, we read how Cupid, to prepare himself for the deceit, took off the wings from his shoulders (I.690), yet they are shown in Tiepolo's painting which not only allows the viewer to recognise the god but also makes an additional visual joke at the expence of the mortal actors in the scene. Aged Carthaginian retainers are the only witnesses, although Virgil's text offered Tiepolo the chance to depict a colourful feast which was one of his strengths. This was not simply a question of space, for the painter chose to include an unnecessarily wide painted frame to his fresco; it is rather that the concentration on one or two figures allows the significance of the scenes to be quickly grasped. The ceiling of this room, now destroyed, showed Venus supervising the drama from her seat in the clouds.

The choice of scenes to be painted by Tiepolo at the Villa Valmarana is, as far as I know, unique. It is not a large building, and were the painted stages which form the basis of his murals to be densely populated with figures it would not have been appropriate. He was also painting on about life-scale so that scenes taking place with action over a large area would also have been impossible. The choice was conditioned by a desire to show the personal crises and the tragic treatment of Virgil's hero at the hands of the gods, and the validity of this interpretation is borne out by a comparison with the selections made from Ariosto and Tasso. Rinaldo is tempted by Armida but is recalled to duty and finally abandons her, a plot which has clear parallels with the story of Dido and Aeneas.

A roughly contemporary cycle by Corrado Giaquinto (1703-1765) to decorate a very different sort of building offers an interesting comparison. Giaquinto had a typical career for his day having been born in Naples, trained in Rome and employed throughout Europe, finally becoming court painter in Madrid in 1753.[16] Both he and Tiepolo were casualties of a change in taste when the Romanised German painter Mengs arrived in Spain in the early 1760s ready to work in the new Neoclassical manner. Giaquinto's Aeneas cycle comprises six oval shaped scenes painted in oil on canvas designed as mural decorations.[17] These pictures are not very large, each being just over a square metre in size. His patrons were the royal household of Savoy, and the series stayed in Turin in the Royal Palace until they were moved to Rome in 1803 to decorate the Quirinal Palace which was to be used during the visit of the German Emperor. They date from the artist's first working period in Turin in the early 1730s. There are six scenes and the dramatic focus is not simply on the most romantic section of the book – the love affair between Dido and Aeneas – as are so many contemporary cycles. Venus' appearance to Aeneas and Achates (*Aeneid* I.314) is included (as in the Valmarana), but Giaquinto next illustrates the moment when the relationship between the two lovers reaches the point of no return. In Book IV Juno forecasts to Venus how she will throw the two of them together as they shelter from a storm whilst hunting (*Aeneid* IV.120 ff.):

> his ego nigrantem commixta grandine nimbum,
> dum trepidant alae saltusque indagine cingunt,
> desuper infundam et tonitru caelum omne ciebo.
> diffugient comites et nocte tegentur opaca:
> speluncam Dido dux et Troianus eandem
> devenient

16. *Atti di convegno di studi su C. Giaquinto* (Molfetta 1971).
17. V. Viale (ed.), Catalogue II 76-77, pls.74 A-B and 75 A-B.

I shall pour down a darkling rain-storm
And hail as well, and send thunder hallooing all over the sky.
Dispersing for shelter, the rest of the hunt will be cloaked in the mirk:
But Dido and lord Aeneas, finding their way to the same cave,
Shall meet.

Virgil's description of this event as it actually takes place follows some few lines later (*Aeneid* IV.160 ff.). In order to economise on space – a familiar problem for decorative painters – Giaquinto conflates these two passages and distorts the text in showing both gods and mortals together, and even suggests some collusion between Juno and Dido as the Carthaginian queen, lightfooted in expectation, appeals heavenwards whilst her future lover plods solidly mortal and rather dull alongside her.

The emphasis upon economical conflation of succeeding episodes from the text into one painted scene is combined with an interest in narrative clarity and heightened visual interest in a scene from Book VIII. Venus prevails upon her husband Vulcan to manufacture arms for her son soon to be embroiled in wars in Latium. She then proudly presents Aeneas with her gifts. She descends, her divinity shining among the clouds about her, and addresses her son in a secluded valley into which he has conveniently withdrawn: 'the radiant arms she had propped up against an oak, before him' (*arma sub adversa posuit radiantia quercu, Aeneid* VIII. 616). As with the *Hunt in the Storm* Giaquinto follows the story only roughly for he includes some of Vulcan's smiths and the impression of their forge. In another scene, *Aeneas offering sacrifice at the shrine of Apollo* (prior to his descent into the Underworld at *Aeneid* VI.55 ff.), Giaquinto includes strong gestures and an elaborate setting to create a mood reminiscent of opera.[18] Indeed, the formula which the

18. Operas on the theme of the *Aeneid* were being produced in the same court circles at Turin at this time; see the sets designed by Galliari in V. Viale (ed.), Catalogue I (Scenografia, pls.49-50. For the connections between mural decoration and opera, see also Levey, *op.cit.* fn.14 above.

painter uses throughout this cycle, with protagonists holding the centre-stage supported by minor figures in the background, contrasts with Tiepolo's purer but also more poetic emphasis on a series of personal crises. Giaquinto presents a sequence of quartets whilst Tiepolo favours the aria.[19]

* * *

We should now move from the problems of illustration to those of inspiration. For many readers a visual response to Virgil's poetry is evoked most strongly in terms of landscape. The story of the *Aeneid* takes place in an assortment of landscape settings: sea-scape and coastal views, hunting country and the pasturelands of Italy. Yet it is perhaps certain evocative passages in the *Eclogues*, which give the clearest expression to a mood of nostalgia, the primitive Golden Age, the now familiar apparatus of conventional pastoral, which seems to characterize a typically Virgilian landscape. The motifs we have come to expect are never described simultaneously in any Virgilian text, and so are not subject to the problems of illustration in quite the same way as the decorative cycles I have already discussed. In the truly Virgilian landscape – one which is always inhabited but rarely dominated by Man – we look for figures in rustic repose beneath a shady tree. We listen for the tinkling brook and occasional – rather amateur – piping music.[20]

This mood, depending upon an expressive treatment of a landscape which completely dominates the figures, is best created in painting by the seventeenth century artist Claude Gellée (1600-1682) from Lorraine (hence often Claude Lorrain), who spent his working life in Italy mostly in Rome working for the aristocratic families attached to the Papal court. More than earlier painters, e.g. Giorgione and Titian, or his contemporary Poussin, Claude masters this mood, as well as the more specific iconography of pastoral poetry, and in

19. The other scenes in Giaquinto's cycle show Mercury appearing to Aeneas in a dream (*Aeneid* IV.557), and Aeneas explaining to Dido that he must leave Carthage for Italy (*Aeneid* IV.333 ff.) – not his arrival in Carthage as labelled in V. Viale (ed.), Catalogue II 76.

20. See M. Kitson, *The Art of Claude Lorrain*, Arts Council Exhibition Catalogue (London 1967) 7.

an important series of paintings after the *Aeneid* shows the limitations of the theoretical distinction between inspiration and illustration of the text which I mentioned above. The paintings were not only stimulated by his own interest in the epic but also painted in response to specific requests from patrons. His landscape scenes leave plenty of scope for the imagination and rely very heavily upon a meticulous attention to composition. It is mood which is Claude's main subject, and we are only confronted by details after closer examination.

In view of this it is perhaps surprising to learn that Claude only came to Virgil quite late in his career. His mythological source material until 1660 was mostly Ovid, and then he moved on to Apuleius and Tasso. But at some stage, perhaps having read the account of Aeneas given by Ovid late in the *Metamorphoses* and keen to extend his knowledge, Claude obtained a copy of the 1623 Italian translation of the *Aeneid*, in unrhyming verse, first published by Annibal Caro in Venice in 1581.[21] This was the purest, most accurate and most widely read version of the text available in Italy in Claude's day. Caro's edition contained only the text itself, a short synopsis at the head of each book and twelve illustrations which Claude seems to have ignored. It was his use of this edition together with the enlightened interest of a small but influential group of patrons which enabled Claude to construct the remarkable series of epic scenes which date from the last decade of his life. In addition to the half-dozen or so finished paintings in this group Claude also made drawings in these same years for at least another five subjects from the *Aeneid*, including Venus disguised as a huntress and Venus giving arms to Aeneas.

Two other paintings inspired by the *Aeneid* date from Claude's earlier years, but only one definitely shows a specific scene, and this was almost certainly selected by the patron who was attracted by the way in which the episode could be interpreted as an allusion to his own experience. This is a picture of 1643 now in New York showing the Trojan women burning the fleet, commissioned by Girolamo Farnese.[22]

21. See M. Kitson, 'The "Altieri Claudes" and Virgil', *Burlington Magazine* 102 (1960) 312 ff.

22. This picture (now in the Metropolitan Museum, New York) has a version in Claude's *Liber Veritatis* (L.V. 71); see M. Kitson, *Claude*

Farnese was the last of a famous family of Roman clerics and art patrons, and he returned to Rome in October 1643 after a spell as papal Nuncio to the Helvetic Cantons, where the local clergy had been quarrelling with the Imperial troops. His mission had involved extensive and arduous travel in the mountains, and one ingenious critic has suggested that the scene illustrated by Claude from *Aeneid* V had a particular significance for his patron.[23] Stranded in Sicily, some seven years after leaving Troy, the women folk are incited by Iris, a disguised agent of Juno, to burn the fleet, which was only then saved by Jupiter sending a rain-storm (*Aeneid* V.659 ff.). The incident was not only a reminder of the painful travelling which both Farnese – and Aeneas – had to endure but also showed the critical moment that followed when the Trojan hero was forced to accept his destiny and press on to the Italian mainland. With morale low in the ranks of his followers Aeneas was required to show considerable powers of persuasion and leadership to guarantee the success of his enterprise, and the scene was therefore a subject which might have appealed to Farnese fresh from his negotiations with the bickering Swiss and the well-nigh impassable Alps. In fact few other subjects from the poem (the carnal love of Dido and Aeneas or the intervention of pagan gods for example) would have been as suitable for a celibate cleric.

The first painting in the late group of works was done almost twenty years later in 1672 for an unidentified French patron. It is in the National Gallery in London and shows an unusual subject: *Aeneas at Delos*, using both Ovid *Metamorphoses* XIII and *Aeneid* III. An inscription on a preliminary drawing makes it clear that Claude is including details from both texts.[24] Aeneas has travelled to Delos to pray for guidance at the shrine of Apollo, and in company with his father Anchises and his son Ascanius meets the king and

Lorrain: Liber Veritatis (British Museum, London 1978).

23. M. Röthlisberger, *Claude Lorrain: The Paintings* (New Haven 1961) vol. I 215-216.

24. The inscription runs: 'Il 13 libro delle Metamorphosi d'Ovidio Anis (for Anchises) preto d'Apollon al tempio di Delphes (*sic* Delos) Anchise Enea Ascanio'; the drawing is now in a private collection in Boston, Mass. and the inscription is quoted by Röthlisberger, *op.cit.* fn. 23 above, vol. I 420-424.

High Priest Anius (*Aeneid* III.80 ff.). Ovid, but not Virgil, makes mention of the Trojans being shown the city and especially the two trees, identified as an olive and a palm, to which Latona clung when giving birth to Diana and Apollo. Claude includes these Ovidian details, but also shows the priest with a laurel crown which is mentioned in Virgil (*Aeneid* III.81).

A drawing for the next scene done in the same year, 1672, was annotated by the artist 'Virgil's book page 10', which gives the evidence for his use of the Caro edition mentioned earlier, that being the only case where the episode *Aeneas Hunting in Libya* figures on that page.[25] The scene was painted for Claude's last really important patron, Paolo Francesco Falconieri, who was both a Florentine nobleman and a Roman prince. Falconieri first employed Claude in 1666 and again for this painting, now in Brussels, and another pendant to it six years later showing *Aeneas and the Cumaean Sibyl* (*Aeneid* VI.1 ff.) for which the painting is now lost although the drawings have survived.[26] These show that Claude's source was Virgil rather than Ovid, and inscriptions on the studies demonstrate the artist's keenness to get his facts right. The oval frame which appears in the drawing is dispensed with in the picture and almost certainly relates to the original shape of the map of the area around Naples which Claude used to get his geographical data properly organised. The cardinal points are marked at the corners of the drawing, and inside the frame are noted the names of the islands of Ischia and Procida, the bay of Baiae, the town of Cumae and the temple there.[27] To the left foreground we see Lake Averno, the Sibyl's own home. In the final version Claude reverts to a conventional shape and lowers his centre

25. 'Libro di Virgilio folio 10' (on L.V. 180), cited by Kitson, *op.cit.* fn. 21 above, 315 and quoted by Röthlisberger, *op.cit.* fn. 23 above 424; the finished picture is now in the Musée Royal des Beaux-Arts, Brussels.

26. L.V. 183 (dated 1673) – a drawing now at Chatsworth, Derbyshire (= M. Röthlisberger, *The Claude Lorrain Album in the Norton Simon Inc. Museum of Art* (County Museum of Art, Los Angeles 1971) 31, no 56).

27. The inscriptions read 'mesedy, ponente, leve^{e}, tramo(nto)' and 'ischia isola, isola prochida, bia, la citta di coma, al tempo (for tempio) coma'.

of horizon to give a more satisfactory proportion between earth and sky and the chance to make more of the spectacular rays of the setting sun.

This same interest in historical geography is revealed in a painting, now at Anglesey Abbey (Plate 5), which shows Aeneas arrived at Pallanteum, the future site of Rome. Soon after he has landed on the coast of Italy at the Tiber's mouth Aeneas orders two boats to be rowed up river. At noon on the second day they approach the future site of Rome. The Trojans row to shore where King Evander and his people, including his son Pallas, have been sacrificing to Hercules. Pallas approaches the strangers, demands their business and asks whether they come in peace (*Aeneid* VIII.115 ff.):

> tum pater Aeneas puppi sic fatur ab alta
> paciferaeque manu ramum praetendit olivae:
> 'Troiugenas . . . vides . . .

> *Then, where he stood high up on the poop, Aeneas answered,*
> *Holding out in his hand an olive branch, emblem of peace:–*
> *We are the sons of Troy that you see here . . .*

In Claude's rendering of the text the only points of deviation are introduced either for clarity or extra effect. The confrontation is centralised with Aeneas high up on the prow, and although Pallas should be alone some supporters are included in the picture to balance the figure groupings within the composition. This painting, which at 1¾ x 2¼ metres is much smaller than the decorative murals by Tiepolo discussed above, was done in 1675 for Prince Gasparo Altieri, who took that surname on marrying into the family and was made Papal Nephew dominating court society in Rome under Pope Clement X from 1670-1676. On the relevant sheet of the *Liber Veritatis,* the notebook in which he entered drawings of his pictures to keep a true record of his output, Claude noted 'the arrival of Aeneas at Pallanteum at Monte Evantino', and on another sheet we hear about the influence the patron had on the

PLATE 1

Giambattista Tiepolo: *Venus departs from Aeneas on the coast of Libya*, 1757, fresco; Villa Valmarana, Vicenza.

PLATE 2

Giambattista Tiepolo: *Mercury appears to Aeneas at Carthage*, 1757, fresco; Villa Valmarana, Vicenza.

PLATE 3

Giambattista Tiepolo: *Cupid disguised as Ascanius is presented to Dido by Aeneas*, 1757, fresco; Villa Valmarana, Vicenza.

PLATE 4

L.P. Boitard: *Mercury*, engraving after a manuscript in the Vatican Museums; from Joseph Spence, *Polymetis* (London 1747).

PLATE 5

Claude Gellée, called Lorrain: *Aeneas arrives at Pallanteum*, 1675, canvas (175.5 x 225 cms.); National Trust, Anglesey Abbey.

PLATE 6

J.W.M. Turner: *The Decline of the Carthaginian Empire*, 1817, canvas (170 x 238 cms.); Tate Gallery, London.

PLATE 7

Claude Gellée, called Lorrain: *Ascanius shooting the Stag of Sylvia*, 1682, canvas (120 x 150 cms.); Ashmolean Museum, Oxford.

PLATE 8

Rhodian School: *Laocoon and his Sons*, probably first century A.D., marble; Vatican Museums, Rome.

choice of subject-matter.[28] The painter notes: 'Prince Don Gasparo has told me he wants the subject of Aeneas showing the olive branch to Pallas as a sign of Peace.' In fact, the patron claimed direct descent from Aeneas – as did a good number of his noble Roman contemporaries – and the subject clearly alludes to the link through marriage forged between his family and that of the Pope, for Gasparo's arms appear as flags on Aeneas' ships. Claude tries to catch the poetic landscape setting accurately as well as illustrate the textual narrative. His Roman landscape is as it is described in the poem, not as on the ground itself. He is not concerned with archaeological reconstruction, and his landscape is firmly set within the poetic mode.

A picture by Claude of *Dido and Aeneas* leaving Carthage to go hunting[29] has often been wrongly labelled as *Dido showing Aeneas Carthage*. A similar mistake was made concerning a painting by Turner exhibited at the Royal Academy London in 1814 and now in the Tate Gallery.[30] The English painter appended lines from Dryden's translation which should have made it clear that the subject was hunting and not, as one contemporary comment implied, the busy scene as Dido supervised the construction of Carthage. Ironically, in the following year and in 1817, Turner produced two scenes of the city.[31] Both loosely Virgilian and with rich allegorical potential, *The Rise* and *The Decline of the Carthaginian Empire* (Plate 6) struck contemporaries as visual *exempla* for the modern British Empire. Gibbon the historian was professor of Ancient History at the Royal Academy during Turner's time there as a student.[32] He was employed to school the young artists in the classical sources which they required for the construction of iconographic programmes for history paintings, and Virgil was, of course, one of the standard sources. To underline the connection between his

28. L. V. 185; Röthlisberger, *op.cit.* fn.23 above, vol. I 436-438.

29. L. V. 186; Röthlisberger, *op.cit.* fn. 23 above, vol. I 438-441.

30. M. Butlin and E. Joll, *The Paintings of J.M.W. Turner* (New Haven and London 1977) 82-83, cat. no. 129, pl.131 with lines from Dryden's translation of the Aeneid (*Aeneis* IV) quoted.

31. *Ibid* 84-85 and 89-90, cat. nos. 131 and 135 (now in the National Gallery, London and the Tate Gallery, London respectively).

32. J. Gage, 'Turner and Stourhead: the Making of a Classicist?', *Art Quarterly* 37.1 (1974) 77 ff.

work and that of Claude on stylistic grounds, Turner later asked for *The Rise of Carthage* to be hung in the National Gallery alongside the painting that inspired it. In theory and in practice Turner's *Rise* and *Decline* were truly epic histories inspired by Virgil.

Claude's very last picture – he died in November 1682 before he could enter a drawing of it into his *Liber Veritatis* – again shows a Virgilian theme. *Ascanius shooting the Stag of Sylvia*, now in the Ashmolean Museum Oxford (Plate 7), is a pendant to the earlier Colonna picture, and is perhaps the most subtle of the whole group in the way it expresses the contrary emotions so typical of the *Aeneid*.[33] Having landed in Latium, Aeneas' son Ascanius goes hunting and is inflamed by Allecto to shoot the pet stag of Silvia, daughter to Tyrrhus, who was warden of the herds of King Latium (*Aeneid* VII.496). Claude has chosen an especially poignant moment: once Ascanius' arrow flies the offence will have been committed and war will be inevitable. The serene, enchanted landscape with its great empty centre and strangely elongated, primitive-seeming figures is filled with tragic implications for those familiar with the story. Once one knows the consequences of Ascanius' innocent action it seems impossible not to detect a chill breeze blowing before the impending storm.

Such is the evocative power of Claude's paintings on Virgilian themes that it seems impossible to imagine a Virgilian landscape presented in any other visual mode. Although the painter's work never approached Virgil's for popularity, despite a great fashion amongst collectors especially in eighteenth-century England, this observation does suggest either a reciprocal current of influence between text and image, or that Claude had a higher degree of Virgilian sensibility than any other artist before or since.

* * *

33. Röthlisberger, *op.cit.* fn. 23 above, vol.I 485-488.

A final Virgilian theme in the history of art takes us away from enchanted landscapes and poetic moments to a debate which took place late in the eighteenth century about textual fidelity and the visual portrayal of emotion and pain. It also takes us away from visual art as such back to where Virgil perhaps more properly belongs – in the realms of literary theory. In a book written by an English clergyman Joseph Spence (1699-1768) called *Polymetis or an enquiry concerning the agreement between the works of Roman poets, and the remains of the ancient artists being an attempt to illustrate them mutually from one another*, which first appeared in 1747, is an engraving of Mercury (Plate 4), taken from an early Christian manuscript of Virgil in the Vatican Collection.[34] Spence's aim is to establish an authentic glossary of images, and he defends his dependence upon such a comparatively late antique source by pointing out that the Vatican illustrations are clearly copies from an earlier and therefore purer manuscript. Spence describes the image as follows:

> It represents Mercury going with his message from Jupiter to order Aeneas to quit Carthage (IV.254 ff.). You see the god passing through the air, in a more natural and easy manner than one generally finds in a modern painting of flying figures. In his left hand he holds his Caduceus: and with his right points to the heavens to show that his commission is from Jupiter. He has his Petasus on his head, and his Talaria on his feet. In a word, it agrees in every respect with Virgil's description of him on this occasion. Excepting that the painter has added his Chlamys which is fastened over his shoulders on his breast; and floats behind him in the air.

Spence states that the reasons for the inclusion of the *chlamys* in the manuscript illustration are obvious and justifiable: first, that drapery is used by the artist to give the impression of speed, otherwise hard to represent against a neutral background and secondly, that many ancient sources mention this

34. J. Spence, *op.cit.* 105-106, n.121, pl.14.5; the engraving is by the Frenchman L.P. Boitard (Plate 4 here).

article of Mercury's attire.[35] Scenes with flying figures by Beaumont of the type mentioned above exemplify the Rococo convention ('modern painting') to which Spence objected: Rococo style draperies are not shown naturalistically but rather for their value as decoration. Turner's image of about one hundred years later shows the same incident in Virgil's text, but completely avoids the tension between nature and decorative artificiality in presenting the god symbolically as a blast of light. Indeed contemporary criticism of the Academy show at which Turner's painting was exhibited centred on his cavalier attitude towards his ancient source.[36]

Spence was concerned with textual fidelity and with the way in which the Mercury illustration showed the figure in motion, but the long debate in the later eighteenth century over the famous sculpted group of the Laocoon, related to Virgil's account of the priest of Neptune in *Aeneid* II, involved more complex arguments about the correct interpretation of the expressions on the faces of the punished Trojan and his two sons. The debate raised three major issues: first, the apparent challenge to naturalism suggested by the very different sizes of the figures, although they all appeared to represent adults; second, because the group was sculpted in the round, the legitimacy of great art being concerned with the body in action; third, a question still partly unanswered, which concerned the priority of the sculpture or the account in *Aeneid* II. The Laocoon group (Plate 8) was discovered on 14 January, 1506 near S. Maria Maggiore, Rome, and quickly purchased by Pope Julius II who ordered a festival of celebration to be held in the following June.[37] The sculpture remained in the Vatican until it was stolen by Napoleon late in 1797. It was returned to Rome after a few years of exile in France. In his *Natural History* (36.37) Pliny the Elder

35. Citing Ovid, *Metamorphoses* II.736 and Statius, *Thebaid* VII.39.

36. Exhibited 1850 and now in the Tate Gallery, London (= Butlin and Joll, *op.cit.* fn.30 above, 247, cat. no. 429, pl.416).

37. For the history of this sculpture and a brief account (with bibliography) of the interpretive arguments, see F. Haskell and N. Penny, *Taste and the Antique* (New Haven and London 1981) 243-247; for full bibliography, see H. Althaus, *Laokoon: Stoff und Form* (Munich 1968) 146-147.

recounts the names of the three Rhodian artists and is lavish in his praise for the work ('of all paintings and sculptures the most worthy of admiration'), but he does not relate the subject-matter with Virgil's description. From the moment of its unearthing various qualities of the Laocoon were almost universally admired: the range or variety of the expression on the faces of the figures which move from suffering to compassion; the technical mastery for which ancient craftsmen were famous exemplified by the realism of the physiognomy and the anatomy; and the organisation of so many forms in movement which was judged a triumphant composition.

During the middle years of the eighteenth century a re-assessment of ancient works of art was undertaken, part of which included the imposition of a canon of taste which recognised a decline in standards after the era of Alexander the Great. For Winckelmann, for example, true beauty demanded a certain tranquillity or stillness despite an element of emotion or passion.[38] This theory could also be applied to poetry: thus Homer describes Jupiter as shaking Olympus with but a twitch of an eyebrow. Winckelmann also found this characteristic in the face of Laocoon who gives vent to an anxious and oppressed groan, rather than the 'fearful shout' which one might expect from Virgil's account (*Aeneid* II.216 ff.):

> post ipsum . . .
> corripiunt spirisque ligant ingentibus; et iam
> bis medium amplexi, bis collo squamea circum
> terga dati superant capite et cervicibus altis.
> ille simul manibus tendit divellere nodos
> perfusus sanie vittas atroque veneno,
> clamores simul horrendos ad sidera tollit:
> qualis mugitus, fugit cum saucius aram
> taurus et incertam excussit cervice securim.

> *Next thing,*
> *They fastened upon Laocoon . . .*
> *. . . and lashed him up in their great whorls.*
> *With a double grip around his waist and his neck, . . .*

38. *Reflections on the Painting and Sculpture of the Greeks* (London 1765) 30 (first German ed. Dresden 1755).

All the while his hands are struggling to break their knots,
His priestly headband is spattered with blood and pitchy venom;
All the while his appalling cries go up to heaven –
A bellowing, such as you hear when a wounded bull escapes from
The altar, after it's shrugged off an ill-aimed blow at its neck.

Winckelmann was undoubtedly anxious to emphasise such aspects of the sculpture's greatness in order to offset the feeling then growing that the muscular contortions of the group of figures were not in accord with the best ancient art: 'the quieter the stance of a body is, the more apt is it to describe the true character of the soul'.[39] In a later book Winckelmann expanded this theory that the central issue raised by the Laocoon group was the conflict between the body wracked by pain and the calm strength of the soul.[40] For Winckelmann the group is not in conflict with Virgil's account in its spirit, although he concedes that there are significant differences between text and image. It is simply that the artists have quite legitimately seen fit to adapt their source material in order to heighten the drama of the piece and create a more moving image.

Lessing wrote his contribution to the debate between the publications of Winckelmann's two books, and he argued that the differences between text and image lay not so much in the latter's moral value but rather in the formal necessity of striving towards perfect beauty. For example, on the question of Laocoon's expression he says: 'in sculpture a merely wide opening of the mouth is a hollow that produces the most repulsive effect in the world'.[41] Behind such statements one can discern Lessing's radical view that the visual arts are concerned with beauty alone. In contrast, poetry is the vehicle of expression and truth, and is accorded a higher place in

39. *Ibid.*

40. *Geschichte der Kunst des Altertums* (Dresden 1764) 2 vols.; see Lodge's tr. (*The History of Ancient Art*, London 1872) I 361 ff.

41. G.E. Lessing, *Laokoon* (1766); see W.A. Steel tr. (London 1903) 13.

Lessing's scheme of the arts which are not to be subjected to one uniform system of analysis as had been traditional. Deviations from Virgil's description are explained as a consequence of visual art's obsession with the attainment of beauty rather than illustrative fidelity. Since the eighteenth century it has become clear that a comparison between the text and the image in the case of the Laocoon group can only hope to produce an aesthetic commentary on the form of the latter rather than a complete analysis or explanation. Although the most recent view dates the group to the later first century A.D. (about one hundred years after the composition of the *Aeneid*) its form is almost certainly dependent upon the older visual tradition in Pergamene sculpture rather than any obligation to give a faithful illustration of Virgil.[42]

Despite his admiration for the group, Goethe firmly rejects the idea of comparing text and image: 'one is most unjust to Virgil and poetry if one compares even for a moment the most complete masterpiece of sculptured art with the episodic treatment in the *Aeneid*'.[43] Goethe's words on the Laocoon form a suitable conclusion to this brief review of the problems encountered by artists who take Virgil as their subject-matter, returning us as they do to the points raised at the beginning of this essay.

* I would like to thank Clare Pumfrey, Dorothy Scruton and Susie Barson for their help in providing the illustrations for this essay. In addition to those works cited in the footnotes the following have also proved useful:

Count Caylus: *Tableaux tirés de l'Iliade, de l'Odyssée d'Homère et de l'Enéide de Virgile* (Paris 1757).

P. d'Ancona: 'Virgilio e le arti rappresentive', *Emporium* (1927) 245 ff.

42. M. Robertson, *A History of Greek Art* (Cambridge 1975) I 541-542.
43. 'Uber Laokoon' in *Propylaeen* (Weimar 1798); tr. M. Bieber in *Laocoon: The Influence of the Group since its Rediscovery* (Detroit 1967) 28.

H. Bardon: 'L'Enéide et l'art des xvie-xviiie Siècles', *Gazette des Beaux-Arts* 6e per. 37 (July 1950) 77 ff.

D.G. Miller 'The Gallery of *Aeneid* in the Plazzo Bonaccorsi at Macerata', *Arte Antica e Moderna* 22 (1963) and 25 (1964).

G. de Tervarent: 'Presence de Virgile dans l'art', *Mémoires d'Académie Royale des Beaux-Arts* s.2 12 (1967) fasc. 2.

Virgil and the Augustans

ANGUS ROSS

> *I question whether in* Charles *the Second's reign, English did not come to its perfection; and whether it has not had its* Augustean Age, *as well as the Latin.*
> Preface to *The Second Part of Mr. Waller's Poems* (1690).

Charles II entered London on 29 May 1660, happily returning from his travels and vowing never to go on them again. A month later, John Dryden published a set of 161 'heroic couplets', one of them characteristically embellished into a triplet, with the title *Astrea Redux: A Poem on the Happy Restoration and Return of his Sacred Majesty Charles the Second*. The title locates the poem in an elevated context. Astrea, goddess of justice, abandoned the earth to the Age of Iron, just as Charles had fled after the battle of Worcester, leaving his kingdoms to the Cromwellian yoke; now, she was returning with the merry monarch to the Age of Gold. The noble imagery, however, is complicated for us. Exercising the historical faculty which the Age of Dryden so successfully nurtured and developed, we remember that three months after the death of Cromwell in November 1658, the same John Dryden had published *Heroique Stanzas Consecrated to the Glorious Memory of his Serene and Renowned Highness Oliver, late Lord Protector, &c.*[1]

Some features of *Astrea Redux*, as a poem, make it relevant to our topic. It has a network of Virgilian references. Dryden gives it an epigraph from *Eclogues* IV.6:

> Iam Redit et Virgo, Redeunt Saturnia Regna

1. Quotations from Dryden's verse are taken from *The Poems of Dryden*, ed. James Kinsley, 4 vols (Oxford 1958); the translation of the *Eclogues* and *Georgicks* in vol. II, of the *Aeneis* in vol. III; most of Dryden's extensive commentary on his translation is omitted. Quotations from Dryden's prose are taken from Dryden, *Of Dramatic Poesy and other critical Essays,* ed. George Watson, 2 vols. (Everyman's Library, London 1962), except for an extensive passage from the Dedication to the *Aeneis*, unfortunately omitted by Watson, which may be restored from Kinsley, *op.cit.* III.1011-1045. The text of Thomson's *Seasons* is most fully available in *The Seasons*, ed. J. Sambrook (Oxford 1981).

Now the Virgin returns, the reign of Saturn returns.

Secondly, for Dryden the theme of Virgil's fourth *Eclogue* was 'a vision of a new golden age under Augustus', and this image of the Restoration informs and concludes Dryden's own poem (321 ff.):

Oh Happy Age! Oh times like these alone
By Fate reserv'd for Great *Augustus* throne!
When the joint growth of Armes and Arts forshew
The World a Monarch, and that Monarch You.

But these closing lines themselves invoke a passage in the *Aeneid*, Anchises' prophecy of the return of the Age of Gold (*Aeneid* VI.791 ff.):

hic vir, hic est, tibi quem promitti saepius audis,
Augustus Caesar, divi genus, aurea condet
saecula qui rursus Latio regnata per arva
Saturno quondam . . .

But next behold the Youth of Form Divine,
Caesar *himself, exalted in his Line;*
Augustus, *promis'd oft, and long foretold,*
Sent to the Realm that Saturn *rul'd of old;*
Born to restore a better Age of Gold.
(tr. Dryden, *Aeneis* 1077 ff.)

In *Astrea Redux* Dryden articulates an image of his own very self-conscious era, and in specifically Virgilian terms inaugurates a new Augustan Age.

The image of Augustan Rome was a powerful resource for English writers during the following years, but it had more than a literary embodiment. Charles II's title, 'Sacred Majesty', has a clear reference to *divus Augustus* and was an innovation. Grinling Gibbons' statue of Charles II as Caesar, presented to the King by his servant Tobias Ruslat, may be seen standing only slightly larger than life-size in Figure Court, the oldest part of the Royal Hospital at Chelsea. The King himself wisely contemplates the Latin inscription over the loggia recording his own part in building the royal foundation for retired and disabled soldiers, and turns his back on the Battersea power station which now closes the noble open axis-vista of Wren's three-sided enclosure. A similar figure of James II, by the same artist, in Roman armour and crowned with laurel, stands at the west end of the National Gallery. It is perhaps Wren's St. Paul's Cathedral, however, that is the best visual correlative surviving from Augustan London of the spiritual, national and intellectual values that the age found relevant to its own development in the triumph of Roman power and culture. This triumph they identified with the career of Augustus from 27 BC onwards. The magnificence of ancient Rome itself haunted the European imagination, both in its vanished glory and in its titanic ruins. When the Great Fire destroyed Mediaeval London in 1666, an opportunity seemed to present itself for Charles II truly to emulate Divine Augustus, who, as Suetonius said in the old common-place, so improved the city of Rome that he justly boasted of finding it brick and leaving it marble. It is an emblem of Stuart aspirations to magnificence that such a vision of London foundered in poverty and the conflict of interests, but not before Wren had built his great classical church. This impressive and apparently 'modern' pile, however, proves on closer inspection to have some strange links with the past and with indigenous English arts and skills. The massive outer walls conceal the old-fashioned flying buttresses found necessary for structural stability. More striking is the construction of the dome, which does not rise according to the mathematics of Michelangelo underlying St. Peter's in Rome; it is instead supported within its double skin by a truncated brick cone, a huge, shortened steeple. So with the age's Augustanism; that, too, is not always what it seems; not always to be interpreted and evaluated by external criteria, whether drawn from what the modern critic thinks ancient Rome 'was' or from what was happening at the time in France and Italy.

It may well have been 'the panegyrics of Virgil, that master publicist, which cast the image for future times'.[2] The English Augustan age revered the scintillating group of writers patronised by Augustus and Maecenas, and who in turn immortalised the emperor's Roman peace and other

2. J.W.J. Johnson, *The Foundation of English Neoclassic Thought* (Princeton 1967) 17.

achievements. Virgil, 'the *vates* of Augustanism',[3] was joined in the pantheon by Horace, Propertius, Livy and the rest. But it is a question just what was drawn from these ancient masters. Modern scholars tend, very naturally, to create a 'real' Virgil, a 'real' Horace. Obviously there are many Virgils, and it is worthwhile asking first what it was that the English Augustans themselves saw in the poetry of their Virgil, before judging whether they had grasped some immutable virtues or values in the text. It seems reasonable, or at least defensible for Thomson to say that 'Dryden's beauties [in translating] however are not at all those of Virgil, *at least as we now feel them*'.[4] But when he goes on to say: 'The classicism of the eighteenth century is therefore for the most part a bad inheritance passed on to us from France, which had gone even further in that direction. But it remains a style and fine work can be and has been done in it. Thus an architect may consider the baroque a bad style, but he will scarcely deny that very fine work has been done in the baroque',[5] the reader's confidence falters. It is surely better to begin by being persuaded by his writing that Dryden is a great poet, of powerful imagination and outstanding skill. To see what he finds in Virgil is important not only in understanding Dryden's own poetry, but also perhaps Virgil's.

Dryden had a wide and profound knowledge of Virgil. The creative use he makes of this in a poem written early in his own writing career has been touched on. His indebtedness extends throughout his life and into other kinds of work. Though this pervasive influence of Virgil on Dryden still requires a full and extended study, his conscious drawing on Virgil's *Aeneid* in his heroic tragedies and other plays to produce an epic effect on the stage has been given some attention.[6] He also constantly makes use in his criticism of

3. L.P. Wilkinson, *The Georgics of Virgil: A Critical Survey* (Cambridge 1969) 43.

4. J.A.K. Thomson, *The Classical Background of English Literature* (London 1948) 204 (italics added).

5. *Ibid* 206

6. R. A. Brower, 'Dryden's Epic Manner and Virgil', *Proceedings of the Modern Languages Association* 55 (1940) 119-38; repr. in *Essential Articles for the study of John Dryden*, ed. H.T. Swedenberg Jr. (Hamden, Conn. 1966).

references and contrasts drawn from Virgil, more than from the works of any other single writer, even including Horace. Dryden held the view, expressed in the Dedication to the *Aeneis*, that 'a Heroic poem, truly such, is undoubtedly the greatest work which the soul of man is capable to perform'. So, naturally, he planned such a noble feat, of which in 1693 in his rambling *Discourse concerning Satire* he gives a 'rude Draught of what I have been long labouring in my imagination'. He intended his great poem, in Virgilian terms, 'chiefly for the honour of my native country'. He relates that he was doubtful whether he should choose the subject that had attracted Milton, that of King Arthur conquering the Saxons, or that of Edward the Black Prince subduing Spain. It was not to be; he was 'encouraged only with fair words by King Charles II, my little salary ill paid . . . and now age has overtaken me; and want, a more insufferable evil, through the change of times, has wholly disabled me . . .'. Yet, a few years later he published the substitute for his unwritten epic, in the form of his grand volume, *The Works of Virgil: containing his Pastorals, Georgics and Aeneis. Translated into English Verse.*

Dryden agreed with Jacob Tonson to translate 'all Virgil' at the end of 1693, and signed the contract on 15 June 1694. The book was to be a subscription venture, and was advertised as printed in June 1697, when Dryden was sixty-six and three years before his death. His translation was not an apprentice task, therefore, but the fruit of his very varied career as a poet. Even more significant than that, translation may be said to have been, apart from his plays, his principal poetic activity; it has been calculated that 'for every line of original nondramatic poetry he wrote two lines of translation from a foreign poet.'[7] There were some personal reasons for this; he became a Roman Catholic convert in 1686, and after the fall of James II in 1688 he could take no significant part in political writing. His theatrical employment was also limited. Even so, he had a strong imaginative drive towards realising in English poetry for the contemporary reader texts that were considered of supreme importance in literary tradition and culture; these included the satires of Juvenal and

7. W. Frost, *Dryden and the Art of Translation* (New Haven, Conn. 1955; rep. Archon Books, 1966) 1 ff.

Persius, poems by Ovid, Lucretius and Horace, as well as 'fables' from Boccaccio and Chaucer. He also needed the money such work earned. The demand of the reading public for translations in the closing decades of the seventeenth century was insatiable, one of the many interesting parallels between that age and the modern world. The demand and its satisfaction are signs of the emergence of a literary market, as we understand it. Dryden's *Virgil* is therefore more than a seminal English text; it is also a monument to the society of the time.

Dryden's methods of working as a translator are easily discovered, and investigation of them shows him to be a good scholar and a conscientious craftsman.[8] This judgement controverts the received opinion of the nineteenth century (which was hard on Dryden), echoed by A.W. Ward in *The Cambridge History of English Literature* (1933) VIII 51: 'From the point of view of exact scholarship, nothing can be said in favour of a method which does not show any reverence for the text, and very little for the style, of the original author'. In rendering Virgil's text, Dryden chiefly used the 'Delphinic' edition of Raueus (de la Rue), printed in Paris in 1675 as one of the texts prepared for the education of the Dauphin, eldest son of Louis XIV. This of course differs in many respects from modern texts, chiefly in the inclusion of passages discarded as spurious by modern editors. Dryden also used other editions, however, and sometimes ventured independent textual judgements characterised by common sense rather than remarkable erudition. The modern reader notices that the translation seems longer than the Latin text. There are of course mistranslations, but many of these and some additional matter come from Dryden's careful use of notes furnished by the editors of the texts he uses, as well as from the Latin prose *Interpretatio* with which, in the style of the Delphinic editions, de la Rue accompanies his text. In his painstaking search for the best possible rendering, Dryden also drew on the verse of earlier English translators of Virgil's works or parts of works, chiefly for rhyme words,

8. J.M. Bottkol, 'Dryden's Latin Scholarship', *Modern Philology* 40 (1943) 241-55; repr. in *Essential Articles for the Study of John Dryden*, ed. H.T. Swedenberg Jr. (Hampden, Conn. 1966).

only occasionally for complete lines.[9]

Dryden outlined his theory of translation in *The Preface to Ovid's Epistles, Translated by Several Hands* (1680), where his lists three kinds of translations:

> Metaphrase, or turning an author word for word, and line by line, from one language to another . . . The second way is that of paraphrase, or translation with latitude, where the author is kept in view by the translator, so as never to be lost, but his words are not so strictly followed as his sense, and that too is admitted to be amplified, but not altered . . . The third way is that of imitation . . .

He amplifies his ideas in the course of several other essays: the Preface to *Sylvae: or the Second Part of Poetical Miscellanies* (1685); *The Life of Lucian*, which the printer prefixed to *The Works of Lucian Translated* (1711); and the Preface to the *Virgil*. The *Virgil* is a paraphrase, or translation with latitude; whatever happens in the translation happens deliberately. An amusing instance of the latitude Dryden allows himself, and a pointer to the service he thought he was giving to his reader, occurs when he translates the final words of *iam pater Aeneas et iam Troiana iuventus / conveniunt, stratoque super discumbitur ostro* (*Aeneid* I. 699 f.) as ' . . . in order sate the rest . . .' (*Aeneis* I.980). He adds in a note: 'This I confess is improperly translated; and according to the modern fashion of sitting at table. But the ancient custom of lying on beds, had not been understood by the unlearn'd reader'.

The splendid folio in which Dryden's *The Works of Virgil* first appeared was the greatest single fruit of a relationship between the leading poet of the age and its principal bookseller, Jacob Tonson (1655-1736; called the elder, to distinguish him from his nephew, also named Jacob). Tonson was well-educated, read Latin and French and could turn passable verses. He was the son of a London cordwainer, one of the founders of the Whig literary group, the Kit-Cat Club, which numbered Addison, Steele, Vanbrugh and Congreve among

9. L. Proudfoot, *Dryden's Aeneid and its seventeenth-century Predecessors* (Manchester 1960).

its members as well as various grandees such as the Earl of Wharton and Walpole. He retired in 1720 to a prosperous life as a country gentleman. In short, he was just the kind of entrepreneur to finance the enterprise of making Virgil English.[10] Tonson's association with Dryden, which it is not too much to call a partnership, went back to 1679, and with ups and downs lasted until the old poet's death. Dryden worked with Tonson to produce the series of verse translations noted above, and these appeared in a skilfully contrived format of *Miscellany* volumes, which by commercial enterprise also gave young poets an opportunity of printing their work, and attracted far wider public circulation than the manuscripts that earlier would have passed round within small groups. Tonson (in association with his elder brother, Richard) advanced two hundred pounds to Dryden during the years he was working on the *Virgil*, and patrons also contributed money and books. The primary finance, however, was built on a foundation of two lists of subscribers to the venture.[11] The first group of a hundred (one more is actually included), each paid three guineas down and two on delivery of the volume printed on fine paper. Each subscriber had his own coat of arms displayed under one of the hundred and two engravings by Hollar of Franz Cleyn's Dutch pictures that embellish the volume. The second (unlimited) group of subscribers paid one guinea down, and a further guinea on delivery of a fine-paper copy; their names appeared in a list. Tonson did not invent subscription publishing, which was much used during the seventeenth century in scientific, theological and law publishing. He had been the first, in the fourth (posthumous) edition of *Paradise Lost*, to use it for an English poem, and with the *Virgil* was the first to use it for the work of a living poet. The *Virgil* with its select company of distinguished, noble and well-born subscribers and its larger group of other supporters was presented as a national and corporate enterprise. It was, however, not the first elaborate appearance of Virgil in English verse. John

10. K. Lynch, *Jacob Tonson, Kit-Cat Publisher* (Knoxville, Tennessee 1971).

11. J. Barnard, 'Dryden, Tonson and the Subscriptions for the 1697 Virgil', *Papers of the Bibliographical Society of America* 57 (1963) 129-151.

Ogilby's *Virgil* of 1654, also a sumptuous venture, had already used the Hollar-Cleyn plates, the pomp of its format contrasting with the flatness of the writing. Dryden's *Virgil* was by contrast a 'realisation' in English of the great Roman poet, in verse by the greatest poet of the day.

Tonson, a life-long Whig, wished the masterpiece to be appropriately dedicated to William III, but Dryden was linked by bonds of religious faith and political loyalty to the *de jure* king, James II, and thus having another Caesar in mind, refused. Instead, he dedicated the *Eclogues* to Lord Chudleigh, the *Georgics* to the Earl of Chesterfield and the *Aeneis* to the Marquess of Normanby. He thus combined the successful pursuit of old-fashioned patronage with the new system of publishing by subscription. The latter innovation Pope was to make more efficient and lucrative in his translation of Homer's *Odyssey* and *Iliad.* Dryden's *Virgil* did not have a uniformly favourable press, and the elaboration of dedications drew Swift's satire in *A Tale of a Tub* (1704), not only in the crazy tophamper of preliminaries to that book, but in the Introduction:

> And indeed it seems not unreasonable, that books, the children of the brain, should have the honour to be christened with variety names as well as other infants of quality. Our famous *Dryden* has ventured to proceed a point farther, endeavouring to introduce also a multiplicity of godfathers* [* See *Virgil* translated, Etc.]; which is an improvement of much more advantage, upon a very obvious account.

The question of dedication, however, points to the importance of politics in the fabric of Dryden's *Virgil.* A political element is clearly important in Virgil's epic. Awareness of this usually comes to the modern reader from commentary. Dryden, by identifying what he thinks was Virgil's doctrine with the contemporary severe and dangerous political struggles of his own day, introduces this strand noticeably into the actual texture of his translation. In the Dedication to Normanby, he devotes a section to the 'defence' of Virgil drawn from the Frenchman J.R. de Segrais and other authorities. In discussing what he calls Virgil's 'moral', that is the conscious doctrine of the poem directly expressed, he compares what he imagines the political state was in Homeric Greece with that of Augustan Rome, and goes on to say:

> But we are to consider [Virgil] as writing his poem in a time when the old form of government was subverted, and a new one established by Octavius Caesar: in effect by force of arms, but seemingly by consent of the Roman people. The Commonwealth had received a deadly wound in the former Civil Wars betwixt Marius and Sylla. The Commons, while they first prevailed, had almost shaken off the yoke of the nobility . . . Thus the Roman people were grossly gulled; twice or thrice over: and as often enslaved in one century, and under the same pretence of reformation . . . the Commonwealth was turned into a monarchy, by the conduct and good fortune of Augustus; . . . Your Lordship will know what obligations Virgil had to [Augustus]: he saw, beside, that the Commonwealth was lost without resource . . . Yet I may safely affirm for our great author (as men of good sense are generally honest) that he was still of republican principles in his heart (*Aeneid* VIII.670)
>
> secretosque pios, his dantem jura Catonem
> *the good set apart, and Cato giving them laws.*

Dryden's intention of drawing a parallel between the politics of the *Aeneid* and contemporary England will be clear from the above passage, a fragment of a longer and more detailed argument. In addition he places himself squarely inside this interpretation of the poem:

> But as Augustus is still shadowed in the person of Aeneas, of which I shall say more, when I come to the manner which the poet gives the hero: I must prepare that subject by shewing how dextrously he managed both the prince and the people, so as to displease neither, and to do good to both, which is the part of a wise and honest man: and proves it is possible for a courtier not to be a knave. I shall continue to speak my thoughts like a freeborn subject

> as I am; though such things, perhaps, as no Dutch commentator could, and I am sure no Frenchman durst . . .

The implication is that Dryden is shadowed in the person of Virgil, and the modern reader will recognise that Dryden had much experience of being a court poet, and of understanding the shifting personal and ideological danger of writing in such a situation. So that, whatever we may think of his actual interpretation of Roman history, we must consider his instinctive feeling for an aspect of the Latin poem unfamiliar to us, but one which is undoubtedly there.

The political 'doctrine' of the *Aeneid* was a matter of passion to the grim conservatism which Dryden had developed in his bitter circumstances which he sketches in the Postscript to the Reader of the *Aeneis*:

> What Virgil wrote in the vigour of his age, in plenty and ease, I have undertaken to translate in my declining years: struggling with wants, oppressed with sickness, curbed in my genius, liable to be misconstrued in all I write; and my judges if they are not very equitable, already prejudiced against me by the lying character which has been given them of my morals.

This kind of political passion was not highly regarded in later times, as may be seen in a comment by Wordsworth (to Walter Scott, 7 November 1805):

> The only qualities I can find in Dryden that are *essentially* poetical are a certain ardour and impetuosity of mind with an excellent ear . . . great command of language; *that* he certainly has . . . but it is not language that is in the high sense of the word poetical, being neither of the imagination nor of the passions; I mean of the amiable the ennobling or intense passions . . . where the language is poetically impassioned, it is mostly upon unpleasing subjects; such as the follies, vices and crimes of classes of men or of individuals. That this cannot be the language of imagination must have necessarily followed from this, that there is not a single image

from Nature in the whole body of his works . . .

It is not the least benefit of considering the importance that Virgil's works had for the Augustans that we may not only, in a European context, see the development of the importance of 'Nature' in English poetry, but also understand the power of passions other than the private, personal feeling which came to dominate Romantic poetry, and value in long historical perspective the poetic achievement of Dryden himself.

One short passage in the *Aeneis* will show how political thinking operates instinctively, if in this case amusingly, in the poem, and has to be accommodated by the reader. In Book I Neptune calms the storm raised by Juno to scatter Aeneas's fleet; his rebuke to the East and West winds prompts an epic simile (*Aeneid* I.148 ff.):

> ac veluti magno in populo cum saepe coorta est
> seditio saevitque animis ignobile vulgus,
> iamque faces et saxa volant, furor arma ministrat;
> tum, pietate gravem ac meritis si forte virum quem
> conspexere, silent arrectisque auribus astant;
> ille regit dictis animos et pectora mulcet:

C. Day Lewis writes in the Foreword to his version commissioned by the B.B.C. 'a translation which is not somehow based upon the language of its own time will never begin to come near the poetic quality of the original', and renders the passage:

> *Just as it so often happens, when a crowd collects and violence*
> *Brews up, and the mass mind boils nastily over, and the next thing*
> *Firebrands and brickbats are flying (hysteria soon finds a missile),*
> *That then, if they see some man whose goodness of heart and conduct*
> *Have won their respect, they fall silent and stand still, ready to hear him;*
> *And he can change their temper and calm their thoughts with a speech.*[12]

12. *The Aeneid of Virgil*, tr. C.D. Lewis (Oxford 1952).

Dryden (*Aeneis* I.213 ff.) makes the passage into:

> As when in Tumults rise th' ignoble Crowd,
> Mad are their Motions, and their Tongues are loud;
> And Stones and Brands in ratling Vollies fly,
> And all the Rustick Arms that Fury can supply:
> If then some grave and Pious Man appear,
> They hush their Noise, and lend a list'ning Ear;
> He sooths with sober words their angry Mood,
> And quenches their innate Desire of Blood.

Proudfoot, whose full discussion of Dryden's *Aeneid and its seventeenth-century Predecessors* has already been cited (fn. 9 above), makes two interesting comments. He is consistently hostile and null in responding to Dryden as a baroque artist, and notes here that '*And all the rustick Arms that Fury can supply* is an inferior rendering. Virgil is condensed, Dryden relaxed.' This of course, as is quite defensible, presupposes that terseness is to be preferred. Dryden has 'realised' Virgil's psychological phrase into a picture of a seventeenth-century country mob armed with scythes and bill-hooks, a potent and terrible scene for his contemporary reader. In the same way Cleyn's pictures present in the illustrations a spectrum of images drawn from Dutch landscape painting. Day Lewis's 'realisation' comes in turn from his nineteen-thirties intellectuals' patronising view of crowds: *hysteria, the mass mind, nastily*. Proudfoot also observes that Dryden expands on 'the anti-popular qualities' in Virgil's image, but the couplets are a neat illustration of the pervasive political strand in the texture of his translation.

It has always been recognised that the greatest influence that Virgil exerted on Augustan poetry lay in the language Dryden developed over the years as he grappled with the task of presenting the Roman in English dress. In his *Preface to the Aeneis*, Dryden has several significant things to say about these linguistic struggles.

> 'Tis true that, when I find an English word significant and sounding, I neither borrow from the Latin or any other language; but when I want at home, I must seek abroad. If sounding words are not of our own growth and manufacture, who shall hinder me

> to import them from a foreign country? I carry not out the treasure of the nation, which is never to return; but what I bring from Italy, I spend in England: here it remains, and here it circulates; for if the coin be good, it will pass from one hand to another. I trade both with the living and the dead, for the enrichment of our native language . . .

The imagery taken from contemporary mercantilist economics stresses in a witty fashion the national status of his endeavour as a translator, and the tone underlines the unity of interest in the publishing enterprise between the poet, his patron and the subscribers, all substantial men. Dryden opened this train of thought a little earlier, when he wrote:

> Words are not so easily coined as money; and yet we see that the credit not only of banks but of exchequers cracks when little comes in and much goes out. Virgil called upon me in every line for some new word: I paid so long, that I was almost bankrupt; so that the latter end must needs be more burdensome than the beginning . . .

Another passage from *Aeneid* I, following the epic simile considered above, is worth reading in the light of these remarks of Dryden's on his language. When Aeneas and his companions after the storm make for the Libyan shore, their landfall is a high point in Virgil's unmatched descriptive art (*Aeneid* I.159 ff.):

> est in secessu longo locus: insula portum
> efficit obiectu laterum, quibus omnis ab alto
> frangitur inque sinus scindit sese unda reductos.
> hinc atque hinc vastae rupes geminique minantur
> in caelum scopuli, quorum sub vertice late
> aequora tuta silent; tum silvis scaena coruscis
> desuper, horrentique atrum nemus imminet umbra.
> fronte sub adversa scopulis pendentibus antrum;
> intus aquae dulces vivoque sedilia saxo,
> Nympharum domus. hic fessas non vincula navis
> ulla tenent, unco non illigat ancora morsu.

This poetic landscape is serviceably rendered by J.W. Mackail:[13]

> *There is a place lies deep withdrawn; an island forms a harbour, thrusting forth its sides, whereon all the waves break from the open sea and part into the hollows of the bay. On this side and that enormous cliffs rise threatening heaven, and twin crags beneath whose crest the sheltered water lies wide and calm; above is a background of waving forest, and a woodland overhangs dark with rustling shade. Beneath the seaward brow is a rock-hung cavern, within it fresh springs and seats in the living stone, a haunt of nymphs; here tired ships need no fetters to hold nor anchor to fasten them with crooked fang.*

Dryden exercises his skill to the utmost and produces a baroque passage, the generous sound of which demands to be read aloud (*Aeneis* I.228 ff.):

> Within a long Recess there lies a Bay,
> An Island shades it from the rowling Sea,
> And forms a Port secure for Ships to ride,
> Broke by the jutting Land on either side:
> In double Streams the briny Waters glide.
> Betwixt two rows of Rocks, a Sylvan Scene
> Appears above, and Groves forever green:
> A Grott is form'd beneath with Mossy Seats,
> To rest the *Nereids*, and exclude the Heats.
> Down thro' the Cranies of the living Walls
> The Crystal Streams descend in murm'ring Falls.
> No Haulsers need to bind the Vessels here,
> Nor bearded Anchors, for no Storms they fear.

The passage has provoked some difference of opinion among critics.[14] Dryden 'realises' Virgil's assemblage and artifice with a disposition of conventions that seems to suggest

13. *The Aeneid of Virgil*, tr. by J.W. Mackail (London 1885; 2nd ed. rev. 1908).

14. W. Frost *op.cit.* fn.7 above, 42 ff.; taking issue with Mark van Doren, *The Poetry of Dryden* (1920; but 1946 refers) 55-6.

either a painting (like one of the plates), or an opera *mis-en-scène*, a Renaissance perspective set. The conventions are not simple, and the composition cannot be judged by pointing to the elements as 'conventions'. The power and decorum of the passage is prompted by Dryden's attempt to meet Virgil's art. The landscape is disposed by contrasts, *briny waters* and *crystal streams*; the chaos of *the rowling Sea* and the order of *a Port secure*; the *Sylvan Scene* (a Miltonic echo from *Paradise Lost* IV.140 alluding to the same passage) and the *Grott*, the former ready for human action to be played out, the latter the shelter of the *Nereids*. Whether this is Virgil's disposition is another matter, but Dryden's translation penetrates at least to the question of the *rationale* of Virgil's passage.

A passage of description like this raises the question of how Dryden's translation of Virgil crystallised his poetic diction, a complex subject which cannot be discussed here, though it is his most important legacy to the eighteenth-century poetic tradition.[15] His imagination works least well for the modern reader in his presentation of psychological states. His conception of Dido, or of the nature of honour seems, perhaps under the influence of the unfamiliar conventions of his heroic drama, to be coarse and thin, too peremptory and abrupt. His art works best in rendering passages of description and in 'realising' what he takes to be the doctrine of the Roman poem. These aspects are fused, because the descriptions offer a poetic or moralised landscape, of importance to the following tradition of art in England, including gardening (e.g. the 'Grott' at Stourhead). He is also good at building straightforward argumentative passages. It is with the influence of such a passage that we leave Dryden's *Virgil*. In Book VI of the *Aeneid*, the shade of Anchises gives a famous prophecy of Roman greatness (*Aeneid* VI.847 ff.):

> excudent alii spirantia mollius aera
> (credo equidem), vivos ducent de marmore vultus,

15. For some brief suggestive remarks, see R.A. Brower, 'Dryden's Poetic Diction and Virgil', *Philological Quarterly* 18 (1939) 211-17; for a hostile discussion, see A. Sherbo, *English Poetic Diction from Chaucer to Wordsworth* (Lansing, Michigan 1975).

orabunt causas melius, caelique meatus
describent radio et surgentia sidera dicent:
tu regere imperio populos, Romane, memento
(hae tibi erunt artes), pacique imponere morem,
parcere subiectis et debellare superbos.

This kind of patriotic self-consciousness spoke to the English nation with increasing power. Dryden's version (*Aeneis* VI.1168 ff.) is:

Let others better mold the running Mass
Of Mettals, and inform the breathing Brass;
And soften into Flesh a Marble Face:
Plead better at the Bar; describe the Skies,
And when the Stars descend, and when they rise.
But *Rome*, 'tis thine alone, with awful sway,
To rule Mankind; and make the World obey;
Disposing Peace, and War, thy own Majestick Way.
To tame the Proud, the fetter'd Slave to free;
These are Imperial Arts, and worthy thee.

Pope drew on this passage and on the Virgilian prophecy to find a fitting close for his *Epistle to Burlington* (1732). He keeps the spirit of the vision but has to turn it upside down. He wishes to outline the future achievements of a princely patron. Also, Britain is to follow Rome in public works while itself leading the world in astronomy (Newton) and manufacture, so the lines on describing the skies or moulding the running mass of metal must be excluded. Pope's lines build on Dryden's; they have a Virgilian tone, but are modified and amplified; they use and comment on his predecessors, Virgil and Dryden, in explaining the moral of 'The Uses of Riches' (*Epistle to Burlington* 191 ff.):

You too proceed! make falling Arts your care,
Erect new wonders, and the old repair;
Jones and Palladio to themselves restore,
And be whate'er Vitruvius was before:
'Till Kings call forth th' Ideas of your mind,
Proud to accomplish what such hands designed.
Bid Harbours open, public Ways extend,
Bid Temples, worthier of the God, ascend;
Bid the broad Arch the dang'rous Flood contain;

The Mole projected break the roaring Main;
Back to his bounds their subject Sea command,
And roll obedient Rivers thro' the Land;
These Honours Peace to happy Britain brings,
These are Imperial Works, and worthy Kings.

* * *

One of the most characteristic manifestations of the development of the literary market at the beginning of the eighteenth century is the initiation, success and continuation of the two essay periodicals, *The Tatler* and *The Spectator*. The 271 numbers of Richard Steele's (Mr Bickerstaff's) *Tatler* appeared thrice weekly from 12 April 1709 until 30 December 1710, with substantial help from Joseph Addison. The first series of Addison's *The Spectator* came out in 555 daily numbers (Sundays excepted) from March 1711 to December 1712, with Steele's collaboration. A second series of *Spectators* was continued thrice-weekly (nos. 556-635) from June to December 1714, wholly by Addison with some assistance from Eustace Budgell. As soon as the runs of each periodical paper were finished, the essays were collected together and printed in volumes. These first collected publications, like Dryden's *Virgil*, were partly subscription ventures. The subscription lists suggest that, like the *Virgil*, the four *Tatler* volumes could have been embellished with a hundred plates bearing the names of well-born, armigerous subscribers; 'cuts' were advertised, but never materialised. The subscribers, at least, to the collected *Spectators* were drawn more from the middle-classes and the professions; the readership certainly was.[16] The collections, and selections from the periodicals, were constantly reprinted throughout the following century and later. The social context of the essays, and the whole publishing venture, is relevant to a discussion of the place of Virgil in the Augustan age.

Up to *Tatler* 41, each number was headed by a Latin

16. The 1139 names of the subscribers to both collections are reprinted in A. Ross, *Selections from The Tatler and The Spectator of Steele and Addison* (Harmondsworth 1982) Appendix B, with some analysis of the make-up of the lists.

motto: '*Quicquid agunt Homines nostri Farrago Libelli* (whatever men do [will make up] the hotch-potch of my book', Juvenal, *Satire* I.85-6). Then for two numbers, *Celebrare Domestica Facta* ('to celebrate actions done at home') was displayed. These two mottoes thereafter recur, but the practice also developed of finding fresh mottoes for many *Tatler* papers. This, perhaps under Addison's direction, became the norm in the *Spectator* run. Finding mottoes for periodical numbers was not an unusual feature of contemporary periodicals, but in the light of what is known of the readership of the essays of Steele and Addison, the selection and distribution of these (chiefly Latin) fragments is not without interest.

It has been noted that 'Virgil and Horace were of course Mr Bickerstaff's favoured authors of all he drew on, save Shakespeare'.[17] Quotations from Virgil are prefixed to 25 *Tatlers*; 5 from the *Eclogues*, 4 from the *Georgics* and 16 from the *Aeneid*. The mottoes serve a number of purposes: acting as a title; pointing to an area of interest; drawing attention to the writer's opinions; defining a tone. They must have been meant to be acceptable to the reader, either because he (or she) recognised them as tags, or because they were drawn from admired writers. They would also nominate writers and passages to be adopted as current references by readers following the fashion. From the 1744 edition of the collected papers, translations were often provided, a neat expression of the didactic and popularising aims of these publications. Addison was, of course, a professional classicist, who specialised in Latin poetry, and the place of Virgil in the literary game of furnishing mottoes for *The Spectator* papers is remarkable throughout the run as a whole. For more than half of the 635 numbers, fragments are drawn from Virgil and Horace, with more than a third from Horace. Even so, the score for Virgil is 126: 24 from the *Eclogues*, 26 from the *Georgics* and 76 from the *Aeneid*. Addison opens *Spectator* 221 (13 November 1711) by giving an account of how he finds and uses these mottoes. Writing as 'Mr Spectator', he says:

17. R.P. Bond, *The Tatler: the Making of a Literary Journal* (Harvard 1971) 106.

> When I have finished any of my Speculations, it is my method to consider which of the ancient authors have touched upon the subject that I treat of. By this means I meet with some celebrated thought upon it, or a thought of my own expressed in better words, or some similitude for the illustration of my subject. This is what gives birth to the motto of a Speculation, which I rather choose to take out of the poets than the prose writers, as the former generally give a finer turn to a thought than the latter, and by couching it in few words, and in harmonious numbers, make it more portable to the memory.
>
> My reader is therefore sure to meet with at least one good line in every Paper, and very often finds his imagination entertained by a hint that awakens in his memory some beautiful passage of a classic author.

In line with this approach, there are several discussions of, or references to, passages in Virgil's works in the *Tatlers,* and many more in the *Spectators*. Pope's *Messiah*, for example, which makes up Steele's *Spectator* 378 is described as 'A sacred Eclogue, composed of several passages of Isaiah the Prophet. Written in Imitation of Virgil's *Pollio* [Ec.4].' In *Spectators* 70, 74 and 85 Addison discusses ballads; in 70 and 74, 'Chevy Chase'; in 85 broadsides and 'The Two Children in the Wood.' Addison has a genuine interest in popular literature, but Virgil is introduced into all three essays as a cultural touchstone, to legitimate the discussion of popular poetry and ephemera. The effect is rather patronising, though the reader senses the intentions to be better (*Spectator* 70):

> *Homer, Virgil* or *Milton*, so far as the language of their poems is understood, will please a reader of plain common sense, who would neither relish nor comprehend an epigram of *Martial*, or a poem of *Cowley*. So, on the contrary, an ordinary song or ballad that is the delight of the common people, cannot fail to please all such readers as are not unqualified for the entertainment by their affectation

> or ignorance; and the reason is plain, because the same paintings of nature which recommend it to the most ordinary reader, will appear beautiful to the most refined.

In *Spectator* 74 Addison juxtaposes passages from the *Aeneid* with stanzas from the ballad under discussion. The judgement in the essays is free, however, and the reader is given stretches of text to work on.

Two citations of Virgil may conclude this note on the Roman poet's place in *The Tatler* and *The Spectator*, a topic worth more extensive consideration. In *Spectator* 514 (20 October 1712) Steele begins with a quotation from *Georgics* III.291 ff.:

> Me Parnassi deserta per ardua, dulcis
> Raptat Amor; juvat ire jugis qua nulla priorum
> Castaliam molli divertitur orbita clivo
>
> *But the commanding Muse my Chariot guides;*
> *Which o're the dubious Cliff securely rides:*
> *And pleas'd I am, no beaten Road to take:*
> *But first the way to new Discov'ries make.*
> (tr. Dryden: *Georgics* III.457 ff.)

He introduces a dream vision, apparently sent in by an anonymous contributor. This opens with a significant paragraph:

> I came home a little later than usual the other night, and not finding myself inclined to sleep, I took up Virgil to direct me till I should be more disposed to rest. He is the author whom I always choose on such occasions, no one writing in so divine, so harmonious, nor so equal a strain, which leaves the mind composed, and softened into an agreeable melancholy, the temper in which, of all others, I choose to close the day. The passages I turned to were those beautiful raptures in his *Georgics* [II.475-89], where he professes himself entirely given up to the Muses . . .

We may set this beside a sentence from Addison's *Spectator* 417 (28 June 1712):

> Virgil has drawn together, into his *Aeneid*, all the pleasing scenes his subject is capable of admitting, and in his *Georgics* has given us a collection of the most delightful Landskips that can be made out of fields and woods, herds of cattle and swarms of bees . . .

Beautiful raptures, agreeable melancholy, the muses, pleasing scenes, delightful landscapes, fields, cattle, bees. This is a Virgil different from Dryden's; we are in the *Georgics* of Thomson's *Seasons*.

* * *

John Chalker in his valuable and detailed book, *The English Georgic: a study in the development of a form* (1969), begins (32 f.) with a contrast between Dryden's translation of the *Georgics* and the anonymous *Essay on the Georgics* which Addison wrote for Dryden's 1697 volume:

> Dryden stresses the complexity and sophistication of Virgil's work, sometimes . . . tending to exaggerate those elements beyond the limits of a strict translation, but not, it could be argued, beyond the spirit of the poem as a whole. Virgil's attitude to his subject is complex, the range of subject extensive and the preoccupations far wider than would be found in a merely preceptive agricultural poem. Addison's attitude is much simpler. For him the chief interest of the *Georgics* is stylistic, how [Virgil] has dressed his precepts in becoming and elegant fashions . . .

The Augustan age produced several more or less straightforward poems which follow the 'rules' of Addison's essay: these include John Philips, *Cyder* (1708), Christopher Smart, *The Hop Garden* (1752), John Dyer, *The Fleece* (1757) and James Grainger's West Indian georgic, *The Sugar Cane* (1764). These works take their starting point in the methodological or technological content of Virgil's poem, whatever mock-heroic or linguistic elaboration the English poets may embody in their pieces. It is James Thomson's great poem *The Seasons*, however, which ranks with Dryden's *Virgil* as one of the most substantial 'realisations' of all that the English Augustan imagination saw in Virgil's work. *The Seasons* started with the publication of the first version of *Winter* in 1726; the complete four-part poem of 1746 is the last version overseen by the poet before his death. The narrative thread of Thomson's vast creation is the farmer's year; this is the structure that holds together the myriad episodes, descriptions and reflections. The second organising principle, which represents another truly Virgilian impulse in the poem, is the voice or sensibility of the poet addressing the reader. It is this second psychological and rhetorical component of *The Seasons* that marks it as a later Augustan development of Dryden's dramatic, even theatrical, presentation. The essays of *The Tatler* and *The Spectator* are a modified, domestic theatre, half-way between. In the Preface to the second version of *Winter* (1726), Thomson declares his relationship to Virgil:

> . . . the best, both Antient, and Modern, POETS have been passionately fond of Retirement, and Solitude. The wild romantic Country was their Delight. And they seem never to have been more happy, than when lost in unfrequented Fields, far from the little, busy, World, they were at Leisure, to meditate, and sing the *Works of Nature*.
>
> That Book of *Job*, that noble, and antient, *Poem*, which, even, strikes so forcibly thro' a mangling Translation, is crowned with a Description of the grand *Works of Nature*; and that, too, from the Mouth of their ALMIGHTY AUTHOR.
>
> It was this Devotion to the *Works of Nature* that, in his *Georgicks*, inspired the *rural Virgil* to write so inimitably; and who can forbear joining with him in this Declaration of his, which has been the Rapture of Ages.
>
> Me vero primum dulces ante omnia Musae,
> Quarum Sacra fero ingenti percussus Amore,
> Accipiant; Coelique Vias et Sidera monstrent,
> Defectus solis varios, Lunaeque labores:

Unde tremor Terris: qua vi Maria alta tumescant
Obicibus ruptis rursusque in seipsa residant:
Quid tantum Oceano properent se tinguere soles
Hyberni: vel quae tardis Mora Noctibus obstet.
Sin, has ne possim Naturae accedere Partis,
Frigidus obstiterit circum Praecordia sanguis;
Rura mihi et rigui placeant in vallibus amnes,
Flumina amem silvasque inglorius.

Which may be Englished thus.

Me may the Muses, my supreme Delight!
Whose Priest I am, smit with immense Desire,
Snatch to their Care; the Starry Tracts disclose,
The Sun's Distress, the Labours of the Moon:
Whence the Earth quakes: and by what Force the Deeps
Heave at the Rocks, then on Themselves reflow:
Why Winter-Suns to plunge in Ocean speed:
And what retards the lazy Summer-Night.
But, least I should those mystic-Truths attain,
If the cold Current freezes round my Heart,
The Country Me, the brooky Vales may please
Mid Woods, and Streams, unknown.

The rotation of the seasons is presented through the weather, and Thomson uses some of Virgil's famous weather signs to produce a passage which is not a translation but a recreation of the ancient poem in modern terms (*Summer* 1116 ff.):

A boding Silence reigns,
Dread thro' the dun Expanse; save the dull Sound
That from the Mountain, previous to the Storm,
Rolls o'er the muttering Earth, disturbs the Flood,
And shakes the Forest-Leaf without a Breath.
Prone, to the lowest Vale, th' aërial Tribes
Descend: the Tempest-loving Raven scarce
Dares wing the dubious Dusk. In rueful gaze
The Cattle stand, and on the scouling Heavens
Cast a deploring Eye; by Man forsook,
Who to the crouded Cottage hies him fast,
Or seeks the Shelter of the downward Cave.

Thomson's lines are rooted in *Georgics* I.356-359 and 374-376:

> continuo ventis surgentibus aut freta ponti
> incipiunt agitata tumescere et aridus altis
> montibus audiri fragor, aut resonantia longe
> litora misceri et nemorum increbescere murmur.
>
> [imber] aut illum surgentem vallibus imis
> aëriae fugere grues, aut bucula caelum
> suspiciens patulis captavit naribus auras . . .

This kind of poetic landscape depends on Thomson finding some linguistic correlative for Virgil's diction. This he does by using Latinate forms and constructions, or by drawing on Milton's diction, which in turn bears this relation to Virgil. Any discussion of Thomson's poetry has to take the *Georgics* into account, and, if it does so, will treat Thomson's text with respect and admiration. The descriptions are not only real, but also 'poetic' or symbolic, related to those assemblages in Claude's paintings in which the elements have subtle and complex relationships to each other, and to which the 'reader' must give time and opportunity for the total effect to evolve. The spirit of such 'reading' is intimately related to the imaginative power which created such actual landscapes as Stourhead for contemplation, compositions of distance, perspective, objects, flora and fauna – and poetry.

As well as the 'poetic spirit' and the descriptive power, Thomson could be said to 'realise' the patriotism of Virgil's complex poem. Just as in Dryden this patriotism takes the shape of political argument, so in Thomson it assumes the form of 'imperialism' seen as a cosmic force. Perhaps the most famous passage of this kind in *The Seasons* is made up of four paragraphs in *Spring* (32-77):

> FORTH fly the tepid Airs; and unconfin'd,
> Unbinding Earth, the moving Softness strays.
> Joyous, th' impatient Husbandman perceives
> Relenting Nature, and his lusty Steers
> Drives from their Stalls, to where the well-us'd Plow
> Lies in the Furrow, loosen'd from the Frost.
> There, unrefusing to the harness'd Yoke,

They lend their Shoulder, and begin their Toil,
Chear'd by the simple Song and soaring Lark.
Meanwhile, incumbent o'er the shining Share,
The Master leans, removes th' obstructing Clay,
Winds the whole Work, and sidelong lays the Glebe.

White, thro' the neighbouring Fields the Sower stalks,
With measur'd Step; and liberal, throws the Grain
Into the faithful Bosom of the Ground.
The Harrow follows harsh, and shuts the Scene.

Be gracious, HEAVEN! for now laborious Man
Has done his Part. Ye fostering Breezes blow!
Ye softening Dews, ye tender Showers, descend!
And temper All, thou world-reviving Sun,
Into the perfect Year! Nor, ye, who live
In Luxury and Ease, in Pomp and Pride,
Think these lost Themes unworthy of your Ear:
Such Themes as these the *rural* MARO sung
To wide-imperial *Rome*, in the full Height
Of Elegance and Taste, by *Greece* refin'd.
In antient Times, the sacred Plow employ'd
The Kings, and awful Fathers of Mankind:
And Some, with whom compar'd your Insect-Tribes
Are but the Beings of a Summer's Day,
Have held the Scale of Empire, rul'd the Storm
Of mighty War; then, with victorious Hand,
Disdaining little Delicacies, seiz'd
The Plow, and greatly independant scorn'd
All the vile Stores Corruption can bestow.

Ye generous BRITONS, venerate the Plow!
And o'er your Hills, and long withdrawing Vales,
Let Autumn spread his Treasures to the Sun,
Luxuriant, and unbounded! As the Sea,
Far thro' his azure turbulent Domain,
Your Empire owns, and from a thousand Shores
Wafts all the Pomp of Life into your Ports;
So with superior Boon may your rich Soil,
Exuberant, Nature's better Blessings pour
O'er every Land, the naked Nations cloath,
And be th' exhaustless Granary of a World!

This carefully orchestrated passage leads on from a transition section in which the sun moves in the zodiac from Aries to Taurus to the metereological accompaniment of the neatly described formation of cirrus cloud. The order which in the *Georgics* Virgil presents by sometimes contradictory and conflicting forces, Thomson embodies also in his fashion. This he does by shifting points of view, offering inconsistency as harmony; Virgil's Roman peace is Thomson's imperial concord given a cosmic dimension by his physico-theological ideas. Virgil's rather mysterious and unplaced voice becomes Thomson's observer's tones. The rhetoric in both poems is recognisably similar and European. Thomson's Virgil is not radically different from Dryden's, and the English Augustan Virgil is, if rather unfamiliar to us, alive and powerfully influential, not dead and displayed *in vitro*.

Virgil and the Nineteenth Century

NORMAN VANCE

The Victorians knew their Virgil well. In educated circles he was read with interest and respect and frequently quoted, even in the House of Commons. The learned Mr Gladstone described his joining the Liberal Party by quoting from the fourth book of the *Aeneid*, seeing himself as the shipwrecked Aeneas being received by Dido. It was to be hoped, he told the House, that the consequences would be more fortunate for the party than they were for Dido. Gladstone seems to have had a special interest in the second book of the *Aeneid*: in verbal duels with his troublesome colleague Robert Lowe in 1866 the two men 'almost exhausted the second book of the *Aeneid*, and left the Trojan horse without a leg to stand on'. The Trojan horse in this case was the prospect of electoral reform.[1]

But Gladstone's admiration for Virgil was tempered with reservations. He greatly preferred Homer, and resented the Virgilian perversions of Homeric tradition, as he saw them, in the *Aeneid*. This qualified respect was not untypical: Matthew Arnold praised Virgil for his elegance, admired him for his pathos and condemned him for his inadequacy, his fumbled attempt to achieve the thorough spiritual mastery of the Roman world and its interpretation in a work of art.[2]

The continuing dominance of the classical curriculum in secondary and higher education in Victorian times ensured that Virgil remained a public property, a cultural monument like the Albert Memorial, charged with significance though possibly a little embarrassing. Public men like Gladstone could adapt him for public and parliamentary purposes not least because his greatest poem elaborated the public theme of arms and the man who was ultimately responsible for the

1. John Morley, *The Life of William Ewart Gladstone* (London 1903) vol. II.204 (*Aeneid* IV.373) and vol. III.481; Herbert Paul, 'The Decay of Classical Quotation' in *Men and Letters* (London 1901) 50.

2. Matthew Arnold, 'On the Modern Element in Literature' (1857) in *Complete Prose Works*, ed. R.H. Super (Ann Arbor, Michigan 1960-77) vol. I.35 f.

Latin race and the walls of lofty Rome. Publicists for cultural values such as Matthew Arnold had to take account of him. Yet for Gladstone and Arnold and many of their contemporaries, reared on romantic conceptions of the poetic, Virgil was at best the vain shadow of Homer, the cultivated and talented poet whose best poem was substantially derived from the truly great poet of antiquity. This negative aspect of the Victorian Virgil needs to be balanced against more positive Victorian perceptions of Virgil as the great poet of public and political themes and as the poet of pathos. This essay seeks to review all three perceptions and to conclude by relating them to Tennyson's imaginative response to Virgil.

* * *

The Victorian Virgil was partly moulded by continental influences. Benjamin Hall Kennedy, one of the greatest of the Victorian classical schoolmasters and compiler of the famous *Latin Primer*, observed judiciously that the Germans had underrated Virgil, the French, characteristically, had overrated him, but English scholars such as Conington could take a moderate and just view 'representing the balanced and impartial judgement of our mixed English race'.[3]

German scholarship, French criticism and English taste, at different times and in different ways, all tended to push Virgil into the shade in the nineteenth century. Germany, the home of massive and meticulous scholarship, pioneered the rigorously scientific approach both to Roman history and to Greek literature in the early nineteenth century. This tended both to glorify Greece and to emphasize the Greek origins of many aspects of Roman culture. The new historical and literary scholarship was animated by an essentially romantic ambition to arrive at origins. Livy was an important source for early Roman history, but what were Livy's sources? Virgil, quite self-consciously, adapted various Roman and Homeric traditions for his own ends in the *Aeneid*, but

3. Introduction to *P. Vergili Maronis Bucolica, Georgica, Aeneis*, ed. B.H. Kennedy (London 1876) xxxii.

what were the origins of these traditions and what status did they have in the consciousness of the nation? Barthold Georg Niebuhr, Professor at Berlin, argued that the legends and traditions about the origins of Rome must originally have been embedded in simple lays or ballads which were handed down by oral transmission until, eventually, they achieved formal literary expression in Livy and Virgil and other writers. Macaulay's *Lays of Ancient Rome* were an imaginative recreation of Niebuhr's lost lays which gave the Victorian reading public easy access to this legendary epoch of Rome. Closeness to the spirit and the detail of ancient but still living traditions became a criterion of value for ancient literature. Homer was celebrated afresh as the poet whose narrative articulated a part of the Greek consciousness preserved by oral tradition. Epic was defined by Niebuhr in the light of this perception as a composition drawing on material 'which has . . . lived for centuries in popular songs and tales as common national property, so that the cycle of stories which comprises it, and all the persons who act a part in it, are familiar to everyone'.

Virgil suffered heavily from this definition of epic since the sources of the *Aeneid* were as much Greek as Italian and the Italian traditions were already buried in oblivion. For Niebuhr the *Aeneid* was a 'complete failure', lifeless, derivative, misconceived from the outset.[4] Theodor Mommsen, a later German historian of Rome, looked more closely at the sources of the Aeneas legend and concluded that it was of comparatively recent origin in Italy and derived largely from Greek sources. By comparison with the Odysseus legend it had few precise connections with specific localities for it had not lived long ages upon Italian soil. A shallow-rooted tradition of this kind was poor matter for a would-be national epic, and Mommsen scornfully linked the *Aeneid* with self-conscious and tedious eighteenth century epics such as Voltaire's *Henriade* and Klopstock's *Messias.*[5] The enormous

4. See Gilbert Highet, *The Classical Tradition* (Oxford 1949) ch.29; B.G. Niebuhr, *History of Rome*, tr. J.C. Hare and C. Thirlwall (Cambridge 1828-42) vol. I.166; *Lectures on the History of Rome*, ed. and tr. L. Schmitz (London 1870) 662.

5. Theodor Mommsen, *The History of Rome*, tr. W.P. Dickson (London 1862-6) vol. I.482-4 and vol. II.458.

expansion of Greek studies, the obsession with origins, the confusion of the primitive with the authentic, all tended to devalue the finished work of art partly parasitic upon Greek traditions and literary modes. Romantic *sturm und drang* was out of sympathy with calm self-conscious literary creation. This German view of Virgil, buttressed by formidable scholarship, was very influential in England where Niebuhr's work attracted the interest of scholars such as the great Dr Arnold of Rugby.

This down-grading of Virgil was reinforced by a parallel English pre-romantic and romantic enthusiasm for the primitive and the craggily original. Thomas Warton complained that while Homer was original like Mount Atlas with its vast rough rocks and gloomy pines and cedars and awe-inspiring torrents, Virgil was derivative like the Capitoline Hill in Rome, covered with the temple of Jupiter which was 'adorned with the spoils of conquered Greece.' If Homer could take much of the credit for the best bits of the *Aeneid* similar debts were due to Hesiod and Theocritus for the *Georgics* and *Eclogues*. Virgil had only his style to commend him, 'the pickle that has preserved his mummy from corruption' as John Pinkerton observed in 1785. Coleridge felt much the same: 'If you take from Virgil his diction and metre, what do you leave him?'[6] Coleridge's *Ancient Mariner* was less highly wrought, or at least less obviously so: it was more 'primitive', closer to the unconscious sources of poetic inspiration, more to the taste of the romantic generation. In fact it exploited the ballad tradition, and the ballad began to supplant the epic as the preferred form of narrative poetry in the nineteenth century. The border ballads of Sir Walter Scott, poems such as *The Lay of the Last Minstrel* and *Marmion*, contrived to incorporate half-forgotten folk traditions in simple, rapid, immediately accessible narrative. It was pointed out that people would read *Marmion* who would not read *Paradise Lost. Marmion* retained its popularity throughout the nineteenth-century despite increasing competition from narrative fiction, which has by now almost eclipsed narrative poetry in any form. In 1866 John

6. See R.D. Williams, 'Changing Attitudes to Virgil' in *Virgil*, ed. D.R. Dudley (London 1969) 127-9.

Conington felt obliged, though with misgivings, to translate the *Aeneid* into the metre of *Marmion* to make sure that it was at least racy and readable.[7] About this time Thomas Hardy, reading the *Iliad* for the first time, exclaimed, without irony, that it was a very good read – almost as good as *Marmion.*[8] It was difficult to make the same claim for the *Aeneid.* Superficially, the greater narrative momentum of the *Iliad* and its apparent artlessness seemed to link it with the best products of the ballad tradition. The new Greek scholarship in Germany encouraged the view that the Homeric poems incorporated the lays of a Greek minstrel. William Maginn, the brilliantly erratic Irish journalist, exploited this in his *Homeric Ballads* of 1850, using Scott's ballad rhythms. This infuriated Matthew Arnold, who winced painfully at the 'detestable dance' of Maginn's verse and complained that this was hardly the grand style of Homer.[9] It may not have been, but it did help to popularize Homer.

Virgil, however, remained a more aloof figure, available through the heroic couplets of Dryden's verse-translation but not so directly accessible. William Morris tried to offer a people's Virgil in his translation into ballad-metre (1876), but whimsical archaisms and a conscious policy of de-sophistication rob his version of epic dignity and poetic subtlety. The opening of the poem is a fair specimen:[10]

> I sing of arms, I sing of him, who from the Trojan land
> Thrust forth by Fate, to Italy and that Lavinian strand
> First came: all tost about was he on earth and on the deep
> By heavenly night for Juno's wrath, that had no mind to sleep:

7. John Conington, *The Aeneid of Virgil translated into English Verse*, (London 1866) x.
8. Robert Gittings, *The Young Thomas Hardy* (1975; and Harmondsworth 1978) 107.
9. Matthew Arnold, *On Translating Homer* (1860), in *Complete Prose Works*, ed. R.H. Super (Ann Arbor, Michigan 1960-77) vol. I.132.
10. *The Aeneids of Virgil*, tr. William Morris (1876), in *Collected Works* (London 1910-15) vol. XI.1.

And plenteous war he underwent ere he his town might frame
And set his Gods in Latian earth, whence is the Latin name,
And father-folk of Alba-town, and walls of mighty Rome.

The French had always admired Virgil, often preferring him to Homer. Voltaire had observed stoutly that if Virgil was the creation of Homer he was his finest work.[11] But the same romantic accusation of inauthenticity, of being merely derivative, began to be heard in the nineteenth century. The most extreme condemnation occurs in a novel, the self-consciously decadent fantasy *Against Nature (A Rebours)* by J.K. Huysmans. The fastidious exquisite Des Esseintes rejects Virgil with an intemperate gusto, in effect rejecting seventeenth-century French classicism with the same gesture:[12]

> Virgil . . . impressed him as being one of the most appalling pedants and one of the most deadly bores that Antiquity ever produced . . . his Aeneas, that irresolute, garrulous individual who strides up and down like a puppet in a shadow-theatre, making wooden gestures behind the ill-fitting, badly oiled screen of the poem . . . He might possibly have tolerated the dreary nonsense these marionettes spout into the wings; he might even have excused the impudent plagiarizing of Homer, Theocritus, Ennius, and Lucretius, as well as the outright theft Macrobius has revealed to us of the whole of the Second Book of the *Aeneid*, copied almost word for word from a poem of Pisander's . . . but what utterly exasperated him was the shoddy workmanship of the tinny hexameters.

The attack on Virgil's prosody, so surprising at first, turns out to be part of a broadly based attack on the restrictions of classical prosody generally. This assault on Virgil has the almost hysterical passion of romantic revolt against the

11. Appendix to the *Henriade*, quoted in W.Y. Sellar, *The Roman Poets of the Augustan Age: Virgil* (Oxford 1877) 67.

12. J.K. Huysmans, *Against Nature*, tr. Robert Baldick (Harmondsworth 1959) 40 f.

institutions of the age. It has a parallel in the writing of Victor Hugo, who had admired Virgil in youth, and translated some of the more romantically horrific episodes of the *Aeneid* into French verse, but came to regard Virgil as a mere copyist, 'the moon of Homer', a good nature-poet perhaps, but definitely a man of talent like Racine rather than a man of genius like Homer or Shakespeare.[13]

This degradation of Virgil to the second class of poets because of his lack of poetic originality was finally and successfully challenged by Sainte-Beuve, perhaps the greatest French literary critic of the nineteenth century. Sainte-Beuve was quite sympathetic to the romantic cult of the primitive and was sufficiently in touch with the new German classical scholarship to have an informed and favourable estimate of Homer. But instead of dividing poets into men of genius and men of talent, Homer *versus* Virgil, he insisted that there were two kinds of poetic genius, primitive poets and studious poets. Homer, Pindar, Aeschylus and Shakespeare belonged in the first category; Virgil, Racine, Horace, Tasso and Pope belonged in the second. Originality and true poetic inspiration could be found in both categories of poetry: neither existed in total isolation from a cultural tradition, though this might be apprehended either intuitively or self-consciously. It was clear to him that Homer was not a completely original poet: he felt sure that he was already following another and earlier Homer. Conversely, the much more obvious and self-conscious exploitation of literary tradition in Virgil and Racine was not inconsistent with the secret and mysterious operations of original genius. This view was developed in a special *Etude sur Virgile* which was widely read and quoted in England as well as in France. Sainte-Beuve still thinks Homer is the greater poet, but maintains that Virgil's deep-seated commitment to the Roman ideal infuses his matter with original inspiration. Where he follows Homer or other writers this is not so much mere copying as an act of recognition of imaginative affinity, a mysterious 'call of the blood' to the strange hidden things that lie behind the writings of more than one great author.[14] This rehabilitation of Virgil

13. Gilbert Highet, *The Classical Tradition* (Oxford 1949) 406.
14. See Ruth E. Mulhauser, *Sainte-Beuve and Greco-Roman Antiquity*

was originally offered to the French public as a series of lectures at the Collège de France. But Sainte-Beuve was shouted down and the lecture-series had to be abandoned. The reason was political rather than literary: Virgil's reputation as the great poet of empire coincided awkwardly with a particularly tense moment in the political history of France.

* * *

Because Virgil's *Aeneid* had apparently been written at the request of Augustus it was almost fatally easy to see Virgil as a mere lackey of imperialism, to see his poem as an unblushing ideological justification of military oppression. This blunt conclusion took no account of the tempering of justice with mercy implied in the sixth book of the *Aeneid* where the special skill of the Romans is foretold in famous phrase as peaceful rule, sparing the humble and beating down the haughty (*Aeneid* VI.861 ff.). But in France the pursuit of empire had involved forsaking the ways of peace for a generation under Napoleon, and when Napoleon III came to power in the 1850s his attempt to revive the spirit and the trappings of empire, if not its substance, was unpopular in liberal intellectual circles. Sainte-Beuve owed his appointment as Professor of Latin Poetry at the Collège de France to the imperial government, and had perhaps unwisely transferred his famous series of critical essays, the 'Causeries du Lundi', to the *Moniteur*, the official organ of the government. Had he chosen to lecture on anything other than Virgil his lectures might have avoided unwelcome attention, but the analogy between Virgil the honoured court poet of the Emperor Augustus and Sainte-Beuve the officer of the Legion of Honour and court-professor of the Emperor Napoleon III was difficult to ignore. There was so much disturbance that only two of the lectures could actually be delivered, in March 1855.[15]

The most determined attack on Napoleon III by any

(Cleveland & London 1969) 196-202.

15. *Ibid* 60 f.; G. McLean Harper, *Charles-Augustin Sainte-Beuve* (Philadelphia & London 1909) 312 f.

literary figure came from Victor Hugo. Amidst the cheers of his fellow-liberals and much favourable comment from the English press he published *Napoléon le Petit*, a scathing lampoon which was immediately translated into English and ran through three English editions in its first year. Hugo's progressive disenchantment with Virgil has already been mentioned. It was closely connected with his politics and came to a head when, inevitably, Hugo found himself exiled from the France of Napoleon III. From that point onwards Hugo repudiated Virgil completely as a mere courtier of the tyrant Augustus.[16]

This political rejection of Augustus and Virgil as the poet of Augustus could be found in nineteenth-century England as well. It was an eighteenth-century fashion to dignify contemporary monarchs and emperors by erecting statues of them in Roman togas and comparing them with Virgil's Augustus. But that opulent and self-indulgent vision of royal magnificence was less popular with revolutionary romantics and down-to-earth middle-class Victorians. Thackeray the novelist, in *The Four Georges*, dismisses the classical image of sovereignty out of hand: 'Augustus is fat and jolly on his throne; he can knock down an ox and eat one almost', but outside the palace 'hunger is stalking about the bare villages . . . ploughing stony fields with starved cattle'. Elsewhere Thackeray describes one of those classical statues in Dublin as 'a pert statue of George III in a Roman toga, simpering and turning out his toes'.[17]

Whether in France or England would-be emperors, aspirants to the imperial dignity of Virgil's Augustus, tended to appear either ridiculous or dangerous to observers of liberal sympathies and classical education. Englishmen had no cause to love the vainglorious swaggerings of Napoleon III in France: no-one liked the threat of invasion they seemed to represent and Napoleon I had provided an uncomfortable precedent. The notion of Empire, given literary currency by Virgil and political currency by Napoleon, seemed to involve European Empire and so threatened British sovereignty. It was not

16. *loc.cit.* fn. 13 above.

17. W.M. Thackeray, *The Four Georges* (1861) in *The Oxford Thackeray* ed. George Saintsbury (Oxford 1908) vol. XIII.704; and *Irish Sketchbook* (1843) in vol. V.20.

until later in the nineteenth century that Englishmen revived the notion of a *British* Empire which might be compared with the old Roman Empire. For the mid-Victorians connections between Rome and ideas of Empire were disquieting rather than stimulating since the very name of Rome could suggest a tradition of religious tyranny not unconnected with the old imperial tyranny. Long ago Thomas Hobbes had proclaimed that 'the *Papacy*, is no other, than the *Ghost* of the deceased *Romane Empire*, sitting crowned upon the grave thereof: for so did the Papacy start up on a sudden out of the Ruines of that Heathen Power.'[18] The temporal power of the Papal states brought Rome into the arena of secular politics: Italian patriots such as Garibaldi who challenged this power had the status of folk-heroes in England.[19] In consequence the poetry of revolt was more popular than the poetry of imperial destiny. In any case, ever since Byron died fighting for Greek independence, if it was more romantic to favour revolution than imperial despotism, it was even more romantic to idealize Greece from Marathon to Missolonghi than to care passionately about imperial Rome. This naturally reinforced the literary enthusiasm for Greece rather than Rome, Homer rather than Virgil, which has already been considered.[20]

But if liberal intellectuals preferred Greece to Rome and Homer to Virgil the men of affairs came to respect the Romans for their administrative competence. As the century wore on the advocates of empire began to thrill to Virgil's celebration of imperial Rome bounding her empire with the earth (*Aeneid* VI.781 f.). They particularly liked Virgil's confident claim that, while other nations might excel in the fine arts, it was the Roman privilege to perfect the arts of government (*Aeneid* VI.848-53). It was almost fatally easy to make this an English Philistines' charter, casting other nations such as the French in the subordinate role of artists and appropriating to the English nation the Roman skills of

18. Thomas Hobbes, *Leviathan* (1651) (Everyman edition, London 1973) ch.47, 381.
19. See John Morley, *The Life of William Ewart Gladstone* (London 1903) vol. II.108 f.
20. See Elizabeth Nitchie, *Vergil and the English Poets* (New York 1919) 197-9.

government. This appropriation did not escape the ironical attention of John Henry Newman. In his historical novel *Callista* his doughty Roman Jucundus is a thinly-disguised earnest Englishman, a type of the 'State's pattern-man' embodying the civic virtues which Newman always scoffed at in relation to the higher seriousness of spiritual claims. Not surprisingly, Jucundus paraphrases Virgil by dismissing the Greeks as unrivalled in the fine arts but of course unreliable in matters of political and constitutional principle.[21] But the connections between Roman and British imperialism were often made quite unironically. The Earl of Cromer, retired Egyptian proconsul, addressed the Classical Association on *Ancient and Modern Imperialism* in 1909. It was clear to him that the Greeks were far too undisciplined to run an Empire properly, but the austere and practical Romans, imbibing the atmosphere of empire distilled in the *Aeneid*, had no difficulties of this kind. The implication was that English colonial administrators, also reared on the *Aeneid*, should be equally competent.[22]

The parallel with Rome was of course a tricky one, for the Roman Empire was known to be founded on slavery, sustained by repression where necessary, and overwhelmed by oriental decadence in the end. This problem is confronted by J.R. Seeley in his Cambridge Professorial lectures on *The Expansion of England* (1883). Seeley partially acquitted England of calculating aggression with his famous remark that the British empire was acquired through absence of mind, but he was honest and realistic enough to admit that the Roman and the British and indeed any route to empire involved a measure of lawlessness and brutality, proceeding by violent and unjustifiable means to the desired end. The best that could be said was that Britain's annals of empire were less bloodstained than some:[23]

> In some pages of these annals there is a real elevation of thought and an intention at least of

21. J.H. Newman, *Callista* (London 1855) ch.8, 62 f.; see Richard Jenkyns, *The Victorians and Ancient Greece* (Oxford 1980) 331-3.
22. The Earl of Cromer, *Ancient and Modern Imperialism* (London 1910) 14.
23. J.R. Seeley, *The Expansion of England* (London 1883) 135.

> righteous dealing, which are not often met with in the history of colonisation. Some of these founders remind us of Abraham and Aeneas.

The comparison is interesting. The colonial pioneer as religiously inspired man of destiny arisen from his country and his kindred like Abraham leaving Ur of the Chaldees and proceeding into the unknown at the behest of a higher destiny dignifies the imperial enterprise without minimising its discomforts or its cost. If *pius Aeneas* can be seen as an Abraham-figure, a man of destiny, rather than an Odysseus-figure, a compulsive wanderer responsible chiefly to himself, then he becomes a more respectable figure altogether. The fourth book of the *Aeneid* sets up a temporary tension between these alternative possibilities, for Aeneas confronts Dido both as an individual and as a man under divine commands. Left to himself, Virgil tells us, Aeneas would have devoted himself to the city of Troy and the sweet relics of his kin (*Aeneid* IV.342 f.), but the unknown Italy must command his love and become his country (IV.347). Virgil's Aeneas takes up the challenge of Abraham, and so did many of Seeley's pupils at Cambridge. They might well have preferred the comforts of Kentish vicarages or a settled life in London to the challenge of empire and the horrors of loneliness and disease involved in colonial administration, but the job had to be done. In India in particular anarchy and plunder were slowly being brought to an end and something like the magnificent authority of the *pax Romana* was being established among two hundred and fifty million human beings.[24]

James Bryce, another late-Victorian academic advocate of empire, traced analogies between the *pax Romana* and the notion of a *pax Britannica* in an essay on *The Ancient Roman Empire and the British Empire in India.* Bryce stressed the relative cultural homogeneity of the Roman Empire induced by the prevalence of the Latin and Greek languages and their classical literatures. Virgil in particular 'became the national poet of the Empire, in whom imperial patriotism found its highest expression'. The British in India lacked this advantage. Neither English nor any other language could claim to be the

24. *Ibid* 305.

common language and the vehicle of a common culture in India.[25]

Both the anti-imperialists like Victor Hugo and the imperialists like Cromer and Bryce simplify the Virgilian vision of empire and iron out the painful but poetically energising tensions which inform it. This is perhaps inevitable when propagandists appropriate public property for their own purposes. But even schoolmasters were tempted to appropriate regardless of context: in 1891 the Assistant Masters' Association was founded, and, conscious of the need to educate youth for empire, it optimistically took as its motto a line from the first book of the *Aeneid: quae regio in terris nostri non plena laboris?* ('what tract on earth is not full of our toil?'), (*Aeneid* I.460). The line is not as self-congratulatory as it may seem. Aeneas has been looking at the record of the world-famous battles around Troy represented on the bronze doors of Dido's temple. This evidence of Trojan fame is at best a consolation for the unspeakable sorrows and suffering associated with the mighty struggle which began at Troy and must continue for years to come until the Trojan remnant can establish a foothold in Latium: *tantae molis erat Romanam condere gentem* ('so massive a task it was to found the Roman race'), (*Aeneid* I.33). The dominant note is of weariness rather than of triumph: after acknowledging the fame of the Trojan remnant Aeneas utters the famous line testifying to the inescapable sadness at the heart of things: *sunt lacrimae rerum et mentem mortalia tangunt* ('tears in the nature of things, hearts touched by human transience'), (*Aeneid* I.462).

* * *

This note of sadness introduces the third aspect of the Victorian Virgil: Virgil as the poet of pathos. The tenderness in Virgil is strangely bound up with the harshness. Professor Seeley's brutal and disenchanting acceptance of the amoral

25. James Bryce, *The Ancient Roman Empire and the British Empire in India* (London 1914) 66 f.

mechanics of empire is somehow shared by Virgil. The *Aeneid* offers disconcerting juxtapositions of glory and grotesque violence, future magnificence and present pathos. This was noted by the saintly and retiring John Keble, a leader of the Oxford Movement, poet of *The Christian Year*, Professor of Poetry at Oxford. In his professorial lectures, dedicated to Wordsworth, Keble admitted he did not like the *Aeneid* very much. But he drew attention to the necessary blend of an almost savage sternness and solemn sadness in the story of Aeneas. Virgil's 'sorrow and sympathy for wretched and weak mortals remind one of a person trying to soothe a child's tears', he observed. But he also pointed out how by closing the *Aeneid* abruptly with the death of Turnus Virgil made no attempt to soften the harshness of death. He compared Homer's account of the death of Hector in the *Iliad*, where death in combat is rendered both nobler and gentler by being placed in the context of heroic friendship provided by the account of the funeral games which follow.[26]

Sternness and gentleness were attributes of Keble himself. Keble's Virgil who 'shrinks back as soon as he approaches those things which, in his judgement, the Gods have shrouded in mystery' also suggests Keble himself, suggests a Tractarian clergyman committed to the principle of decent reticence or reserve in imparting religious knowledge. Keble goes on to say that 'the last great dread of all', whether one encounters it on a Christian deathbed or before the massy gates of Virgil's underworld, is the supreme test of 'reverent modesty' in anyone who would seek to write about it.[27]

The solemn sadness, the sternness, the reverent modesty of Keble's Virgil go a long way towards outlining a poetic personality derived from the poems. This Virgilian personality emerges more and more as a dreamer, a poet of personal and national nostalgia, drawing his truest inspiration from childhood memory and the legendary intimations of the first beginnings of the Roman state. In the *Georgics* the celebrations of spring and fertility are associated with the springtime of the world and the frugal simplicity of life in

26. John Keble, *Lectures on Poetry* (1844), tr. (from the original Latin) by E.K. Francis (Oxford 1912) vol. II.267 and vol. I.135.
27. *Ibid*. vol. II.462 f.

the childhood of Romulus and Remus before the seven hills of Rome were built upon. Even when Virgil looks into the future, in the fourth *Eclogue*, in the sixth book of the *Aeneid* when he envisages Rome's coming glories, his imagery is shaped by that which is already past. His future golden age is like that forgotten time when Saturn ruled; his future national destiny is one in which the already legendary Alban kings are joined with Julius and Augustus and great rulers still to come. This affectionate turning back to memories of the early world and the first beginnings of life naturally reminds Keble of Wordsworth's *Ode on the Intimations of Immortality* and echoes of it in some of Newman's *Parochial Sermons*. Heaven lies about us in our infancy because vivid impressions are received innocently, unreflectingly, to surface in after years from deep wells of memory and acquire significance as the vestiges of primal joy. Keble lovingly analyses the visual imagery of the *Eclogues* and the *Georgics*, which interest him far more than the *Aeneid*, and attributes special felicities in the poetry to sights which had fascinated Virgil as a child, impressions sunk deep into his being together with half-forgotten emotional associations which flood back to enrich the poetry with a kind of mystery.[28]

This intensely romantic, Wordsworthian Virgil, ally of the aesthetic branch of the Oxford Movement, can be discovered also among the pages of Newman, particularly in his theological and psychological *Essay in Aid of a Grammar of Assent* (1870), written after he had become a Roman Catholic. Emotion recollected in tranquillity, intimations of significance from a lost or forgotten world, can be found in Virgil not only because the poetry is mysteriously enriched by memories from the childhood of the race and of the poet but because the poetry itself has become part of growing up, a structure for childish or at least adolescent emotion. Newman is obviously thinking of his own bookish boyhood when he describes how the words of some classic author[29]

> at length come home to (the reader), when long years have passed, and he has some experience of

28. *Ibid* vol. II.450-8.
29. J.H. Newman, *An Essay in Aid of a Grammar of Assent* (London 1870) 75 f.

> life, and pierce him with their sad earnestness and vivid exactness. Then he comes to understand how it is that lines, the birth of some chance morning or evening at an Ionian festival, or among the Sabine hills, have lasted generation after generation . . . Perhaps this is the reason of the medieval opinion about Virgil, as if a prophet or magician; his single words and phrases, his pathetic half-lines, giving utterance, as the voice of Nature herself, to that pain and weariness, yet hope of better things, which is experience of her children in every time.

This is the Virgil of the fall of Troy and the death of Dido and of the funeral of Pallas, the melancholy Virgil which co-exists strangely with the other Virgil of heroic conquest in Latium. In the sixth book of the *Aeneid* the tragedy of unfulfilled possibility is most painfully present: we see mighty-hearted heroes and unwedded girls and sons placed on the pyre before their father's eyes, the unburied ones who stand on the banks of the Styx longing, perhaps in vain, to reach the further shore (*Aeneid* VI.313 f):

> stabant orantes primi transmittere cursum
> tendebantque manus ripae ulterioris amore.

> *So they all stood, each begging to be ferried across first,*
> *Their hands stretched out in longing for the shore beyond the river.*

Later Aeneas himself encounters the pain of death's separation, the pang of a longing that cannot be fulfilled. Three times he seeks to fling his arms round the neck of his father Anchises, but three times the insubstantial shade flees from his hands (*Aeneid* VI.701 f.):

> ter frustra comprensa manus effugit imago,
> par levibus ventis volucrique simillima somno.

> *Three times the phantom slipped his vain embrace – it was like*
> *Grasping a wisp of wind or the wings of a fleeting dream.*

There is a point of intersection between the romantic religious temperament of Newman, pierced with sadness and looking beyond a beautiful but doomed world to a heavenly city and the hope of better things, and the religious melancholy of Virgil, poising his Aeneas between pain and promise, ruined Troy and the vision of a greater city. One of the links between Virgil and Newman is St Augustine. Newman's friend Keble points out how the tone and temper of Virgil penetrated into the very heart and soul of the boyish Augustine.[30] From Virgil Augustine inherited the imagery of glory and of desolation. At the beginning of *The City of God* Augustine makes the *Aeneid* the supreme literary celebration of the rejected and now crumbling earthly city, once-glorious Rome now penetrated by Alaric and the Goths. For Augustine the Virgilian doctrine of Roman destiny, mercy for the vanquished and chastisement for the haughty, was a neat summary of 'the swollen spirit of human pride (which) claims for itself this high prerogative, which belongs to God alone.' God's prerogative is asserted in Holy Scriptures in terms parallel to Virgil's claims for Rome, Augustine observes: in *Proverbs, James* and *I Peter* it is written that 'God resisteth the proud and giveth grace to the humble'. Augustine deplores, where Virgil merely records, the endless wars of Rome, wars against external foes and civil wars, all undertaken to gratify the dangerous lust of sovereignty at a frightful human cost.[31] The tension between glory and misery is delicately balanced in Virgil, so that it is easy for Augustine and his disciple Newman to respond sympathetically to the sadness of the Roman poet for the world as it is and to identify themselves in part with his vision of future peace when the gates of war are closed and impious rage shall sit within with fettered hands (*Aeneid* I.293 ff.).

This sadness of Virgil pierced more secular Victorian minds as well. The story of Dido had always been popular and her suffering appealed to the Victorians as to earlier generations. Music helped to bring it home to them. Purcell's opera *Dido and Aeneas* had been little known, had remained

30. John Keble, *op.cit.* vol. II.469.
31. Augustine, *The City of God*, tr. D.B. Zema and G.G. Walsh (Washington 1950) I (preface) and I.2; see also III.12-14.

in manuscript, in fact, until 1840, when it was published by the Musical Antiquarian Society. This soon stimulated amateur performances in London, Liverpool, Manchester and other more provincial centres. Novello, the music publishers, produced an inexpensive edition of the score so that more and more choral societies added it to their repertoire. While the *Aeneid* had long been public property among the classically educated the increasing musical fame of Dido's lament, acknowledged as one of the great things in music, helped to degrade Aeneas in the eyes of a wider public who might have had little contact with the poem itself. Aeneas is curiously marginal in the account of Dido's passion and sorrow even in the *Aeneid*, and in Purcell's opera the feelings of Aeneas are dealt with only in a few bars of recitative. When the two lovers sing together at the end this is merely to allow Dido to fling insults at Aeneas. While Purcell's Dido was often compared to a Shakespearian tragic heroine Purcell's Aeneas was little more than a functionary of plot.[32]

This downgrading of Aeneas assisted the appropriation of the *Aeneid* as a series of vignettes of private emotion. For poets of romantic and melancholic tendency Dido's sorrow held more interest than the deeds of Aeneas and the walls of lofty Rome. Matthew Arnold's sensibility winced at the brassy notes of martial endeavour associated with the war in Latium, but savoured the poem's more private moments. In 'The Scholar Gipsy', his poem of retreat, the proud and angry Dido spurning her faithless lover supplies an image and a vocabulary of withdrawal: Arnold deliberately echoes Virgil's language *oculos aversa tenebat* 'she kept her gaze away from him' (*Aeneid* VI.469) by urging the Scholar gipsy to withdraw from contact with modern life:

> Averse, as Dido did with gesture stern
> From her false friend's approach in Hades turn,
> Wave us away, and keep thy solitude.

For Arnold as for many Victorian critics the Dido episode was the most interesting because the most directly dramatic and moving episode of the *Aeneid*. But the poem is not a

32. W.H. Cummings, *Purcell* (London 1881) 33; J.A. Westrup, *Purcell* (1937; rev. ed. London 1975) 116 and 123 f.

drama, even though Arnold wished it was. Somehow Arnold contrives to enrol Virgil among the company of noble literary and personal failures, a kind of Augustan Arthur Hugh Clough almost, whose best work should have assumed a different form and attempted a less daunting subject.[33]

> Virgil, as Niebuhr has well said, expressed no affected self-disparagement, but the haunting, the irresistible self-dissatisfaction of his heart, when he desired on his death-bed that his poem might be destroyed.

Haunting irresistible self-dissatisfaction and a despair of fully mastering the world about him are really more the characteristics of Arnold than of Virgil. By looking for lyrical and dramatic fragments in the *Aeneid* Arnold fails to take account of the overarching structure of historical continuities reaching from the walls of Troy to the triumphs of Augustus. Because Arnold could no longer really believe in unity and peace and historical continuity in a problematic age of social and political disruptions he refused to listen properly to a poet who did.

As the nineteenth century drew to its close and elegant and cultured despair at the end of the age became the fashion it was natural that Virgil as poet of pathos should be assimilated to the taste of the time. F.W.H. Myers wrote wistfully[34] that

> all his emotions seem to have fused or melted into that *Welt-Schmertz* . . . so familiar to our ears . . . The so-called modern air in Virgil's poems is in great measure the result of the constantly-felt pressure of this obscure home-sickness – this infinite desire.

This is only part of the truth. The sense of separation from an earlier and more fortunate time is present in the poem, particularly when Aeneas recalls comrades and family who have perished, but this sadness and regret is contained within a larger structure of historical continuity and manifest destiny. Among the Victorians only Tennyson really

33. Matthew Arnold, *Poems*, ed. Kenneth Allott (London 1965) 342, line 208; *Complete Prose Works*, ed. R.H. Super (Ann Arbor, Michigan 1960-1977) vol. I.35 f.

34. F.W.H. Myers, 'Virgil' in *Essays Classical* (London 1883) 144.

understood: he comes closer than most of his contemporaries to the Virgil of the *Aeneid* because his own imagination combines Virgilian pathos and responsiveness to natural things with an acute sense of inevitable historical process.

* * *

The death of Tennyson's King Arthur is essentially Virgilian. It is sad and strange but it is also caught up in the larger movement of history as the old order changeth giving place to new. This helps to contain the sadness, to make it possible to sustain the heavy sense of loss; whether Arthur comes again or not there is a sense of future possibility and a new day dawning. Sir Bedivere looks along the water into another age: even his hesitation recalls the language and atmosphere of *Aeneid* VI.451 ff. (*The passing of Arthur* 464):[35]

He saw,
Straining his eyes beneath an arch of hand,
Or thought he saw, the speck that bare the King,
Down that long water opening on the deep
Somewhere far off, pass on and on, and go
From less to less and vanish into light.
And the new sun rose bringing the new year.

The tone is melancholy, but the sense of historical succession may possibly recall a much more jubilant celebration of renewal in Virgil's *Eclogue* IV.4 f.:

ultima Cumaei venit iam carminis aetas;
magnus ab integro saeclorum nascitur ordo.

Ours is the crowning era foretold in prophecy:
Born of Time, a great new cycle of centuries
Begins.

Tennyson's *Idylls of the King* is formally a series of pictures rather than a full-scale epic, almost as if the steady heroism and sustained purpose of epic narrative were no longer possible in troubled and fragmented times. But the

35. All Tennyson quotations are from *Poems*, ed. Christopher Ricks (London 1969).

Aeneid looms as a huge shadow behind Tennyson's poem. There are many verbal echoes of Virgil, as there are elsewhere in Tennyson. It would be tedious to examine these in detail: John Churton Collins, who scrutinized all Tennyson's supposed classical borrowings, probably deserved the poet's alleged rebuke that he was 'a louse on the locks of literature'.[36] Tennyson's treatment of Virgil, like Virgil's treatment of Homer, is not plagiarism but creative adaptation and transformation of public and private themes. The echoes resonate with significance. When Bedivere falters in the *Idylls*' final episode, *The Passing of Arthur*, he is described (228) as 'dividing the swift mind', which is a literal translation of Virgil's phrase for Aeneas' hesitation when Mercury tells him he must leave Dido (*Aeneid* IV.285). The point is that in both cases business of epic importance presses upon the individual: Bedivere must dispose of the sword Excalibur, not keep it from the waters whence it came, so Arthur may die in peace. Aeneas must obey Mercury and proceed to Latium despite the seductions of Dido. The passing of Arthur is both an end and a beginning of a new order; the departure of Aeneas from Carthage is the end of his love but is necessary so that he can inaugurate the new order from which the greatness of Rome was to spring. Other echoes, particularly of the Dido episode which provides a model for Merlin's seduction by Vivien and for other emotional encounters throughout the *Idylls*, serve a similar purpose. Not only do they wrap the experience in dignified epic language: they recall the central importance of order, of the noble idealism of the round table, which pervades the poem just as the destiny of Rome pervades the *Aeneid*.

For Tennyson the Dido story, for all its pathos, is not merely passionate lyric or dramatic episode: it belongs in a context of epic destiny. Rome is not merely a distant prospect for Aeneas, something which will come after him:

36. Discussed by Theodore Redpath in 'Tennyson and the Literature of Greece and Rome', in *Studies in Tennyson*, ed. Hallam Tennyson (London 1981) 211, n.10; classical influences on Tennyson are studies in W.P. Mustard, *Classical Echoes in Tennyson* (New York 1904); W.P. Mustard, 'Virgil's Georgics and the British Poets', *American Journal of Philology* 29 (1908) 1-32; Douglas Bush, *Mythology and the Romantic Tradition in English Poetry* (Cambridge, Mass. 1937) 206-228.

it is a moral ideal, the supreme goal and justification for the strivings of arms and men, the ideal which is enshrined in the peace of Augustus and the practice of vanquishing the proud and showing mercy to the humble. Like Rome, Camelot is both physical location and moral ideal, just as the quest of the Holy Grail is both physical journey and encounter with moral vision. When Gareth sets forth with his companions for Camelot the fair city disappears in the mist and the companions feel it is a city of Enchanters, built by fairy kings (*Gareth and Lynette* 203):

> Lord, there is no such city anywhere,
> But all a vision.

This is prophetic, for Camelot itself seems to disintegrate by the end of the *Idylls*: the ideal cannot be sustained in practice against inner dissensions and betrayal, though the vision itself remains. The poem operates in a twilit zone between dream and waking reality, between the visionary world and the actual world. The image of a city looms through the half-light, and that city is not Camelot but heaven itself. Percival thinks he has found the Grail in a mighty city 'Pricked with incredible pinnacles to heaven' (*The Holy Grail* 423), but this turns out to be a ruinous city. If he finds the Grail there he can be sure it will crumble into dust. But there is a city which will never perish: later, in a moment of vision, he catches a glimpse of the heavenly city. Like Virgil, like St Augustine, Tennyson has the imaginative capacity to encompass both the ruined city and the glorious city which is yet to be (*The Holy Grail* 524):

> . . . I saw the least of little stars
> Down on the waste, and straight beyond the star
> I saw the spiritual city and all her spires
> And gateways in a glory like one pearl –
> No larger, though the goal of all the saints –
> Strike from the sea; and from the star there shot
> A rose-red sparkle to the city, and there
> Dwelt, and I knew it was the Holy Grail,
> Which never eyes on earth again shall see.

Tennyson's *Idylls* are a series of episodes, not a continuous epic, written over a long period and only retrospectively grouped into twelve books like the *Aeneid* and *Paradise Lost*. Yet they enshrine a moral vision, an ideal of order for the contemporary world, set about with difficulties as was the quest of Aeneas and the founding of Rome, drawing on dim legends of an earlier time touched with strangeness as well as sadness, like Virgil's poem. They represent the noblest tribute of the nineteenth century to the high seriousness of the *Aeneid*.

The affinities between Virgil and Tennyson can be exaggerated. Tennyson is too much of a romantic to be simply the English Virgil. Some of his most haunting lyrics are rich in a melancholy which uses Virgilian language but taps romantic rather than classical sources of feeling. 'Tears, idle tears', a poem about causeless despair catches up the *lacrimae inanes* of the *Aeneid*, but where the sorrows of Aeneas have specific causes in his memories of lost companions or the life of Troy which can never return, Tennyson laments to explore an emotion for its own sake (*The Princess* IV.39)

> Deep as first love, and wild with all regret;
> O Death in Life, the days that are no more.

But in *The Passing of Arthur* personal melancholy and public disaster, the lyrical world of dreams and shadows and the epic world of violent action come together as they come together in the sixth book of the *Aeneid*. Tennyson mingles (*The Passing of Arthur* 108)

> Shocks, and the splintering spear, the hard mail hewn,
> Shield-breakings, and the clash of brands

with the wintry desolation and swirling mists of the waste sand by the waste sea in 'this last, dim, weird battle of the west' (*The Passing of Arthur* 94). In *Idylls of the King* Tennyson had an imaginative encounter with lofty moral idealism, with the possibility of disaster and yet of hope beyond it. This gave him the authority and the right, supreme among living poets, to pay tribute to his master in 1882. In his poem *To Virgil* he stresses disaster and suffering as well as idealism and new beginnings: both Virgil and he had encountered such things (*To Virgil* 1 ff., 11 ff. and 19 ff.):

Roman Virgil, thou that singest
Ilion's lofty temples robed in fire,
Ilion falling, Rome arising,
wars, and filial faith, and Dido's pyre; . . .

Thou that seest Universal
Nature moved by Universal Mind;
Thou majestic in thy sadness
at the doubtful doom of human kind;

Light among the vanished ages;
star that gildest yet this phantom shore;
Golden branch amid the shadows,
kings and realms that pass to rise no more; . . .

I salute thee, Mantovano,
I that loved thee since my day began,
Wielder of the stateliest measure
ever moulded by the lips of man.

For Tennyson, as for Dante in the *Purgatorio* where he is again addressed as 'Mantovano' ('man of Mantua'), Virgil is the poet of supreme intuition, the familiar guide through the dark places of the imagination, the means of access to mystery and to wisdom.

The *Eclogues* and the Pastoral Tradition

LAURENCE LERNER

What are Virgil's *Eclogues* about? They are such a miscellaneous group of poems that the question may at first seem unanswerable. Of their two titles, *Eclogues*, the common one now, means 'selections' and probably does not go back to Virgil himself. It tells us nothing, but the other title, *Bucolics*, songs about herdsmen, may well be Virgil's own. The obvious answer to the question is that the poems are about country life, and that is of course the usual definition of pastoral, but it does not tell us much. First, we must add that the countryside is present both for its beauty and for its economic activity: wild nature is occasionally described, but it is above all the *farmed* countryside that we are shown. It is a land of sheep and goats, corn and vines and orchards and bees. Here for instance is the landscape that Corydon wanders through when sick for love of Alexis (*Eclogue* II.8-13):

> nunc etiam pecudes umbras et frigora captant.
> nunc viridis etiam occultant spineta lacertos,
> Thestylis et rapido fessis messoribus aestu
> alia serpyllumque herbas contundit olentis.
> at mecum raucis, tua dum vestigia lustro,
> sole sub ardenti resonant arbusta cicadis.

> *This is the hour when even cattle seek the coolness of the shade; when even the green lizard lies hidden in the thorny brake; when Thestylis brews a fragrant soup of pounded garlic and wild-thyme for the reapers wearied by the scorching heat. Yet I am wandering in the paths that you have trod, under the burning sun, while the orchards echo to the harsh cicadas' notes and mine.*
> (tr. E.V. Rieu)

Heat and shade are a practical contrast – they affect the way you work – as well as a pleasing aesthetic juxtaposition. The only detail unconnected with farming (the green lizards) is exactly what the reapers might notice. It is a landscape of farming, pure and simple.

But it is not only the economy of the countryside itself that we are made aware of, it is the wider context too: what happens on your farm – whether you *have* a farm – depends on external forces, and the first *Eclogue* is concerned with these. There can be no doubt that this poem is partly about politics, though scholars have not been able to settle exactly what it is telling us. Octavian, like other politicians before him, settled his soldiers, when the civil wars were over, on farms partly acquired through confiscation. We do not know how much biographical basis the poem has: we do not know whether Virgil himself or his family lost their Mantuan farm. Who was the youth whom Tityrus saw when he went to Rome, who saved his farm for him and whom he will now always revere as a god? Some editors maintain that an unimportant slave like Tityrus could never have met Octavian, probably would not even have heard of him. But we do not need to read the poem so literally: these fictitious, symbolic shepherds would obviously see the appropriate person in Rome, and that is certainly Octavian, who as ruler of the city would be the one person that could be called a god. If the poem was written as an act of homage by a Virgil grateful that his farm had been restored to him, then the youth would obviously be Octavian, though it might not, in that case, have been tactful to lay so much stress on the miseries of the dispossessed. There is no reason to identify Virgil with Tityrus more than with Meliboeus, and the interaction between them is what the poem is about. Are we not meant to realise (though we are never told explicitly) that the youth who gave Tityrus liberty and land was the same man who was responsible for the eviction of Meliboeus?

This first poem, then, places the rural setting in the context of contemporary politics; this is enormously important to the subsequent history of pastoral in two ways. First, it sets a precedent for the moralising pastoral, the use of shepherds' conversations to comment on contemporary abuses. Almost all the Renaissance pastoralists do this – Mantuan in Latin, Marot in French, Spenser in English. The eclogues of Spenser's *Shepherds Calender* are divided by E.K. in his General Argument into three kinds: plaintive, recreative ('such as all those be, which contain matter of love, or commendation of special personages') or moral ('which for the most part be mixed with some satirical bitterness'). Here in the first *Eclogue* we see the origin of the moral.

And also of the plaintive. It is not quite clear what EK means by the term, but it cannot just refer to love laments, since 'matter of love' is placed among the recreative; certainly it has something to do with melancholy. Now the first *Eclogue* began with Tityrus lying at ease under the beech, playing his pipe, while Meliboeus has to leave his beloved fields (*Eclogue* I.4-5):

> nos patriam fugimus; tu, Tityre, lentus in umbra
> formosam resonare doces Amaryllida silvas.
>
> *We flee our native home; you, Tityrus, relaxed in the shade, teach the woodlands to echo (the name of) beautiful Amaryllis.*

Here we are, near the beginning of European pastoral – apart from Theocritus, *at* the beginning – and the opening lines of the very first poem give us an idyllic scene steeped in melancholy. It is not the bleak landscape and the farmer's struggles that arouse melancholy; it is the happy scenes, because of their fragility. The end of the poem returns us to the same theme. Meliboeus' last and longest speech ends with a picture of what he is losing (*Eclogue* I.75-6):[1]

> non ego vos posthac viridi proiectus in antro
> dumosa pendere procul de rupe videbo.
>
> *Henceforth I will not lie stretched out in a green cave, watching from afar my goats hanging from the bushy rock.*

I find these lines memorable not so much for felicitous detail but for their emotional impact. This is what Tityrus will be able to do: its beauty is heightened by the poignancy of loss, so it is the evicted Meliboeus who says it.

The final speech belongs to Tityrus. At least you can stay tonight, he says, under my roof: I have got some good apples, chestnuts, lots of milk. This has never struck me as a tactful reply: what is Tityrus trying to do: rub in to Meliboeus the

1. Wordsworth incidentally singled out the word *pendere* ('hang') as a particularly splendid stroke of imagination; *Preface* to 1815 Edition of his Poems (= *Poetical Works*, ed. A. de Selincourt (Oxford 1952) vol. II.436).

happiness he is losing? Or is he savouring it himself, taught now to appreciate it even more fully? And then come the last two lines (*Eclogues* I.82-3):

> et iam summa procul villarum culmina fumant,
> maioresque cadunt altis de montibus umbrae.
>
> *Now the roofs of the farmhouses over there are sending up their smoke and longer shadows are falling from the mountain tops.*

Is this reassuring and peaceful, or sinister and slightly threatening? The shadows are growing longer: so it is all the better to have a comfortable house (which Meliboeus has not). Or are they not just material shadows? Is there not always a chill threat about encroaching darkness?

No less than five of the *Eclogues* end with evening – each time leaving us in ambiguous shadow – reassuring and frightening, recurrent but with a hint of finality, and nowhere more perfectly than near the end of *Eclogue* II (66-67):

> aspice, aratra iugo referunt suspensa iuvenci,
> et sol crescentis decedens duplicat umbras.
>
> *look where the oxen are drawing home the hanging ploughs by the yoke, and the declining sun has doubled the growing shadows.*

First, a simple descriptive line on the farm at evening, then a line that plays with the paradox of evening: the sun is going down, the shadows are getting longer. Evening means both a coming and going.

Beauty can be vulnerable because threatened: hence sadness. Or the unreal can be beautiful with an intensity it would not attain, unless it was the result of longing: hence the acute sadness of awakening. The two emotional effects are similar, and both are found in the *Eclogues*. There are no moments of happiness more intense than those of Gallus in *Eclogue* X, dreaming of the girls he might have had instead of Lycoris, or of hunting to forget his sorrows (*Eclogue* X.58-61):

> iam mihi per rupes videor lucosque sonantis
> ire, libet Partho torquere Cydonia cornu
> spicula – tamquam haec sit nostri medicina furoris,
> aut deus ille malis hominum mitescere discat.

> *I see myself already, climbing the crags: I hear the echoes as I thread the woods; a Cretan arrow flies from my Parthian bow – and I am happy. As though such things could be a cure for my disease, or the god of love could learn to soften at the sufferings of men.*

The sadness of the beautiful, the close association between happiness and its vulnerability is prominent in the *Eclogues* and central to the pastoral tradition, but one hesitates to see it as the influence of Virgil. It seems more like part of an emotional make-up. There is of course no way of distinguishing these, since that tradition is one of the factors that has gone into the make-up. For a later example, we can turn to a single very famous line.

'What is it in these six simple words of Milton', asked Housman in his famous lecture, 'that can draw tears, as I know it can, to the eyes of more readers than one? . . . I can only say, because they are poetry, and find their way to something in man which is obscure and latent, something older than the present organisation of his nature'.[2] The six words are the opening line of the last song in *Arcades*, but we shall need to quote at least half a dozen lines:

> Nymphs and shepherds dance no more
> By sandy Ladons lillied banks.
> On old Lycaeus or Cyllene hoar,
> Trip no more in twilight ranks,
> Though Erymanth your loss deplore,
> A better soil shall give ye thanks.

Housman's tears seem to have caused him, on the literal level, to ignore Milton's point (I will not say to miss it, since he remarks that the 'sense' of the line is gay). And so F.W. Bateson has riposted:[3]

> Milton's injunction to the nymphs and shepherds was not, in fact, to stop dancing, but to 'dance no more *By sandy Ladons lillied banks*'. The nymphs

2. A.E. Housman, *The Name and Nature of Poetry* (Cambridge 1933) 46.
3. F.W. Bateson, *English Poetry: A Critical Introduction* (London 1950) 15.

> were only to transfer their dances from Arcadia to Harefield in Middlesex . . . Housman's tears came from taking Milton's line out of context and giving it a meaning it was never intended to have.

I know few neater examples than this of the difference between a poet's reading and a scholar's reading. Would Milton – who after all was both – have treated Housman's tears with such learned disdain? Is it, for instance, an accident that his first line sounds so self-contained? Or that it has such a delicate ambiguity, between personal and historical regret – any given group of nymphs and shepherds will cease dancing, for death, too, is in Arcadia; and in this late age of the world the woods of Arcady are dead, and the dancing over. It is very like the ambiguity of Eliot's line in *The Waste Land*, 'the nymphs are departed', which means either 'the young ladies have gone home' or 'who would describe this landscape in pastoral terms?' Eliot's point is the same as Milton's, and so is his technique; only his mood is different, for his anti-romanticism has renounced the plangent overtones of 'no more' – he does not care to bring tears to anyone.

All this is achieved by Milton in one line; and it reverberates through four more before it is finally pushed aside. These four lines list the places in which the dance has ceased, now Greece has lost her pastoral tradition. With cumulative sadness they make it clear that the historical and not the personal meaning is the one that matters, building up a sense of loss that line 6 can now push aside into a graceful compliment – indeed if we really feel the pathos of Erymanth's loss, an almost desperate compliment – to the Countess of Derby. The dispute between Housman and Bateson is actually enacted by the movement of the song.

It is this, the nostalgia so central to later pastoral, that led to the belief that pastoral poetry should be set in the Golden Age. There was a good deal of quibbling in the 18th Century on this point. 'Pastoral', said Pope, 'is an image of what they call the golden age . . . We are not to describe our shepherds as shepherds at this day really are, but as they may be conceived then to have been; when the best of men followed the employment';[4] he carefully guarded himself, we may notice,

4. Pope, *A Discourse on Pastoral Poetry* (1717): Twickenham ed.

from any suspicion of levelling! Dr Johnson dismissed this view with scorn: 'I cannot easily discover why it is thought necessary to refer descriptions of a rural state to remote times'.[5] As a staunch Ancient, Johnson assumes that pastoral poetry is what is found in Theocritus and (especially) Virgil; and since there is no Golden Age in the *Eclogues*, that is that. Perhaps this sturdy empiricism can be seen as parallel to the anti-pastoralism of Crabbe, for whom the age of pastoral is (or ought to be) over (*The Village* (1783) 39-48):

> I grant indeed that fields and flocks have charms
> For him that grazes or for him that farms;
> But when amid such pleasing scenes I trace
> The poor laborious natives of the place . . .
> Then shall I dare these real ills to hide
> In tinsel trappings of poetic pride?

Johnson is against idealised rustic description because he believes it is not found in Virgil; Crabbe is against it because it – and, he might have added, Virgil too – are escapist. The difference of opinion over pastoral should not be allowed to conceal a great similarity of tone and even of politics.

Now there *is* a Golden Age in the *Eclogues,* but in an unusual form. The Golden Age belongs to the beginning of human history, as in Hesiod (*Works and Days* 109 ff.):

> First of all the deathless gods who dwell on Olympus made a golden race of mortal men who lived in the time of Cronos when he was reigning in heaven. And they lived like gods without sorrow of heart, remote and free from toil and grief; miserable age rested not on them; but with legs and arms never failing they made merry with feasting beyond the reach of all evils. When they died, it was as though they were overcome with sleep, and they had all good times; for the fruitful earth unforced bore them fruit abundantly and without stint.
>
> (tr. *Loeb Classical Library*)

There is nothing moral or political about the fact that the Golden Age gave place to a Silver Age, then a Bronze, then a

of *Works* (London 1961) vol. I.25.

5. Johnson, *The Rambler* 37 (24 July 1750): *Works* (London 1820) vol. IV.239.

4th and finally a 5th 'when men never rest from labour and sorrow by day, and from perishing by night'. The gods simply imposed this decline on mankind; we can do nothing about it, and the motive for thinking and writing about the Golden Age is simply nostalgia.

In *Eclogue* IV, Virgil places the Golden Age in the future and connects it with the birth of a child. This poem is in many ways distinct among the *Eclogues*: it is the only one without any named shepherds or any dialogue, and it announces in its opening lines that it is to be read with special awe. *Eclogue* VI does also begin with an apology for sticking to pastoral and not writing on a heroic subject; but IV remains unique, beginning with a request to the Muses: *Sicelides Musae, paulo maiora canamus* ('Sicilian Muses, let us sing on somewhat loftier themes', *Eclogue* IV.1). The glorious future that the birth of a child will bring is not however the kind of Utopia that is brought in by revolution and political bosses. In his marvellous contrast between the Arcadian and the Utopian, W.H. Auden sets out the difference between a nostalgic paradise and the fierce political idealism of the visionary (*Vespers* in *The Shield of Achilles*; 1955):

> In my Eden our only source of political news is gossip; in his New Jerusalem, there will be a special daily in simplified spelling for non-verbal types.

It is certainly Eden and not the New Jerusalem that Virgil announces. The earth is going to yield gifts without cultivation. Goats will run around oozing milk. The sheep will grow coloured wool, so that we shall not need dyes. No-one will sail on the sea. And it is all to happen effortlessly: no revolution, no Day of Judgement, will intervene. Only one line in the poem suggests politics: *pacatumque reget patriis virtutibus orbem* ('he (the child) will rule over a world pacified *patriis virtutibus*', *Eclogue* IV.17). Now here is an ambiguity. If *patriis uirtutibus* means 'by the prowess of his father', then there is going to be some political cleaning up by the child's father – Antony, Octavian, or Pollio, or whoever it is – to make things ready; such cleaning up, as Auden brilliantly reminds us, is Utopian, not Arcadian:

> When lights burn late in the citadel, I (who have never seen the inside of a police-station) am

> shocked . . . He (who has been beaten up several times) is not shocked at all, but thinks: 'One fine night our boys will be working up there'.

But if, on the other hand, it means 'by our ancestral virtues', then Octavian's boys are not going to be working late in the citadel, for the line is about the past only.

Certainly this is the only political line in the poem, the only line which Pope leaned on very heavily for his free rendering of *Eclogue* IV (*Messiah: A Sacred Eclogue* (1712) 57-60):

> No more shall nation against nation rise,
> Nor ardent warriors meet with hateful eyes,
> Nor fields with gleaming steel be covered o'er;
> The brazen trumpets kindle rage no more.

All that is squeezed out of *pacatum*. Pope set out to rewrite Virgil in the light of Isaiah, and to show 'how far the images and descriptions of the Prophet are superior to those of the Poet'. This meant turning Arcadia into Utopia, and he even called his version 'Messiah'.

Virgil, however, has not left the Arcadian world: his first line was at least partly misleading. If he is writing prophecy, it is not Messianic prophecy: looking into the future he sees the original Golden Age. The Virgil of the *Aeneid* is a long way off: even the Virgil of the *Georgics* is not yet present.

The *Georgics* are nature poems. They tell of crops and weather, of the planting of trees and vines, of the raising of cattle and bees. They are almost a practical handbook, by a poet who prided himself on his knowledge of the country-side. They also contain (*Georgics* II.458 ff.) a long praise of rural content, contrasted with the restless life of soldier or merchant, and seen as a thing of the past (*Georgics* II.532-3):

> hanc olim veteres vitam coluere Sabini,
> hanc Remus et frater.

> *This was the life which the ancient Sabines once led, or Remus and his brother.*

So the Golden Age is naturally mentioned; but when Virgil speaks of it at length, he speaks of its end (*Georgics* I.129-30):

> ille malum virus serpentibus addidit atris
> praedarique lupos iussit pontumque moveri

> *He (Jupiter) gave deadly poison to the black snakes, and ordered wolves to pillage and the sea to rage in storms.*

Not the Golden Age itself but the evils that have followed it is the theme of the *Georgics*; not Saturn's earth that yielded crops *nullo cultu*, but the details of husbandry rendered necessary by the reign of Jupiter; not pastoral but nature.

Each of Virgil's three poems has its version of the Golden Age; and that in the *Aeneid* is different again. They had no agriculture, not because their life was easy but because it was hard; they were not able to lay up store, but lived off hunting and fruit: *sed rami atque asper victu venatus alebat* ('it was the branches and tough hunting that provided a livelihood', *Aeneid* VIII.318). This stern existence no doubt fits the epic spirit; and it puts Virgil (for the moment) among the 'hard primitivists'. I take the term from Lovejoy and Boas's useful contrast between soft primitivism (which delights in the freedom of primitive man to do as he pleases, in the dream 'of a life with little or no toil or strain of body or mind') and hard primitivism (which praises the austerity and stern character training of primitive society).[6] The finest example of hard primitivism in English poetry is the eighth book of Wordsworth's *The Prelude*, in which he contrasts the life of classical or Mediterranean shepherds with those of Cumberland (*The Prelude* (1850 text) VIII.173-5):

> Smooth life had flock and shepherd in old time,
> Long springs and tepid winters, on the banks
> Of delicate Galesus.

But the bleak life of the Lake District produces 'a free man, wedded to his life of hope, / And hazard' – austere, difficult and imaginatively far richer (*Ibid* 244-6):

> The lingering dews of morn
> Smoke round him, as from hill to hill he hies,
> His staff protending like a hunter's spear.

Hard primitivism is unpastoral: goes, even, with its explicit rejection. The shepherds of the Golden Age leapt from no

6. A.O. Lovejoy and George Boas, *Primitivism and Related Ideas in Antiquity* (Baltimore 1935) 9 ff.

rocks, battled through no mists, but spent their hours (*Ibid* 205-6) –

> In unlaborious pleasure, with no task
> More toilsome than to carve a beechen bowl.

Wordsworth is the great unpastoral poet in English – not anti-pastoral in the sense of Touchstone and Sidney, rejecting country for court, but unpastoral in his concern with incidents and situations from common life: a poet of the direct, not the mediated provincial. So it is appropriate that he finds soft primitivism slightly unreal and not altogether admirable.

* * *

Turning to the language of the *Eclogues*, we should be able to move to some understanding of what style has become associated with pastoral poetry. We have learnt to associate pastoral poetry with simplicity: its attraction lies in the contrast it offers with urban or courtly sophistication. The style of the *Eclogues* however is certainly not simple and the manner of presentation is highly self-conscious. The fact that Virgil is imitating Theocritus – and sophisticated readers were meant to notice this – removes spontaneity; as do the singing contests. Little seems to be known about whether the shepherds of Sicily actually did hold such contests; in the *Eclogues*, they certainly seem to raise our consciousness of the fact that we are reading poems, not listening to actual countrymen. Probably the most self-conscious of the *Eclogues* are VI and IX. In IX we are given a discussion of the poems of Menalcas by two of his friends and admirers: a few fragments are quoted, along with some discussion on how good they are, and on the usefulness of poetry (it is no use at all: Lycidas' belief that Menalcas had saved the district by his verses is dismissed with the observation that poetry can do nothing against armed men); Lycidas mentions that he is a poet too, and advances that as a claim to hearing more of Menalcas' stuff. This can surely be described as meta-poetry; but even this is not as self-conscious as VI, in which Silenus sings his song of creation. We are not given an account of creation such as you find in Lucretius, or a retelling of myths such as you find in Ovid. There is a preface, apologising for the kind of poetry Virgil writes; then an account of how Silenus, the poet, was found and captured, and only then consented to sing; the song itself is presented in indirect speech 'he repeats', 'he adds', 'then he sings of'; none of the stories is really told, they are hinted at. It is a poem about writing a poem.

It may seem that this high degree of self-consciousness puts paid to all claim to rustic simplicity, revealing Virgil as the most urban and sophisticated of poets. Before accepting this point, we must utter one warning. Self-consciousness and primitiveness are by no means incompatible. Self-conscious narrators and concern with the act of composition itself are as old as poetry (they are as prominent in *The Odyssey* as in Sterne or Proust), and elaborate ritual, concern with the process as well as the product, are quite as characteristic of primitive tribes as of modern *literati*. So the acute consciousness of, say, Menalcas' place in the hierarchy of poets, and his impact on the world around him – driving out Menalcas' actual poems – does not necessarily remove us from the traditional culture of the rural world.

For perhaps the richest and most complex exploitation of the self-consciousness of the pastoral tradition in English, we can turn to Matthew Arnold. Both his great pastoral elegies are explicit about their relation to the tradition, and *Thyrsis*, the second, is even explicit about its relation to *The Scholar Gipsy*, the first. *Thyrsis* must be one of the most nostalgic poems in English, impregnated with a sense of loss; when we pause to ask what has been lost, we see the sophistication. For we are overwhelmed with answers.

First, the historical loss: we are no longer in the ancient world – not, as it happens, Mantua now, but the Sicily of Theocritus, 'when Dorian shepherds sang to Proserpine' (*Thyrsis* 97-8):

> She loved the Dorian pipe, the Dorian strain.
> But ah, of our poor Thames she never heard . . .

This stanza is based on the *Lament for Bion*, in which the Greek poet imagines that he will be able to bring back his friend from the underworld, since the 'Maiden' who presides there (Proserpine) is Sicilian like him, and will respond to his songs. Ingeniously, Arnold sighs that he has lost that 'easy access', and the sigh of regret becomes an apology, that England is not Sicily. It is the exact opposite of Du Bellay's famous sonnet, *Heureux qui comme Ulysse a fait un beau voyage*, in which the moment to praise the Loire most eloquently is when he is comparing it to the Tiber, and with defiant provinciality preferring his own culture.

The second loss is that of Clough, for whom the elegy is written. This turns out to be a double loss: Clough left Oxford and the academic life and was absorbed into the 'strange disease of modern life', as it is designated in *The Scholar Gipsy*; and now he is dead. The reference to Clough's death is strangely perfunctory, for the true grief is for the way his restlessness drove him from 'the shepherds and the silly sheep' (from country to town; from pastoral tradition to writing the sophisticated *Amours de Voyage*). And then, casually, as if it followed naturally from all this, 'he is dead'.

This makes Clough's loss a parallel to the poet's own: Arnold too has left the fields of Oxfordshire (*Thyrsis* 40-1):

> Too rare, too rare, grow now my visits here!
> But once I knew each field, each flower, each stick . . .

The poet is a townsman, but a townsman who once felt he belonged in the Oxford countryside. This reminds us that pastoral is an urban genre, but with a special immediacy. There are no enamelled meads here, but the particularity of the actual countryside (we shall return to this point).

Least obvious, but most important of all for the actual writing of the poem, there is the loss of the pastoral tradition itself. Arnold, writing in the Romantic tradition, makes the psychological basis of the poem explicit: he begins from his own personal situation, and builds the symbolism (elm tree and Scholar Gipsy) in front of us. It is because he has started from himself that he feels entitled to use the tradition (*Thyrsis* 81-90):

> Alack, for Corydon no rival now! –
> But when Sicilian shepherds lost a mate,
> Some good survivor with his flute would go,
> Piping a ditty sad for Bion's fate,

And cross the unpermitted ferry's flow,
And relax Pluto's brow,
And make leap up for joy the beauteous head
Of Proserpine, among whose crowned hair
Are flowers, first open'd on Sicilian air,
And flute his friend, like Orpheus, from the dead.

It is hard to be sure whether this is a stanza of pastoral poetry, or a stanza about it. Telling us what the Sicilian shepherds did, he re-enacts it for himself, for he feels he has now earned the right – a right that Milton, say, took for granted – to use the convention.

One stylistic device is particularly important in this poetry, if only for the enormous subsequent influence it has had: it combines spontaneity and self-consciousness in paradoxical form. This is the pathetic fallacy. When Mopsus is lamenting the death of Daphnis in *Eclogue* V, he says that nobody has led his cattle to the stream, no beast has drunk from the river or cropped the grass; the wild mountains and the woods speak of how the African lions lamented the death of Daphnis (*Eclogue* V.24-8):

non ulli pastos illis egere diebus
frigida, Daphni, boves ad flumina; nulla neque amnem
libavit quadripes nec graminis attigit herbam.
Daphni, tuum Poenos etiam ingemuisse leones
interitum montesque feri silvaeque loquuntur.

In these days Daphnis, none have brought their pastured cattle to cool streams; no beast has drunk the river water or touched the meadow grass. Daphnis, the wild hills and woodlands tell how even the lions of Africa lamented your passing.

Under the stress of a strong emotion, you project the same feeling onto nature. When in love, you hear birds rejoicing and the stream laughing; when jilted, you hear the dove mourning and the stream sobbing. This device was brought into lyric poetry by the Hellenistic poet Bion in his lament for Adonis, and by the anonymous author of the *Lament for Bion* (30-4):

For your death trees dropped their fruit; the flowers all withered. For sorrow that you are lost

> the trees have cast their fruit on the ground, and all the flowers are withered away. The flocks have given none of their good milk, and the hives none of their honey; for the honey is perished in the comb for grief.

The device was not actually named until the 19th Century, by Ruskin, who did not understand it very well. He thought that fallacies damaged poetry, because he held the absurd view that poetry must, on any level, tell the truth.[7] But it needed no Ruskin to tell us that the pathetic fallacy is a fallacy: we have always been meant to realise that. It has the paradoxical function of testifying to the overwhelming power of an emotion that can lead one into such palpable untruths – an extreme of spontaneity – and at the same time of showing the strength of a stylistic tradition imposing itself on a fresh poem – an extreme of sophistication.

To illustrate the pathetic fallacy in the English pastoral tradition I choose a piece of Milton (*Lycidas* 39 ff.):

> Thee, Shepherd, thee the woods, and desert caves,
> With wild thyme and the gadding vine o'ergrown
> And all their echoes, mourn:
> The willows and the hazel copses green
> Shall now no more be seen
> Fanning their joyous leaves to thy soft lays.
> As killing as the canker to the rose,
> Or taint-worm to the weanling herds that graze,
> Or frost to flowers, that their gay wardrobe wear
> When first the white-thorn blows;
> Such, Lycidas, thy loss to shepherd's ear.

Lies, lies, lies. The woods are not mourning Lycidas, because trees cannot mourn. There are no desert caves or gadding vines in Southern England anyway – we have been tricked away into an Italian landscape. And Lycidas was no shepherd, he was a student, potentially a poet and a priest. The second sentence recovers from the obvious lie it seems to tell, so that there is an element of factual truth in the statement that the woods will not respond to Lycidas' song any more: but they

7. Ruskin, *Modern Painters* (1856) vol. III, part 4.

were not really joyous, and it was not the lays that fanned their leaves. Lycidas' death is simply reminding us that a poetic fancy is a fancy.

After these beautiful lies, another note breaks in (*Lycidas* 50 ff.):

> Where were ye, Nymphs, when the remorseless deep
> Closed o'er the head of your loved Lycidas?
> For neither were ye playing on the steep
> Where your old bards, the famous Druids, lie,
> Nor on the shaggy top of Mona high,
> Nor yet where Deva spreads her wizard stream:
> Ay me! I fondly dream –
> Had ye been there – for what could that have done?
> What could the Muse herself that Orpheus bore,
> The Muse herself, for her enchanting son,
> Whom universal nature did lament,
> When by the rout that made the hideous roar
> His gory visage down the stream was sent,
> Down the swift Hebrus to the Lesbian shore?

What is the effect of this exclamatory break (*Ay me, I fondly dream!*) which introduces one of the most moving passages in all English poetry? Literally, it says that Nymphs could not have helped Lycidas even if they had been there, since even the Muse herself could not save Orpheus. But when such an exclamation irrupts into such tightly conventional and elaborate writing, its effect is certain to be much greater. 'I fondly dream' – not only through believing the Nymphs could have helped, but perhaps through mentioning Nymphs, through getting caught up in the old stories of Druids and Welsh legends, even through writing a pastoral elegy. Of course Milton is not really rejecting the conventions, and he goes on to tell the very old story of the murder of Orpheus by the Thracian women, but in the age-old tension between spontaneity and artifice, we can see that the obvious artificiality of the pathetic fallacy has a useful function. It conveys an awareness of artifice even in the very act of being swept away by passion, and it makes possible an outburst of rejection (*Ay me, I fondly dream*) whose overtones spread far wider than the literal content.

*   *   *

I have pointed out the element of self-consciousness in the style of the *Eclogues*. In conclusion I wish to distinguish between two different forms of self-consciousness. I have talked so far about consciousness of the process of composition, but not about consciousness of the nature of rural life itself. If pastoral is self-conscious, it must know surely that the countryside is not the town, and if the pastoral poet is a townsman, his reasons for loving the rural scene will be external, they will be motives he has brought with him from outside. This then offers the possibility of two different kinds of rural poetry, that of direct response to nature, and that of escape. Examples are here drawn from Shakespeare (*As You Like It* II.1.1 ff.) and from Thomson (*Spring* (1728) 529 ff.):

Now my co-mates, and brothers in exile
Hath not old custom made this life more sweet
Than that of painted pomp? Are not these woods
More free from peril than the envious court:
Here feel we but the penalty of Adam,
The seasons' difference, as the icy fang
And churlish chiding of the winter's wind,
Which when it bites, and blows upon my body
Even till I shrink with cold, I smile, and say
This is no flattery: these are counsellors
That feelingly persuade me what I am:
Sweet are the uses of adversity
Which like the toad, ugly and venomous,
Wears yet a precious jewel in his head:
And this our life exempt from public haunt,
Finds tongues in trees, books in the running brooks,
Sermons in stones, and good in everything.
I would not change it.

Fair-handed Spring unbosoms every grace:
Throws out the snow-drop, and the crocus first;
The daisy, primrose, violet darkly blue,
And polyanthus of unnumbered dyes;

The yellow wall-flower, stained with iron-brown;
And lavish stock that scents the garden round:
From the soft wing of vernal breezes shed,
Anemonies; auriculas, enrich'd
With shining meal o'er all their velvet leaves;
And full ranunculus of glowing red.

The first of these passages is a central example of Renaissance pastoral. Nothing in it is an attempt to see the countryside as it is. The one point that runs through it all is that the country is not the court: the contrast with 'painted pomp', with 'flattery', with 'public haunt', determines every detail. Real toads are not venomous and carry no jewels, but to the Duke this does not matter: Arden is not the actual countryside but belongs in the Golden Age, where toads point a moral and adorn our nostalgia. We would stop there if the Duke was a real poet: since he is a fictitious figure, devised by Shakespeare, we have learned by the time the play is over to look with some irony – but only some – at his simple pastoral impulse. Orlando finds kindness in the forest, but at the hands of courtiers not countrymen; the lovers' courtship ends happily, but then they leave the forest. And however much the Duke may like Arden, once he is offered his kingdom back he naturally takes it. 'I would not change it' is what exiled Dukes are supposed to say, but we are to realise that he does not actually *mean* it.

I have set against this a passage of nature poetry that attempts to see the countryside as it is. The attempt to render the infinite variety of natural appearances, announced (but not carried out) by Wordsworth, entered poetry as a central concern only with the 19th Century: it runs through Keats, Tennyson and Hardy to the Georgians. If there is any earlier example, it is James Thomson's *Seasons*, one of the purest examples of descriptive poetry in existence, and for that reason more interesting in extracts than as a whole. Once the abstraction of the first line is cleared out of the way, these lines are an attempt to see the natural scene direct, unencumbered by the emotional concerns of the nostalgic courtier. To set that against the Duke's speech is to see the simple contrast between pastoral poetry and descriptive nature poetry: but this contrast will no longer serve to cover what is most interesting in the poetry of the countryside since the Romantics, as we see if we turn to Wordsworth (*The Recluse*, 'Home at Grasmere' 126 ff.):

> What want we? Have we not perpetual streams,
> Warm woods, and sunny hills, and fresh green fields,
> And mountains not less green, and flocks, and herds,
> And thickets full of songsters and the voice
> Of lordly birds, an unexpected sound
> Heard now and then from morn till latest eve,
> Admonishing the man who walks below
> Of solitude, and silence in the sky.

Virgil lies a good way behind this. A more immediate ancestor is Milton, and the dignified praises of Eden uttered by Adam and Eve. The rhetorical movement of 'Fresh green fields / And mountains not less green' is purely Miltonic. Now Milton, for all his famous artificiality, was a step on the road to this aspect of Wordsworth, for he began to internalise the landscape, and he even lies – remotely – behind the one marvellous and utterly Wordsworthian line in this passage, which is of course the last: 'Of solitude, and silence in the sky'. The solemnity and generalisation of this (Wordsworth at his best is utterly remote from that 'infinite variety of natural appearances' he used to claim to be offering) combine introspection and observation in a peculiarly Wordsworthian formula. What is omitted is a conscious setting of the scene, a planning of poetic art to fit the elegant point of pastoral – the very thing that *As You Like It* does so wonderfully. Two details make this clear. The first is 'unexpected'. The voice of birds might be unexpected to the Duke, but it would be because it recalled the country to someone who was at that moment thinking of court, and made him exclaim, in pleased surprise, 'This is no flattery'. To Wordsworth however the word is meant quite literally – the man who is out walking had not noticed the bird till it began singing. The other detail is 'man': would a pastoral poet have missed the opportunity to call him 'one that hath been a courtier', or a 'brother in exile' or at least shepherd, or forester? For Wordsworth he is any man – which is to say, himself.

With this distinction we have, I must confess, left Virgil

behind. The two traditions, of pastoral poetry and nature poetry, both derive from the *Eclogues*, but Romanticism of this sort comes from a later age. The world of the *Eclogues* is the real countryside, its details lovingly described as they are; at the same time it is related to a wider world. But because the perspective is not yet the outsider's, that relationship is not simply one of contrast. I will end therefore with one last quotation, from *Eclogue* I. Tityrus has been to Rome, and found it overwhelming. He had known Rome was a town, but thought it was like the local market town, only bigger. The experience, when he got there, introduced a new dimension (*Eclogue* I.19-25):

> urbem quam dicunt Romam, Meliboee, putavi
> stultus ego huic nostrae similem, quo saepe solemus
> pastores ovium teneros depellere fetus.
> sic canibus catulos similis, sic matribus haedos
> noram, sic parvis componere magna solebam.
> verum haec tantum alias inter caput extulit urbes
> quantum lenta solent inter viburna cupressi.

> *I was a simpleton, Meliboeus, I thought the town called Rome was like ours, where we shepherds are always driving the tender offspring of our sheep. I knew that puppies are like dogs, that kids are like their mothers, so I judged big things by comparing them to little things. But I tell you, this town stands out above all others as the cypress does above the bending undergrowth.*

It is a tantalising passage. Is Tityrus a straw-chewing yokel swept off his feet by the big town? And if so, can we trust his judgement? What does the passage tell us about rustic values? He still seems blissfully happy to lie in the shade and teach the words to echo the beautiful Amaryllis; he still seems to think all an evening's hospitality needs is apples, chestnuts and milk, though they would not think much of that in Rome. Are we being told that Rome is a wonderful place but just for visits – tourism in reverse, and then you return to the countryside? To end on such an ambiguity reminds us that Virgil is the ancestor of both pastoral and nature poetry, and shows the rich mysteriousness that gave these lucid poems their unique place in European literature.

* Some of the material in this chapter first appeared in the author's *The Uses of Nostalgia*, published by Chatto and Windus.

Virgil at the Turn of Time

STEPHEN MEDCALFE

. . . Fferyllt (who learned from the Sibyl the Change and the Turn of Time) . . .

David Jones, *The Hunt.*[1]

Virgil died,
Aware of change at hand, and prophesied
Change upon all the Eternal Gods had made
And on the Gods alike.

Rudyard Kipling, *The Last Ode.*[2]

I
Darkness in Virgil

To walk round the lake at Stourhead on a hot bright day, a day as near as one can find to an Italian summer's day, brings you into the heart of one man's reading of Virgil.[3] Over the temple of Flora is the inscription *procul o procul este profani*, which expresses the awe with which the Sibyl introduces Aeneas' descent into the underworld (*Aeneid* VI. 258, 'Far hence be souls prophane' – Dryden). At Stourhead the awe is to be felt for the shrine of the goddess of gardens and for the garden round about. The same temple, by its placing in relation to water, a bridge, and the Pantheon across the water, evokes Claude Lorrain's picture of *Aeneas at Delos*, and therefore, perhaps, the oracle given there (*Aeneid* III.94-6; Dryden, *Aeneis* III.126-30):

Undaunted Youths, go seek that Mother Earth
From which your Ancestors derive their Birth.
The Soil that sent you forth, her Ancient Race,
In her old Bosom, shall again embrace.

On the other side of the water a cave opens unexpectedly on to impenetrable darkness: but if you walk resolutely in, the passage twists, and you are in a luminously dim grotto

1. D. Jones, *The Sleeping Lord* (London 1974) 66.
2. R. Kipling, *Debits and Credits* (London 1926) 395.
3. I am much indebted in what follows to K. Woodbridge, *Landscape and Antiquity* (Oxford 1970).

with a chill that delights. Here beneath the statue of a sleeping nymph the river Stour rises, making actual what was written over the original pedimented entrance to the grotto (*Aeneid* I.166-7):

> intus aquae dulces vivoque sedilia saxo,
> Nympharum domus.

Dryden's expanded translation is particularly appropriate (*Aeneis* I.235-40):

> A Grott is form'd beneath, with Mossy Seats,
> To rest the *Nereids*, and exclude the Heats.
> Down thro' the Cranies of the living Walls
> The Crystal Streams descend in murm'ring Falls.

The cave represents then the cave of the nymphs, which is Aeneas' first landfall. In its darkness are sweetness, life, silence and springing waters.

It seems however that the maker of the gardens, Henry Hoare, also associated his grotto and lake, as the inscription at the temple of Flora suggests, with Avernus. For, he says, the gradually descending path he made to the grotto 'will make it easier of access facilis descensus Averno'.[4]

Still, there is nothing hellish in the darkness of the grotto. Rather, after obeying the instruction in front of the nymph, 'drink in silence or in silence lave', you see across the cave another statue, the figure of Aeneas' dream on the night before he sets out for the site of Rome (*Aeneid* VIII.31-4; Dryden, *Aeneis* VIII.45-8):

> Then, thro' the Shadows of the Poplar Wood,
> Arose the Father of the *Roman* Flood;
> An Azure Robe was o'er his Body spread,
> A Wreath of shady Reeds adorn'd his Head.

The statue, like Tiber in the poem, evokes the future: he waves the traveller up out of the cave to the Pantheon or Temple of Hercules, as in the poem he directed Aeneas to Rome and the sacrifice made to Hercules by Evander. The darkness of the grotto and the waters that pour from it into

4. Henry Hoare to Lord Bruce, 23 December 1765; Woodbridge, *op.cit.* 35.

the lake become associated with rebirth and a vision of the greatness of Rome to come. Henry Hoare added further associations, mediaeval buildings already existing, transported or created, to apply these thoughts to the birth of England, and in an inscription above the lake dedicates the whole to King Alfred. If furthermore he associated his lake and his cave with Avernus, his sense of the Virgilian underworld and its darkness as the womb of rebirth would seem to have been very powerful.

Although one does feel this at Stourhead, the Virgilian image of darkness has not generally been taken to be so benign in our day. R.S. Conway suggested a concrete origin in a real landscape for Virgil's underworld, in the tunnels made during Virgil's lifetime leading out of Naples under Posillipo, and from Cumae to Lake Avernus itself.[5] It would be curious to know if Henry Hoare had any experience of these, but, although he travelled in Italy, there is no evidence of where he went. And the stress laid by Conway is on the constriction and blindness of the tunnels as the precondition of the sense of release as one emerges from them, suggesting the emergence of Aeneas and the Sibyl to the Elysian fields (*Aeneid* VI.640-1), the ampler sky, and new sun.

In Henry Hoare's Virgilian fantasia, that light plays back even on the darkness of the entry to Hades. In some modern readings of the *Aeneid* the darkness of Hades at its most malign infects the whole poem. William Golding's novel *Darkness Visible* (1979) relates itself deliberately to the three great epics of the tradition which issues in *Paradise Lost*: by its title to *Paradise Lost* itself and to Milton's imagination of hell; by its epigraph *sit mihi fas audita loqui* (*Aeneid* VI.266; 'may divine law allow me to say what I have heard') to Virgil's invocation of the gods of the underworld, just before Aeneas' descent, and just after the line of which Henry Hoare gave so much more benign a reading in setting it over Flora's temple, *procul, o procul este, profani;* and finally to the *Iliad* by a pitifully twisted evocation at the end of the novel, of the most pitiful passage in the epic, Priam's plea to Achilles by the thought of his own father τηλίκου ὥς περ ἐγών (*Iliad* XXVI.487, 'an ald man, as I am')

5. Alexander Mackay, *Vergil's Italy* (London 1971) 126.

to give Hector's body back. And although the novel ends in a salvation, its image of darkness is connected with horror and the running down of the universe.

Independently, so far as can be known, W.R. Johnson chose *Darkness Visible*[6] as the title of his sensitive, though at times perverse, account (1976) of how it feels to read the *Aeneid* for an American in the disillusionment consequent on the war in Vietnam – independently, but not by mere coincidence, since clearly the phrase does convey a certain characteristically modern response to Virgil and to the world. Johnson perhaps best expresses it in one of his most perceptive critiques, that on the passage following Golding's epigraph (*Aeneid* VI.268-72; Bridges, *Ibant Obscuri* 268-272):[7]

> ibant obscuri sola sub nocte per umbram
> perque domos Ditis vacuas et inania regna:
> quale per incertam lunam sub luce maligna
> est iter in silvis, ubi caelum condidit umbra
> Iuppiter, et rebus nox abstulit atra colorem.

> *They wer' amid the shadows by night in loneliness obscure*
> *Walking forth i' the void and vasty dominyon of Ades;*
> *As by an uncertain moonray secretly illumin'd*
> *One goeth in the forest, when heav'n is gloomily clouded,*
> *And black night hath robb'd the colours and beauty from all things.*

The simile, says Johnson, 'appeals to the eye only by methodically depriving it of the images that it presents and . . . enhances this deliberate failure of vision with an extraordinary musicality' in its spondaic movement. Virgil 'was interested in trying to imagine, *and to show the difficulty of imagining,* the incomprehensibility' not only of the underworld as a natural place in his narrative, but also of hell 'as a mode of existing which cannot be described or even perceived in terms

6. W.R. Johnson, *Darkness Visible* (University of California 1976).
7. *Poetical Works of Robert Bridges*, 2nd ed. (Oxford 1953) 448-465.

of the ordinary categories that belong to the realities of time and space . . . Thus, though the sentence begins with a verb of motion and though this verb is clarified by *quale iter est per lunam*, there is no real sense of motion'.[8]

Virgil must have been well aware of both the senses of darkness, Henry Hoare's and that of Golding and Johnson. After all, he created the cave of the nymphs, the night in which Tiber appears and the entry to the underworld. It is a singular fact too that the first poem and the last of the strict canon of his poetry, the first *Eclogue* and the *Aeneid*, both end with shadows, with the words *umbrae, umbras.*

Shadows make an appropriate ending. But there is evidently a contrast, in the *Eclogue* and in the *Aeneid*. The first *Eclogue* ends (82-3; Paul Alpers, *The Singer of the Eclogues*):[9]

> et iam summa procul villarum culmina fumant
> maioresque cadunt altis de montibus umbrae.
>
> *Already the rooftops in the distance smoke*
> *And lofty hills let fall their lengthening shade.*

Here we have just those benign effects of shadow which Henry Hoare and after him Blake and Samuel Palmer took from Virgil, 'the glimpse', as Palmer put it, in describing Blake's woodcuts of the *Eclogues*, 'of that rest which remaineth to the people of God'.[10] Even here of course it is possible to find a note of warning, though at the end of a Mediterranean summer day it is hard to think it: the close of the last *Eclogue* remarks reasonably enough that shadows can be harmful to crops, or if you sit late singing in them, and some would transfer the chill back here, though I do not think it can be more than an ambiguity or undertone. Of the shadows at the end of the *Aeneid*, on the other hand – *vitaque cum gemitu fugit indignata sub umbras* (*Aeneid* XII.952; 'and with a moan his life, resentful, fled to Shades below' – Allen Mandelbaum, *The Aeneid* XII.1270-1).[11] –

8. Johnson, *op.cit.* 88-90.
9. P. Alpers, *The Singer of the Eclogues* (University of California 1979) 15.
10. R. Lister, *Samuel Palmer: A Biography* (London 1974) 48f.
11. A. Mandelbaum, *The Aeneid of Virgil* (University of California 1972).

one might use Johnson's words about the fury that besets Turnus before his death: 'She represents and brings with her into the poem and its closure the full fruition of the evil, incomprehensible darkness that has drifted through the poem but has never, until now, overwhelmed it.'[12]

This malignant darkness, and the twist of self-consciousness by which Virgil shows 'the difficulty of imagining' it, are further related, by Johnson's way of it, to what an older American critic, Kenneth Rexroth, calls the '*sfumato* and suggestiveness' of Virgil's images.[13] This may be allowed to be true of the fights by night, the dreams and monsters, or such a tremendous set of images, as those by which Mezentius is compared in his onset first to a whirlwind, then to a constellation that is also a giant (*Aeneid* X.762-8).

Yet one might equally extend the benignity and light of Henry Hoare's Virgil to another feature of his style, to the loving clarity caught in a few words of his landscapes. This is more evident, not unexpectedly, in the *Georgics* than in the *Aeneid*: e.g. *fluminaque antiquos subter labentia muros* (*Georgics* II.157: 'and rivers gliding under ancient walls') with its alternating flow and rest of dactyls and spondees, the little ripple of the elided – *que*, the interdependence of the alternating words for water and walls, the suggestion even of the reflection of the walls in the water, and the co-inherence of stability and change. But there is a line in the *Aeneid* which echoes it both in sound and pattern of sense, in the description of Tiber flowing past Marcellus' burial, with the same vivid relation of monument and river: *quae, Tiberine, videbis / funera, cum tumulum praeterlabere recentem* (*Aeneid* VI.873-4; 'what death-rites seest thou there, / O Tiber, as thou glidest by his new-wrought tomb and fair!' – William Morris, *The Aeneids of Virgil*).[14] There is too something of the same effect of conjoined peace and movement in the relation of a thing to its reflection, in the voyage upriver in Book VIII – *variisque teguntur / arboribus, viridisque secant placido aequore silvas* (*Aeneid* VIII.95-6; 'and sail beneath the shade of varied trees / and cleave green woods

12. Johnson, *op.cit.* 130.
13. K. Rexroth, *Classics Revisited* (Chicago 1968) 87.
14. William Morris, *The Aeneids of Virgil* (London 1876).

reflected in calm water' – Mandelbaum, *The Aeneid* VIII. 123-4). That voyage also provides two of the clearest images of benign darkness in the *Aeneid*: the night in which Tiber appears to Aeneas, as sculpted at Stourhead, and the magical night in which he holds his waters back to allow Aeneas' ships free passage. Altogether, with its images of darkness, its landscapes and its story of the beginnings of Rome, Book VIII gives us most fully Henry Hoare's reading of Virgil.

The two interpretations, of the late twentieth and of the eighteenth centuries, cleave in two a single whole: their contrast indeed looks like the Virgilian version of the Nietzschean balance of formgiving light and unformed urgent darkness, Apollo and Dionysus. The problem however about Virgil is that, in the *Aeneid* at least, while he exhibits now Apollo, now Dionysus markedly dominant, more often than he displays them in absolute balance, so that one can pick and choose to make his poem seem wholly Apollonian or wholly Dionysiac, there is yet a coherence about his poetry which makes one want to give a single account of it.

II
A Fuller Sense of Virgil

This sense of coherence in Virgil's poetry is partly the result of metre: it is hard to think of another poet of the first rank the whole of whose strict canon, varying so much in mood and genre, is in one metre. But metre is bought at a price, embodies in itself (as Lytton Strachey said of Pope and the heroic couplet) an individual's 'poetic criticism of life'.[15] Virgil's hexameter does seem to constitute such a criticism, majestic and inexorable but also capable of infinite variations, the rise and fall of the quantitative movement counterpointed by the variation of stress, hard and soft at once, supporting an amazing auditory imagination. It is one and the same medium that is concrete enough to persuade me at any rate that I can hear the sticking of earth to the hands in the ns and ms and clotted plosives and sibilants of *sed picis in morem ad digitos lentescit habendo* (*Georgics* II.250 'but grows sticky like pitch under the fingers in the handling') and to persuade

15. Lytton Strachey, *Literary Essays* (London 1948) 'Pope' 90.

T.E. Page four lines earlier that the repeated t-sounds of *et ora / tristia temptantum sensu torquebit amaro* (*Georgics* II. 246-7; 'with its bitter flavour distort the wry mouths of those who make the trial' – Page) 'mark the feelings of a person who has tasted something which he desires to spit out'.[16] Yet the same medium has sufficient power over abstractions and general propositions to make something magnificent of *Romanos, rerum dominos gentemque togatam* (*Aeneid* I.282; 'The Roman folk, the togaed men, lords of all worldly ways' – Morris) and something untranslatably melancholy out of *sunt lacrimae rerum et mentem mortalia tangunt* (*Aeneid* I. 462; 'Lo here are tears for piteous things that touch men's hearts anigh' – Morris). Here one sees how much Virgil is the poet who draws the utmost power out of Latin, and its peculiar capacity for attaching emotion to abstractions: neither of these last two lines goes very happily into English at all, and the word *rerum* demands something – noun, or noun with adjective – more concrete, defined or picturesque than 'things'.

There is necessarily much that is extremely personal in such responses: but this is precisely the power of Virgil, that after two thousand years people of another language and culture cannot give a just account of him without calling on their most elusive, and personal feelings. Ronald Knox puts the point very well in *Let Dons Delight*: 'Virgil – he has the gift, has he not, of summing up in a phrase used at random the aspiration and the tragedy of minds he could never have understood; that is the real poetic genius'.[17]

This universality of Virgil is presumably connected with his own powers of variation as well as with the potentiality in him of vastly differing interpretations. It is because of these qualities that, although he is the poet of law and empire who said that a Roman's business was to rule *pacique imponere morem* (*Aeneid* VI.852; 'and to set the stamp of civilised usage upon peace' – R.G. Austin),[18] nevertheless in looking for the single model for understanding Virgil that I think he requires, I choose Keats. The capacity for

16. T.E. Page, *P. Vergili Maronis Bucolica et Georgica* (London 1898) 264.

17. R.A. Knox, *Let Dons Delight* (London 1939) 197f.

18. *Aeneid VI*, ed. R.G. Austin (Oxford 1977) 263.

identification with others which Keats said was characteristic of his kind of poet – 'The setting Sun will always set me to rights – or if a Sparrow come before my Window I take part in its existence and pick about the gravel'[19] – is exactly expressive of what Virgil gives us in such passages as the following (*Georgics* I.383-7):

> iam variae pelagi volucres et quae Asia circum
> dulcibus in stagnis rimantur prata Caystri
> certatim largos umeris infundere rores,
> nunc caput obiectare fretis, nunc currere in undas
> et studio incassum videas gestire lavandi.

> *At such time you may see all kinds of seabirds, and the kinds that pick about the Asian watermeadows of Cayster in the pools that delight them, trying to outdo each other in pouring masses of water over their shoulders, now ducking their heads against the waters, now running into the billows, revelling in bathing for nothing but the joy of it.*

Keats translated the whole of the *Aeneid* before he was sixteen, albeit into prose. That version, I think, would have told us something about Virgil: even without it we may learn something from its traces, and from a certain natural affinity of Keats with Virgil. Near the beginning of *Hyperion* (5-7, lines omitted in the revised *Fall of Hyperion*), Saturn is found

> Still as the silence round about his lair
> Forest on forest hung about his head
> Like cloud on cloud.

That is partly Miltonic: Keats will have had in mind *Paradise Lost* IV.137-42:

> Insuperable highth of loftiest shade
> Cedar, and pine, and fir, and branching palm
> A sylvan scene, and as the ranks ascend
> Shade above shade, a woody theatre
> Of stateliest view.

19. *Letters of John Keats*, ed. M. Buxton Forman, 3rd ed. (Oxford 1947) (22 Nov. 1817).

But it is also Virgilian, and Virgilian to a degree that Milton is not here. Milton's passage owes something to the lines which introduce the cave of the nymphs (*Aeneid* I.164-6; Mandelbaum, *The Aeneid* I.230-4):

> aequora tuta silent; tum silvis scaena coruscis
> desuper, horrentique atrum nemus imminet umbra.
> fronte sub adversa scopulis pendentibus antrum;
>
> . . . *tranquil water lies / silent and wide: the backdrop – glistening / forests and, beetling from above, a black / grove, thick with bristling shadows. Underneath / the facing brow: a cave with hanging rocks.*

From this passage, Milton has taken the ranks of trees overhead, and the baroque conceit of the theatre: Keats has taken the ranks of trees from Milton, omitted the theatre, and put back two things that were in Virgil, the stillness and the peculiarly Virgilian word 'hung'. It was a commonplace among critics, which Keats may well have known, that Virgil had a special fondness for *pendere*; and various critics had wrestled with it as a means to discovering what poetic language and imagination are. Charles Rollin in his essay *De la Poésie* discusses ten examples of Virgil's uses of the word to show how poetry, 'which is a speaking painting', uses words like colours to paint things with life and nature.[20] Wordsworth, in marked contrast, picks out the line in the first *Eclogue* where goats are seen hanging from a rock, and observes that goats do not really hang 'as does the parrot or the monkey': rather, 'presenting to the senses something of such an appearance, the mind in its activity, for its own gratification, contemplates them as hanging'.[21]

Owen Barfield in our own day has used the same example to show that words have a 'soul' over and above their mere definitions: and that that soul is found out by a poet in juxtaposing one word with another in ways which may be revealing of the poet's own nature.[22] This would seem to be

20. C. Rollin, *The Method of Teaching and Studying the Belles Lettres . . . Translated . . .* bk ii, ch ii, art. 2, pt. 2, 2nd ed. (1737) 305-6.

21. W. Wordsworth, *Preface* to the 1815 ed. of *Lyrical Ballads: Poetical Works,* 2nd ed. (Oxford 1952) II.436.

22. O. Barfield, *Poetic Diction* (London 1928) 130f.

to the point here: Virgil loves the word *pendere* because of the overtones he finds in it of suspense, of the ominous, of dependence – the ship hanging on a wave in the first book of the *Aeneid*, Dido hanging on Aeneas' story – as well as for its sheer pictorial power and beyond that the empathetic sense of dizziness it conveys; Keats, feeling similarly for its English equivalent, uses it here. The result is something which recalls a Virgilian simile in Milton, when the fiend is seen 'As when far off at sea a fleet descried / Hangs in the clouds' (*Paradise Lost* II.636-7) and Virgil's own description of Atlas, *cinctum adsidue cui nibibus atris / piniferum caput* (*Aeneid* IV.248-9; 'whose head is always girt with clouds and carries pines'). These, which may or may not have entered Keat's head, confirm a quality which is pervasive in *Hyperion* and make it, and even more its revised version, with its darkness, its rich music, its romantic development from Miltonic diction, its pain and questioning, and if one follows Charles Martindale the 'soft focus' of its similes,[23] perhaps the most Virgilian thing in English.

It may in fact be that when Keats was struggling in the last days of his poetic life towards a new style he was struggling still nearer Virgil. In the melancholy lines of the introduction to the revised *Hyperion* Keats not only embodies one of Virgil's characteristic moods, but by the repetition of a plural word as singular achieves Virgil's peculiarly Latinate power over abstractions (*Fall of Hyperion* 147-9):

> 'None can usurp this height,' returned that shade,
> 'But those to whom the miseries of the world
> Are misery, and will not let them rest.'

It would be wholly characteristic of Virgil's power that he should preside over such a turn in Keat's life: one finds something similar in the history of the reading of Virgil at the great turns of culture, not I think because there is something in him to provoke change, but because the qualities of universality and range which we have pointed to in him, qualities which he shares with all great poets, are in him peculiarly adapted to breast the changes of time. We have seen an instance of this in the contrast between the Virgil

23. In this volume, *supra* p.11.

read, as by Henry Hoare, by a governing gentry, half rural and half imperial, with a certain touch of the financier, who saw, with some justification, a similarity between Virgil's milieu and their own, and the republican liberal Virgil of W.R. Johnson's reading, whose Aeneas suffers from the delusion 'that it will be possible for him to perform the role that destiny has thrust on him and to preserve the integrity of his personal sensitivity and decency'.[24] But these Virgils are the same Virgil: Virgil is not a poet who will allow us, to elude the difficulty of his universality by calling him simply 'myriad-minded'. One Virgil is always present, telling us the story even when he is at his most dramatic.

Something similar may be observed of Virgil at other great turns in time, at the turn from the later Middle Ages to the Renaissance, or from the Roman Empire to the Dark Ages. Indeed a consideration of what happens to Virgil at these times is a support to the belief in radical changes, which a sophisticated historiography undermines. It suggests a very profound change when one finds the idea of a literal translation of the *Aeneid* replacing that of adaptation and retelling with Octovien de Saint-Gelais in France in 1500 and Gavin Douglas in Scotland in 1513: we realise that we are observing the development of the idea that the ancient world is dead, and ought to be revived as our model. Conversely, the change in the response to Virgil in the centuries before and after the fall of Rome, from a sophisticated reading that assumes him as one of the givers of life to a desperate love-hate that clings to him as the exemplar of dying civilisation, brings new life to that sense of the perilous beauty of civilisation which in the twentieth century seems to flicker, flare up and fade.

Part of the advantage of touching on such a study is that it illuminates Virgil more fully. Response to Virgil is not infinitely various, and some factors recur in odd combinations. The Renaissance humanist tradition for example took Aeneas as Gavin Douglas did, a perfect, static ideal of 'all wirschip, manheid and nobilite' (Prologue to Book I of his *Aeneid*, 324). Those readers who found him flawed, as in his treatment of Dido, were disturbed by it. Modern interpretations on the contrary rejoice in his flawedness and insist on

24. Johnson, *op.cit.* 74.

the development of his character. But then so did the mediaeval interpretations that begin with Fulgentius and see Aeneas' progress as an allegory of the life of man, strained as their details appear today. Evidently profound differences about what literature is, and about the relation of story to ideal are involved here.[25]

III
Civilisation and Gentleness

Another variation in response to Virgil which shows some odd turns concerns the idea of civilisation. 'Civilised' can mean many things: but in this case I think of a society that can afford and cherish a certain gentleness, even though this may be no more characteristic of its rulers than it is in any other society. Imperial Rome, that cherished and spread the gladiatorial games throughout its empire, was in some ways a radically horrible society, and of course traces of that appear in the *Aeneid*, notably in the aesthetic decadence of Euryalus' death. But Horace talked (*Satires* I.10.44) of Virgil's *molle atque facetum*; in so far as that refers to the *Eclogues*, as it probably does, I suppose one must render it as 'sensitive and witty', or perhaps more strongly as 'pitying and witty'. But I think Horace has also in mind Virgil's general personality and, if so, the best translation might be Wordsworth's phrase of Charles Lamb, 'the frolic and the gentle'.[26] Virgil has commonly appealed to people who valued those qualities.

Alcuin casts this same response into a distinctively mediaeval shape when he quotes Virgil to Charlemagne as supporting the New Testament precept of mercy:

> It is read that one of the old poets said when – if I recall correctly – he sang the praise of the emperors of the Roman kingdom, and how they should be, 'spare the conquered and strike down the proud,' which verse blessed Augustine presented with great

25. I owe this point to Jerome Singerman, whose thesis on Virgil in the Middle Ages will I hope soon be published.

26. Wordsworth, *Extempore Effusion upon the death of James Hogg, Works* IV.277.

> praise in his book *The City of God*, although much more should we attend to the Gospel precepts than to Virgilian verses. For Truth Himself said, 'Blessed are the merciful: for they shall obtain mercy'.[27]

It is not surprising that Alcuin is hesitant in introducing Virgil here, for in later life he was much against reading any but the divine poets. *Unde te habemus, Virgiliane?*, (which I take it implies 'Where your loyalties, you follower of Virgil rather than Christ?') he said to one Sigulf who was trying to read Virgil with his sons in secret, but not secretly enough to elude Alcuin.[28] He told a story, according to the *Life*, that when he was eleven he loved Virgil very much, until one night when he was sharing a cell with a 'tonsured rustic' who turned on his other side and went on snoring when he heard the signal for the night office. Horrible spirits came in and beat him, and Alcuin, shivering for fear the same should happen to him, prayed from the bottom of his heart, 'Lord Jesus, if you save me from the bloody hands of these creatures, and I am not in future eager for the vigils of your church and the ministry of praise, and any longer love Virgil more than chanting psalms, may I have a flogging like this.' The devils seeing him 'most carefully wrapped up, body, head and all in the bedclothes, breathing almost imperceptibly' said 'as he is only a boy we shall not punish him with sharp blows, but only by cutting with a knife at his feet where the skin is hard.' Their hands had already bared his feet when Alcuin crossed himself and said the twelfth psalm, at which the fiends vanished and man and boy rushed into church.[29]

The detail about cutting the horny part of the boy's feet suggests a vision less than a hazing such as schools in many societies have given to the lazy or the overfond of their books: the schools of York where this happened must have seen many such. One might suspect the hand of whoever allowed this odd couple to share a cell, which Alcuin implies was unusual. Whether it was such a joke or not, it began a conflict in his mind that was never resolved. For though he

27. *Alcuini Epistolae* CIX; Migne, *Patrologia Latina* C, column 330.
28. *Alcuini Vita* ch. X; Migne, *op.cit.* 101.
29. *Alcuini Vita* ch. I; Migne, *op.cit.* 91-2.

might officially condemn Virgil, his poems never lack Virgilian echoes. One of the very last has an image – *nos nunc velivoli pelagi spectamus in horis, / Quando dei adveniat, quando serena dies* ('And now, / Beside the shore of the sail-winged sea / I wait the coming of God's silent dawn' – Helen Waddell[30]) – which is most likely to derive from the moment at *Aeneid* I.223 when Jupiter looks down from heaven on *mare velivolum terrasque iacentis* ('the sailwinged sea and outspread lands'), and promises Venus the coming of peace and the ripening of time.

Alcuin's divided mind is common enough among the churchmen of the Middle Ages. But the feeling that Virgil represents civilisation does not die. Abelard, for example, three hundred years after Alcuin, casts a similar positive response into the same tradition of finding in literature a repository of moral types, when he singles out *tolerantia* (endurance) and *pietas* (in the sense of Aeneas' feeling for Anchises and Ascanius) as qualities which Virgil specially teaches, besides calling us to religion and away from the love of what is not lawful.[31] Virgil was in dark times a standard, a rallying point for civilisation in the sense of gentleness. A hundred years before Alcuin, only a short time after the conversion of England, Aldhelm writes to the first English scholar king, Aldfrith, probably not long after his accession in 685, comparing himself, because he is introducing the study of poetry to England, to Virgil who brought Hesiodic poetry to Rome. And something similar appears in what the *Aeneid* may have meant to the author of *Beowulf*, writing most probably at Alcuin's time or else Aldhelm's. There is no conclusive evidence that the poet had read the *Aeneid*, yet he has suggestively similar turns of phrase, and it is *prima facie* probable enough. Perhaps it is added evidence that he ends his poem, I think uniquely among heroic poems, with a praise of its hero's gentleness. (That one of the three speeches made at Hector's funeral is Helen's praise of him for having been gentle to her, marks the difference: for that is an individual and personal praise. It is not like the close of the

30. H. Waddell, ed. F. Corrigan, *More Latin Lyrics* (London 1976) 147 and 202-3.

31. Text, cited as unedited, by T.B. Haber, *A Comparative Study of the Beowulf and the Aeneid* (Princeton 1931) 6.

whole story on 'they said that he was of the kings of the world the mildest and gentlest of men, the kindest to his people and the most eager for praise'). Tolkien remarks that 'the smaller points in which imitation or reminiscence might be perceived are inconclusive while the real likeness is deeper and due to certain qualities in the authors independent of the question whether the Anglo Saxon had read Virgil or not . . . We have the great pagan on the threshold of the change of the world: and the great (if lesser) Christian just over the threshold of the great change in his time and place: the backward view: *multa putans sortemque animo miseratus iniquam* . . . In fact the real resemblance of the *Aeneid* and *Beowulf* lies in the constant presence of a sense of many storied antiquity, together with its natural accompaniment, stern and noble melancholy'.[32]

Something of the same affinity appears in the first great English historian, Bede, who loves to decorate his history with Virgilian quotations. But he also has Alcuin's divided mind about pagan Rome; when he writes a poem in praise of a virgin, saint and queen, Aethilthryth he says *bella Maro resonet, nos pacis dona canamus / munera nos Christi, bella Maro resonet* ('Let Maro wars resound, I will not cease / To sing the gifts of Christ, the gifts of peace').[33] But it is possible that even here, since what he specifies are the rape of Helen and the war at Troy rather than Aeneas' martial glory, that he is not condemning Virgil for praising war, but rather for choosing war as a subject at all. If he did not recognise how much Virgil is a poet of the pity of war, he missed something which is present in one of his principal sources, Gildas. For Gildas, writing little more than a century before Aldhelm, resorts to Virgil in recounting the struggle to preserve civilisation by the Britons against those whose descendants – Bede, Aldhelm, Alcuin – would use Virgil in the attempt to recreate civilisation. His quotations come above all from *Aeneid* II and the narrative of the war at Troy, and they are used for the most part to express the wolf-like ferocity of men of war, the terror of their onset, and the pitiful dismay

32. J.R.R. Tolkien, 'Beowulf, the monsters and the critics', *Proceedings of the British Academy* 22 (1936) 24-5 and 49.
33. Bede, *Ecclesiastical History* IV.20.

of their victims; *multa deos orans, oneravitque aethera votis* (*Aeneid* IX.24; 'Praying the Gods, and laid a load of vows upon the air' – Morris) is an exception that proves the rule, for though it comes from Book IX and the wars of Aeneas in Italy, it picks out the doomed prayer of Turnus.[34]

IV
Civilisation and Self-Consciousness

In dark times the simple appeal of Virgil's gentle civilisation, the need to defend it, appears. But civilisation is also complex and inclusive, is aware and respectful of other civilisations, other epochs, to the point where weaknesses appear, because awareness of cultural relativity, of layer upon layer of meaning in literature, culture and language disables belief. Civilisation goes with self-consciousness. We have already touched on aspects of Virgil's self-consciousness, on his awareness of 'many-storied antiquity', and on the disabling self-consciousness which W.R. Johnson finds in him, set in the terrified and superstitious world of late antiquity. In his analysis of the approach to the underworld Johnson finds three layers of consciousness: first, the contemplation of an incomprehensible journey taken by Aeneas and the Sibyl in the story into the empty kingdoms; secondly, the provision of a simile for that which works by negation; and thirdly, an awareness of the imaginative activity itself and its difficulty in contemplating these successive unthinkables.

This is a perception characteristic of our time. I suppose *The Waste Land* particularly embodies the kinds of self-consciousness we have mentioned: and a quotation from the *Aeneid* in that poem to which T.S. Eliot draws attention is suggestive. At the beginning of *Part II,* a lady is sitting in a room 'where the glass / . . . / Doubled the flames of seven-branched candelabra / Reflecting light upon the table as / The glitter of her jewels rose to meet it;' and her perfumes 'troubled, confused / And drowned the sense in odours; stirred by the air / That freshened from the window, these ascended / In fattening the prolonged candle-flames, / Flung

34. Gildas, *The Ruin of Britain*, ed. M. Winterbottom (London 1978) ch. 25, 10, 28 and 98.

their smoke into the laquearia, / Stirring the pattern on the coffered ceiling.' Eliot draws our attention in his notes to the lamps that hang from the *laquearia* in Dido's palace at *Aeneid* I.726. But it seems to me that at the back of his mind and much more important there must have been another passage about light and *laquearia*, where the doubleness, reflection and confusion that he attributes to both light and odour is given full expression. This is the simile that describes Aeneas' doubt at the beginning of Book VIII, the doubt that is resolved by the vision of Tiber (*Aeneid* VIII. 20-5; Mandelbaum, *The Aeneid* VIII.26-32):

> . . . animum nunc huc celerem nunc dividit illuc
> in partisque rapit varias perque omnia versat,
> sicut aquae tremulum labris ubi lumen aënis
> sole repercussum aut radiantis imagine lunae
> omnia pervolitat late loca, iamque sub auras
> erigitur summique ferit laquearia tecti.
>
> *his racing mind is split: it shifts here, there / and rushes on to many different plans, / turning to everything: even as when / the quivering light of water in bronze basins / reflected from the sun or from the moon's / glittering image glides across all things / and now darts skyward, strikes the roof's high ceiling.*

There is evidently a strong similarity, enhanced by the fact that if Eliot is building on Virgil, Virgil in turn is building on the lovely simile of Apollonius Rhodius (*Argonautica* III. 751-760) in which, as Johnson points out, what is at issue is not the utter confusion of Aeneas, but the clear-cut anxiety and conflict of Medea in love with Jason.

That simile reflects a concern that pervades the *Aeneid*, a concern with moments of crisis that ask for decisions reaching into the inmost secrets and potentialities of the personality. Throughout the poem Virgil seems to be forcing himself to deal with such decisions, which do not concern him in the *Eclogues* or the *Georgics*. Book II may be seen as Aeneas' making up his mind to leave Troy, and Book IV as his making up his mind to leave Dido, while the whole poem ends on his decision to kill Turnus. In each case the decision is presented as difficult and obscure, and Aeneas' personal part in it as hard to discern, and perhaps not important: things seen (that is omens, messages from Venus or Jupiter, and finally the belt of Pallas) overwhelm him, as he either doubts, or, in the matter of leaving Dido, conceals from himself what he must do. The simile of reflected light suggests how much Virgil is exploring a kind of dazzling, the dazzling found by introspection when it looks for the roots of decision (a dazzling which can be equally imaged as darkness or depth), in which he has not much guidance from earlier writers, even the Greek tragedians. It is worth asking how much Augustine's magnificent introspections partly derive from his childhood steeping in Virgil, and how much therefore Virgil stands as the fountainhead of the tradition of intensifying introspection which passes through Augustine and later through Montaigne and Shakespeare down to T.S. Eliot and others in our time.

But a large distinction may be noted. The quotation given above from *The Waste Land* is distinctly more confusing than that from the *Aeneid*, even though in the interest of brevity of quotation I have simplified Eliot's syntax. Eliot remains, in this passage, in control: but the control is much more strained than in Virgil; the strain, in fact, of self-consciousness, of making one's eyes, as Eliot puts it in *The Death of St Narcissus*, 'aware of the pointed corners of one's eyes' is more embodied in the syntax. Perhaps one could put it this way: that in describing the approach to the underworld, one should add to Johnson's three levels of consciousness a fourth and reigning consciousness, that which with none of the obscurity, uncertainty and effort of the inferior three which it includes, sees steadily and finally.

It is in metre and syntax that this becomes clear. In other parts of *The Waste Land*, in *Gerontion* or *The Hollow Men* the equivalent of that fourth consciousness also finds a broken and bewildered expression, in breaks of the rhythm and still more in those breaks of the syntax which may be compared to the synapses of the nervous system.

Now it must be significant that of all ancient poets, Virgil comes closest to this, in some of his 'pathetic half-lines'. But even if those are deliberate, and not the accidental result of Virgil's death, or if they are the result of some final unease in Virgil that would never have been satisfied and so a real product of his inspiration, still there is no case where one could be sure of this. One undoubtedly can be sure with Eliot. The extremities of self-consciousness in Virgil do not reach to breaking the syntax.

The nearest approach to a self-consciousness like that of *The Waste Land* or *The Hollow Men* comes perhaps in such fallings back before a universe that may be ultimately chaotic and malign, as one has in the half-line *inimicaque Troiae / numina magna deum* (*Aeneid* II.622-3: 'great shapes of the powers of the gods, hating Troy'). And the fear of the draining away of meaning which Virgil sometimes expresses by *inanis* – the *inania regna* ('empty kingdoms') of Hades, or the chilling *dat inania verba* ('it gives empty words') of the simulacrum of Aeneas at *Aeneid* X.638 – this too has something of the Eliot of *The Hollow Men*. Yet these kingdoms and these words are only parts of the universe; they do not seem to engulf it. Except perhaps in the phrase *numina magna deum*, which does engulf the universe, and the metre echoes the engulfing, Virgil does not seem to abandon the steady Apollonian consciousness, embodied in the metre, with which he normally sees, even when *what* he sees is chaos and old night. There is nothing blurred in the actual prayer at the entry to the underworld *sit mihi fas audita loqui, sit numine vestro / pandere* . . . ('may the Law allow me to say what I have heard: may it be allowed by your divinity to unclose . . .') even though the sentence ends . . . *res alta terra et caligine mersas* ('things sunk in darkness and the deep earth').

V
Epiphanies

The Renaissance, the humanist tradition of reading Virgil, so to speak lived with the topmost, the Apollonian level of his awareness. At its finest, this reading perceived in Jupiter, the serene god beyond all the storms he contemplates, the god of Stoic philosophy explicitly described in Anchises' speech in the end of Book VI. It imagined the lesser gods as the beautiful beings which the sculptors and the poets from Homer to Callimachus had made them, and as the Epicureans supposed they must be to account for dreams of them. Marlowe offers marvellous fragments of translation from *Aeneid* I to present these stately deities: in *Dido Queen of Carthage* Aeneas says to Venus, disguised as a nymph, 'But whether thou the Sun's bright sister be / Or one of chaste Diana's fellow-nymphs / Live happy in the height of all content' and as he recognises her in the moment of her vanishing 'I know her by the movings of her feet' (*Dido Queen of Carthage* I.I.193-5 and 241). This makes a lovely picture; but I doubt if one feels that Marlowe believed in Virgil's Venus. The humanist tradition, in its neglect of Virgil's complexity and his ability to encounter not only flowery tenderness but darkness, did impoverish him in the end. The Enlightenment reduced his gods to epic machinery, mere names for human emotions. Modern critics who try to save their reality, as does W.R. Johnson, tend to reduce them to dark demonic forces. One needs to do justice to both sides, the Apollonian beautiful image and the Dionysiac unseen demon. Chaucer perhaps catches something of this by taking Venus as the kind of spirit he understands, and rendering *venatrix dederatque comam diffundere ventis* (*Aeneid* I.319) as 'going in a queint array / As she had been an hunteresse / With wind blowing upon her tresse' (*House of Fame* I.228-30), which suggests one of the faery hunt.

But really to apprehend a Venus with at once the beauty and the believability required for a full reading of Virgil, one must go back behind Gildas, to the still secure Roman civilisation of fourth century Britain. There is in Taunton museum (illustrated as frontispiece to this volume) a mid fourth-century mosaic from Low Ham in Somerset which tells the story of Dido and Aeneas. Unfortunately this is now displayed upright against a wall and not as it was found on the floor at the entrance to the villa's *frigidarium*, and is therefore easy to misread.[35] As you entered the *frigidarium* you saw a spectral Venus naked but for some jewellery and 'a semicircular diadem or crown, the mark of Venus Genetrix (mother of Aeneas and foundress of the Julian House)'.[36] She is drawing Cupid in the form of Ascanius towards Dido. Over Ascanius' head Aeneas is casting a sidelong glance at Dido,

35. For a slightly different interpretation, to which I am nevertheless much indebted, see J.M.C. Toynbee, *Art in Britain under the Romans* (Oxford 1964) 241-6.

36. Toynbee, *op.cit.* 243.

who stands with her finger at her mouth 'in the familiar Roman gesture expressive of such emotions as wonder, admiration, bewilderment or confusion';[37] her stance seems to be that of one unwilling but fascinated. On the left is a scene of ships arriving, at right angles to the observer except the foreground, ingeniously twisted so that one sees Achates fetching Ascanius from the ships and receiving gifts for Dido – *colloque monile / bacatum, et duplicem gemmis auroque coronam* (*Aeneid* I.654-5; 'a necklace hung with pearls and a double coronet of gems and gold'). To the right and at right angles is the hunt, with only three figures, Aeneas looking back at Dido who looks to him, and beyond them, eager and regardless, Ascanius galloping. There is an odd flavour of caricature about the drawings in this panel, Dido being a little like one of Thurber's predatory women, and Ascanius one of Thelwell's little girls on horses: I think this is because the two side panels, the voyage and the hunt, are cramped because meant to be viewed obliquely.

But the hunt one saw better from the final viewpoint, when one turned to see once again Venus dominating the scene; but now from a separate panel, central to the whole pavement, above the panel containing the lovers. She is apparently about to shroud herself in a black cloak. To her left a Cupid kneels, his eyes turned towards her, holding up a flaming nuptial torch and holding a ribbon from Venus' cloak. To her right another Cupid stands, who seems by the posture of his head and legs to be shuddering back, his eyes shut as if weeping or not to see, his torch pointing downwards, which 'spells death'.[38] The Cupid with the nuptial torch stands over Aeneas, the Cupid with the torch of death over Dido. Dido and Aeneas clasp one another, her arms about his neck, his arms about her shoulders. She thrusts forward with her head and breast, pushing with the toes of her left foot. He stands upright, one foot slightly askew. A tree frames them on each side, seeming to push them in, Aeneas' tree however having a main branch that ultimately points away, Dido's only compelling her forward. The hunt, now on the left, leads up to this, the ships now on the right are going away,

37. Toynbee, *op.cit.* 243.
38. Toynbee, *op.cit.* 245.

I think doing duty for Aeneas' departure.

The governing themes seem to be the inevitability of it all, the instrumentality of Ascanius, and the presiding will of Venus, not only, not even primarily, as Aeneas' mother, but as love and perhaps death. I do not think one feels her as malevolent, but as delighting in the exercise of her being: a beautiful and deathly personality, her reality taken for granted, herself as much an integral though controlling part of the action as the lovers are. The treatment is in the most enduring tradition among readers of Virgil. The boy Augustine will have been weeping over Dido's fate at something like the time when this mosaic was installed. The pictures resemble those in the somewhat later Vatican manuscripts of Virgil. Yet, with all the turns of time that have come between, one can still respond to its sad beauty, and to the uncanny epiphany of Venus. It is appropriate therefore that its subject is one of the turns of time that are part of Virgil's text, portrayed spatially in the transformation between the two principal viewpoints, the growing love of the first, the doomed love of the second.

But close as I believe this mosaic pavement is to Virgil's purposes, another, twenty years older, from Lullingstone in Kent offers something quite different and also plausible. Here Jupiter in the form of a bull is seen carrying away Europa while two Cupids, both flying merrily, beckon him on and hang on to his tail. Above is an epigram:

> Invida si tauri vidisset Iuno natatus
> Iustius Aeolias isset adusque domos.

It is immensely allusive, literary and sophisticated, a comment on Juno as she appears in the opening of the *Aeneid*. She persecuted Aeneas without justice, causing Aeolus to rouse the winds against him; she would have had some justice if she tried to prevent her husband the bull from raping Europa. The *invida* is neatly placed, both in coming first and in its contrast with *iustius* at the beginning of the second line. In the wit, at once bitter and brittle, with which it condemns Juno and Jupiter with her, combined with the gaiety of the picture, and the extreme literariness of the whole, there seems to be the decadent hyper-civilisation of a disillusioned paganism. It may seem to make either for Johnson's, or the

Enlightenment's view of Virgil's gods, demonically amoral, or mere epic machinery and subjects for epigram.

But there is a curious further point. The *triclinium*, in whose apse this pavement lies, was built and decorated ca. 330AD. About twenty years later, the kitchen attached to the *triclinium*, and two or three further rooms, were transformed into a Christian house-church. What kind of turn in time was this? If the villa was now occupied by a Christian household, had it changed hands? Or was the disillusioned pagan of the epigram now to be found as depicted on the walls of the church, his hands stretched out in prayer in the presence of a Chi-Rho wreathed in laurel, the symbol of Christ's Resurrection? – *tendebantque manus ripae ulterioris amore* (*Aeneid* VI.314; Their hands stretched out in utter love for that far-lying shore – Morris).

To read Virgil is to come continually across lines that seem to have a fatal capacity for translation into Christian terms: to be in the presence of the kind of Roman who in the centuries to come found Christianity irresistible and indeed, as the legend of Dante's *Purgatorio* said of Statius, was perhaps sometimes helped to do so by reading Virgil. The picture of Virgil suggested by W.R. Johnson would reinforce this point: for there is great probability that the dark blurred milieu of superstition and scepticism, which characterises Virgil, as it characterised late antiquity, helped the Christians, unafraid of demons or divine possession and secure in the faith of an eternal triumph, to win their converts. And yet again: can this Virgil be reconciled with the believing poetic paganism suggested with at least equal plausibility at Low Ham or recalled, even if with a less full understanding, at Stourhead?

VI
Time

One possibility is that Virgil created a structure of symbols so open that anyone can appropriate them. But this is not in fact true – Virgil's poetry is very much more easily appropriated by some people than by others – and, moreover, when it is appropriated takes on shapes that suggest strongly the degree to which it has been distorted in the process.

Virgil's poetic personality is strong and idiosyncratic. And it is in one of his idiosyncrasies that I think part of the answer lies: in his obsession with time, and his belief, or at least readiness to believe, that a new epoch with a radical shift in the nature of things, was happening in his own time.

I have already suggested that Low Ham conveys, spatially, as one turned to look back at the pavement, the sense of the turn in time in the story of Dido and Aeneas. Now the poignancy of their story is due to the fact that another outcome is imaginable, even if not possible, an outcome in fact associated with Venus' instrument, the boy Ascanius, Dido's affection for him and even his attractive freedom from the gloom around him. Dido hoped to bear Aeneas another son; her plea for that possibility is the only occasion in the whole *Aeneid* where the diminutive, the emblem of affection, is used of or to a person (*Aeneid* IV.327-30: Mandelbaum, *The Aeneid* IV.440-5):

> saltem si qua mihi de te suscepta fuisset
> ante fugam suboles, si quis mihi parvulus aula
> luderet Aeneas, qui te tamen ore referret,
> non equidem omnino capta ac deserta viderer.

> *Had I at least before you left conceived / a son in me: if there were but a tiny / Aeneas playing by me in the hall, / whose face, in spite of everything, might yet / remind me of you, then indeed I should / not seem so totally abandoned, beaten.*

Virgil had once presented something very like that as a real possibility: and the words here, *suboles, parvulus,* with the picture of the child playing before its mother recall the occasion in the fourth *Eclogue: cara deum suboles* (*Eclogue* IV.49; 'dear son of the Gods'); *incipe, parve puer, risu cognoscere matrem* (*Eclogue* IV.60; 'begin, little boy, to recognise your mother with a smile').

In the *Aeneid*, personal affection must give way to fate, and to reasons of state. In the *Eclogue*, the other story, which implies a world where reasons of state, personal affection and fate are one, the story that a child is being born whose life will be the return of the Golden Age, is told. In fact, in the *Eclogue*, one of the central symbols of Christianity is adumbrated, the identity between a newborn child and divine strength that sways the heavens.[39] How Virgil thought this would happen, and why he thought it, is immaterial to our present purpose. The essential point is that in the fourth *Eclogue* Virgil played with the idea that what he (later) denied to Aeneas might become a reality in his own lifetime. And twice in the *Aeneid* he posits the kind of change in the ordinary nature of things that the fourth *Eclogue* demands, a change that requires the interposition of a god or, more fundamentally, a change in the nature of the gods themselves.

One such change happened before Aeneas' time. Hercules delivered the Arcadians on the site of Rome from Cacus: *attulit et nobis aliquando optantibus aetas / auxilium adventumque dei* (*Aeneid* VIII.200-1 'Time brought even to us in our longing at last the help and advent of a god'). *Aetas*, time itself, is the agent here, and the whole episode that follows (as Evander tells Aeneas of the Golden Age, points out the ruins of that time, built by Saturn and Janus, and, both unknowing, leads him over the places that are to be important to Rome in Virgil's day), is dense with Virgil's feeling for time and with a pointing to his own day.

The nature of time is in question too with the other change, the one promised by Jupiter in that speech which we have noted as possibly contributing to Alcuin's imagery for awaiting the coming of God. Jupiter tells Venus (*Aeneid* I. 279-82);

aspera Īuno,
quae mare nunc terrasque metu caelumque fatigat,
consilia in melius referet, mecumque fovebit
Romanos rerum dominos, gentemque togatam.

Sour Juno even who now wearies earth and heaven with terror, will take a better mind, and with me will cherish the Romans, lords of the world, the people of the toga.

The Juno whom Virgil took from Homer, who, Zeus says in the *Iliad*, will never be satisfied till she has eaten the Trojans

39. See *The Classical World*, ed. D. Daiches and A. Thorlby (London 1972) art. 'Virgil's Aeneid'.

raw, the goddess who for Virgil seems to concentrate in herself the horror of the heroic age, even she will change. How, is suggested by a significant echo, that of the word *aspera* twelve lines later: *aspera tum positis mitescent saecula bellis* (*Aeneid* I.291; 'the sour centuries, wars laid aside, will turn ripe'). Juno seems to be identified with the bitterness in the heart of things which will ripen.

That Virgil regarded the wars and sufferings of the heroic age and of his own lifetime with horror is clear. But it is also clear that he did not regard this as an irremediable condition of the world, nor necessarily as one that would last very much longer. Perhaps, though he leaves the timescale a little vague, the happy time began when Augustus closed the temple of Janus and there was no more war. Perhaps the death of Marcellus shows that the bitterness is not yet passed. But the faith in *aetas* and *saecula* remains in the *Aeneid*, as it was in the *Eclogues*. David Jones and Kipling, in the epigraphs to this essay, are right. Virgil learnt the turn of time from the Sibyl, and he did expect the gods themselves to change. In this belief lies some of the secret of his appeal to Christendom, and of his reconciliation of light and dark.

Moreover, if one single cause can be found for the fact that beneath the broken half-lines, the images of darkness, the realisation of pain and perplexity, and the fear of emptyness, the lover of Virgil finds a perpetual spring of life, and a living repose – *intus aquae dulces vivoque sedilia saxo* – it is because in various forms he believes in time. He loves the motion of rivers, the endurance of walls, the antiquity of things human and natural (Quintilian I.7.18 rightly calls him *amantissimus vetustatis*), the history of Rome, the growth of crops, the succession of the constellations – what enjoyment there is in the opening of the *Georgics: quid faciat laetas segetes, quo sidere terram / vertere* (*Georgics* I.1-2; 'What culture crowns the laughing fields with corn / Beneath what heavenly signs the glebe to turn' – Joseph Warton).[40] In the *Georgics*, he even admires the way in which *improbus labor*, work without limit, in the end conquers everything. Even in the lines where his melancholy and his hope are most sharply

40. *The Works of Virgil in Latin and English*, ed. J. Warton, 3rd ed. (London 1778).

juxtaposed, when the dead rush on, it is the *motion* – the fall of leaves, the gathering of the birds and the coming of autumn – that is the delight, and all reflected in the movement of the lines (*Aeneid* VI.309-12):

quam multa in silvis autumni frigore primo
lapsa cadunt folia, aut ad terram gurgite ab alto
quam multae glomerantur aves, ubi frigidus annus
trans pontum fugat et terris immittit apricis.

It is hard not to unbalance the melancholy and the hope in these lines. Does one prefer Bridges' melancholy:

Countless as in the forest, at a first white frosting of autumn
Sere leaves fall to the ground; or like whenas over the ocean
Myriad birds come thickly flocking, when wintry December
Drives them afar southward for shelter upon sunnier shores

or Gavin Douglas' cheerful:

Als gret number thiddir thikkit in feir,
As in the first frost eftir hervist tyde,
Levis of treis in the wod doith slyde;
Or birdis flokkis our the fludis gray
Onto the land seikand the nerrest way,
Quhom the cald sesoun cachis our the see,
Into sum benar realm and warm countre?

I think myself that of the second simile the right note is caught by Keats, at the very end once more of his poetic life with the ode *To Autumn* 'And gathering swallows twitter in the skies'; the first perhaps we must allow to Milton's 'Thick as autumnal leaves that strew the brooks / In Vallombrosa'. But that full contrast of tone is certainly there in Virgil, and it is the sense of time and season that holds it together.

It may be that in this love of time we may find a context too for Virgil's exploitation of time, his mastery of metre: and in his awareness that time itself is changing, something to explain the peculiar capacity of his words to extend their meanings to match the turns of time. For the poem that follows I do not claim anything more than that it states what I should want to say on this subject:

IN MEMORIAM JAMES REEVES

Old friend, when you died on May day,
You who saw clearly, and dimly, as any man alive
What did you see?
It's hard to recognise a man is dead, whose voice
Being printed, echoes in one's eyes
Harder to realise
There's no time now, to talk of all we meant to.
Virgil died at the turn of the year
Turning into darkness at the turn of the year
In the childhood of Mary, not far from her birthday,
On the day of Librá, when day and night
Hang in the balance.
At the further end of winter he saw the edge of darkness:
He saw
Light between trees and a flaw of wind
In the embryon leaves and a veil of green
And the eyes of a girl in the breeze and the emerald
(Bright where the light shone through,
Dark on the mossèd bark
Of uncountable years reborn)
And – so bright that it blocked his sight
Incessu
A foot on the edge of the tomb
And a hand with a signal, white
White with a vein of red,
Vexillum: he could find
A word for that in his mind
Pietate insignis et armis – but
Pietas, virgo, dea – he stumbled
On what the least in the kingdom
Of our lord of two thousand years
Calls *charity* and *lady*.
The wind from the forest
Breathed in his dying mouth:
'I have seen such things', he said,

'As make all I have written like straw' –
Straw for the burning:
Straw for the warming
Of a speechless child. He saw
And stammered '*Parvule, princeps.*'
He went in the wood of Eden, and his epic down
the winds of time.
Written in the sunlight, when you were called away
In lapses of our conversation.

*Vergil Dying**

GABRIEL JOSIPOVICI

I

This essay is different in kind from the others in this book. I have been asked to write not about Virgil and the Twentieth Century but about a play of my own. I could not have written an essay of the former kind because I do not know enough, and I hesitated before agreeing to write this one, for a writer should not look too closely at the way he creates or he will be in danger of producing works which fit in with theories rather than following where his instincts lead him. And in art as in life instincts tend to be better guides than theories. Yet two considerations led me to accept the invitation. The first was that I owed much, if not everything, in my play to Virgil, and if, in this bimillennial year of his death, I could contribute even a tiny fragment to the celebrations in his honour I felt I should do so. The second was the thought that perhaps the editor of this collection of essays had not been wholly eccentric in asking me to contribute this particular piece. For the expected essay, though it might have appeared to fit in with the general pattern of the book, would not in fact have done so. We are still right in the Twentieth Century, and a mere survey of the books influenced by Virgil in the past eighty years would not really have told us much about the place of Virgil in our imagination. It is perhaps only by focussing on a specific work and examining it in some depth that we can see whether Virgil still has something to say to us today, and my excuse for focussing on my own play is that at least I know more about it than anyone else. I hope that what I have to say will throw light on Virgil and on the general theme of the volume, and so will be of interest to those who do not know my play and have no particular interest in my work.

* The play *Vergil Dying* by Gabriel Josipovici was first presented in a broadcast on Radio 3 on 29 March 1979, and subsequently published by SPAN, the Windsor Arts Centre Press.

II

I must begin with a confession. I have had no classical training and, until five years ago, had very little interest in Virgil. Homer seemed more alive, Dante spoke to me more immediately. Virgil seemed to be a poet who could only be appreciated if one was thoroughly at home in Latin and in the classical tradition, very much a poet's poet or, at least, a scholar's. I myself did my schooling in Egypt, spending more hours on the study of Arabic even than English, and none at all on Latin. When, faced with the daunting task of taking O-level Latin in one year (along with three A-levels) in order to get into Oxford, I was sent to a crammer, he told me bluntly: 'I can either teach you Latin or get you through O-level. I cannot do both'. Since I had to get my O-level there was really no choice, and the result is that though I can now work through Latin poetry with a crib, I still do not know Latin.

And yet one can never tell what has made a profound impression on one, or what will surface at unexpected moments. At a certain point in my life and under pressure of a specific creative task, I discovered that Virgil meant far more to me than I had realised. In order to explain how and why this was so I need to go back some fifteen years and sketch in my peculiar relation to the theatre.

Until about 1967 I was totally uninterested in the theatre. To me the theatre was a place where large overdressed families passed chocolates to each other with a great noise of crinkly paper, while on stage overdressed actors mouthed phrases as they crawled towards dénouements which the average five year old could have seen coming from a mile away. But around 1967 things began to change. The first little theatres and pub theatres sprang up in Britain, and one of the first and best of these was the Brighton Combination. Its theatre consisted of a room in which at most fifty people could congregate, sitting on upright chairs, and the first play there was a one-man show by Tutte Lemkow. It was a double bill, the first part of which was a performance of Kafka's story, *A Report to an Academy*. This is the story of an ape who, captured off the African coast and brought back to Europe, manages, by dint of a mighty effort of will, to master human speech – not in order to say anything in particular, but in order to escape his inevitable fate of being put in a zoo and stared at by human beings. The story consists of a lecture given by the ape, late in life, to honoured members of the Academy, recounting his story. Lemkow entered furtively, dressed in a frock coat and an overlarge pair of trousers, hurried up to a person sitting in the front row, shook his hand, made a rush for the lectern, gripped it, and began. He managed to convey at one and the same time a nervous lecturer and an animal. He would catch us up in the pathos of his story, and then, when we were wholly gripped and starting to forget who it was who was speaking to us, crumple the page he had finished reading from with one fierce uncontrolled gesture and drop it to the floor. Apart from that his only action was the occasional tense gripping of the glass of water that stood on a table by the lectern, and the banging of it on the table when he got over-excited at the memory of some injury that had been done him. The only 'event' was the shattering of the glass in a moment of particular excitement. Yet that play and performance rivetted me in a way I had never been rivetted in the theatre. There was no plot, no dénouement, but by the time the hour was up we had all been through a very great deal – something had been happening there before us in that small room – something which would not be possible on the page or at the cinema. I went back the next day and the day after that. I went every night the play was on. I had understood what the theatre could be about.

Shortly afterwards Nick Woodeson, the best student actor we have ever had at Sussex, now a well-known professional, asked me to write him a brief lunch-time monologue. I wrote a piece called *One*, which he acted magnificently, and which showed me what I could do in the theatre, and taught me how great is the pleasure of moving people and making them laugh.

The play has since been performed professionally once or twice, but it was too short, at twenty minutes, ever to enter the repertory. However, it was published in a collection of seven stories and short plays of mine, *Mobius the Stripper*, and seven years later, when I had practically forgotten it, I heard through a mutual friend that it had greatly appealed to Paul Scofield, who had thoughts of doing it himself if he ever, as he hoped, put on his own one-man show. Did I, the friend wondered, have something else to go along with it and which might fill out a solo evening?

I did not, but the thought of writing something excited me even though I had no idea what I might do. I wrote to Scofield, asking him if he was interested in my trying to write something to go along with *One*. He wrote back that he was. Did he have anything in mind? I asked him. Modestly he said that he, a mere actor, would not dream of suggesting anything. When I pressed him he said that perhaps, since *One* was short and tense, and would keep the audience on the edge of their seats, the ideal companion piece should perhaps be slower, more expansive, giving the audience a chance to sit back. I had never thought in these very physical terms about an audience, and was grateful for the suggestion. I set my inner clock and began to think about a piece.

But though one may have the will and the desire, nothing may come. Of course I could simply have my character tell a story of a certain length. But that was of no interest to me. I felt that a monologue in the theatre should be something unique to the theatre, and that anything I wrote should explore that uniqueness. The trouble was that my original monologue, *One*, was precisely such an exploration, and what I found happening was that, as I tried to write a companion piece, I was merely rewriting *One* in different guises, and naturally less well, since I no longer had the original impetus.

However work, even if it goes very badly, does generate ideas. As Proust remarked, after a lifetime of beating on all the doors, which do not open, suddenly a door you never knew was there swings open and you fall inside. I had not been working in vain on the play for a lifetime but for a bare three months, yet it was frustrating enough to have tried so hard and got absolutely nowhere. I was beginning to feel I might never get anywhere. And then, in accordance with Proust's law, the thing happened. I woke up one morning and seemed to catch the last traces of a dream: a voice seemed to be giving me traffic directions: 'Left', it was saying, 'then left again, and again. Always turn first left and you can't go wrong'. At once, for no reason that I could or can fathom, I thought, simultaneously: 'Virgil in the underworld!' and: 'My play!'

When a totally new and unexpected idea comes to one it is always a little frightening. You are not sure if you are fooling yourself or not: Will the whole thing disintegrate when you examine it a little more closely? Should one hold back and not destroy whatever is there by premature exploration? Or will holding back at this moment only lead to the disappearance of the idea? Is it not better to press on before it vanishes?

Gingerly, I probed at it, waiting for it to disintegrate. Virgil in the underworld? But it was Aeneas who went down there. So was I identifying Virgil with his hero? Would that hold up? And why did I think of the underworld as a labyrinth (for I had quickly realised that my traffic directions were the classic description of the way to get to the heart of a labyrinth)?

I recalled that years before I had started to read Hermann Broch's novel, *The Death of Virgil*, with great excitement. I had been reading Kafka, Rilke, Musil, and I had read – in Maurice Blanchot I think – that Broch's novel was a masterpiece, on a par with Mann's *Dr. Faustus*. But – at least in translation – I soon grew disillusioned with it. It seemed to me more like Hesse's *The Glass Bead Game* than like a Mann novel: allegory and theory not too happily combined. But now memories of Broch's novel came back to me, and strengthened me in the feeling that at least there was a subject here.

Broch's novel, as I remembered it, turned on the fact that Virgil, according to Donatus, had asked for the *Aeneid* to be destroyed as he lay dying. The parallel with Kafka (not, I think, made by Broch) was striking. Almost the best-known fact about Kafka is his mysterious injunction to his friend and executor, Max Brod, to burn all his unpublished work on his death. Yet, though the fact seems to be indisputable, the reasons for this remain baffling, and I had in recent years been much concerned with the problem. Yet did anything in Virgil's writings warrant one in thinking of him in this way? Was one not foisting much too modern a view of art and the artist upon an ancient author? If Donatus was right and Virgil did ask for the *Aeneid* to be destroyed, was this not simply the perfectionist in him showing himself unwilling, in the end, to let a work go out to the world which he had not quite been able to complete? Or was he voicing a deeper unease?

Only a thorough re-reading of the works could settle that question. Meanwhile, one thing was obvious: this subject at any rate would fulfil my requirement about pace. And not only was it likely to turn into something large and expansive, totally different from *One*, it also seemed to be a subject eminently suited to the grandeur and dignity of Scofield's style of acting and delivery. And yet doubts remained. If there was a play here, was I the person to tackle it? Did I want to, even? I had always felt closer to a writer like Beckett than to, say, Thomas Mann. That is, I have never been interested in historical reconstruction, or in 'reading up' a subject in order to write about it. I have always felt that one must write about whatever is close to one, about those things which demand to be spoken but for which there are no words. This at any rate is what excites me, and only in this way do I feel I can be true to myself – and thus, ultimately, to others.

And yet (such are the paradoxes of art) a part of me has always felt that Beckett's stance, admirable though it is, could become something of a trap. Sometimes one discovers what is really close to one only by going far away; to remain only with one's immediate instincts might be to impoverish oneself.

At moments then I thought that the idea of a play which would have something to do with Virgil was a pretentious undertaking; at others it seemed something that might be interesting but was not suited to my talents. After all, how could I make the necessary identification with Virgil to carry the thing off? Yet at others I thought that if *I* couldn't quite conceive the grandeur and dignity of the great ancient writer, I had in Scofield the only English actor who might actually be able to convey this. So I turned and twisted, wondering whether to plunge in or not. What finally decided me was this: the *excitement* of the initial moment, when I had woken up and thought: 'My play!' stayed with me. And when that happens I know that there is something to discover, something that needs working on. In other words, a real subject. So I started to work.

III

I spent a year reading and re-reading all of Virgil. I was surprised to discover how constant Virgil's themes had been despite the fact that every work of his belonged to a totally different genre. Even the *Culex* (which most scholars today regard as a forgery) struck me as echoing his central obsessions: with snakes, with the underworld, with pastoral peace. And I read every scholarly book I could lay hands on, indiscriminately, but with an instinct that grew sharper as I went on for what would be useful to me. The two most interesting from my point of view were Cruttwell's *Virgil's Mind at Work*, which deals in marvellous detail with metaphorical and imagistic patterns and parallels in the *Aeneid*, and Weinstock's *Divus Julius*, about Julius Caesar's self-creation as an emperor and a divine being.[1]

As I worked, quite instinctively, jotting down quotations whenever they seemed important to me, certain very clear lines began to emerge. My initial excitement, you will remember, had had to do with the parallel I had sensed between Virgil and Kafka. Now, reading Donatus, I was surprised and delighted to find not one but a whole series of parallels: both men were said to have been reserved, even shy; both were solitary; both sickly, probably tubercular; and both, their contemporaries insisted, flowered when they came to read their own work in public. Emboldened by this I began to think I might introduce into the play, in the midst of Virgil's own words, extracts from Kafka's letters, as a challenge both to myself and to the audience to try to spot where Virgil ended and Kafka began, so to speak.

But all this was only superficial. What really convinced me that I had a subject which was both close to my heart and out there in Virgil was my growing realisation that so much of Virgil's work, like Kafka's, was about *exile* and *doubt*. As I read and reread the poems and recent scholarly work on them I realised that the popular image of Virgil as a proud

1. Robert Cruttwell, *Virgil's Mind at Work: an analysis of the symbolism of the Aeneid* (Oxford 1947); Stefan Weinstock, *Divus Julius* (Oxford 1971).

Roman classic was simply false to the facts. What was intriguing and moving about Virgil was precisely that in him, more than in any other classical writer, there seemed to be profound, even unacknowledged, doubts and contradictions. Was he for war or against? For conquest or against? For sexual passion or against? For Roman *pietas* or against? And all these doubts and contradictions were bound up, from the *Eclogues* on, with the question of exile: exile from the countryside, from the fatherland, from tradition, from the fullness of life itself.

Now I had myself just finished a novel called *Migrations* for whose epigraph I had chosen a phrase from Micah: 'Arise and go now for this is not your rest'. In Micah this is addressed to the Jews, but for me it had come to have universal significance. In the novel I had explored not so much the public world of migration, exile, and separation, which has been the lot of so many in our century, but the inner world of modern man, exiled from the certainties of his fathers. And it is a fact of creation that a big work carries others in its wake. *Vergil Dying* is very much bound up with *Migrations*, even if it is not quite so obviously connected with it as 'The Hollow Men' is with *The Waste Land.*

The theme of *Migrations* is that it is our condition in life to be always on the move, that to imagine there is a point at which we can arrive from which we will be able to look down on our lives free from time or contingency is nothing but a myth, though one deeply rooted in the human psyche. As I wrote *Migrations* I began to understand that this too could be seen as the burden of Kafka's work and, to some extent, of Rilke's. Now I began to see that it was also central to Virgil. And, grasping this, I felt I had grasped, however vaguely and intuitively, the real link between Virgil's last decision (and Kafka's) and the central themes of his work. What precisely the link was it would be the task of the play to discover.

I found, too, in Virgil an echo of another element, the relation of exile to land. In order to explain an aspect of my play and why it was important to me I will have to become personal once again. I will have to talk about my Jewishness.

Although I am Jewish I have been to a synagogue only

once in my life and that was by mistake. I had not even really thought of myself as Jewish – until the 1967 Arab-Israeli war. Suddenly, with Israel threatened on all sides and liable at any moment to extermination, I experienced a profound feeling of identification with other Jews. I find this difficult to understand, but it has stayed with me. And this of course has made it all the more painful for me to see what has been going on in the Middle East since that time, the holding on to land which was not hers by Israel, and the justification of this by some, including Menachem Begin, by reference to Israel's God-given right to the land they now occupy. As I re-read Virgil in preparation for my play I was amazed to find that in talking about Aeneas and his men he was talking about Israel. The Christian Middle Ages had of course seen the *Aeneid* as a (if not *the*) pagan counterpart to the Bible, but that kind of patterning was surely something we could no longer take seriously. Yet here was Virgil writing about precisely the same kind of situation as we are now seeing in the Middle East. And the question the *Aeneid* asks is this: does anyone ever own land by right, even by divine right? Aeneas and the Trojans triumph, but the poem leaves us with a profound sense of the horror of the dispossession of the land of those who had lived in Latium all their lives.

Virgil's way is not to provide answers. He is as ambivalent about the right to land as he is about sexual passion. But ambivalence, I began to realise, is not a weakness but a strength in Virgil. And it effects every aspect of his work. Cruttwell's book alerted me to a whole series of ambiguous images, images which function in opposite ways yet are also closely related: urn and house; ashes and spirit; tomb and womb. Two images in particular I found significant. The first is the image of the snake which, all the way through Virgil's poetry, is a force both for life and for death. In a mysterious but beautiful passage in the first *Georgic* it seems even to be suggested that it is the helical shape of the snake that is at the source of the entire universe (*Georgics* I.234-237; tr. C. Day Lewis):

> Five zones make up the heavens: one of them in the flaming

Sun glows red for ever, for ever seared by his fire:
Round it to right and left the furthermost zones extend,
Blue with cold, ice-bound, frozen with black blizzards:
Between these and the middle one, weak mortals are given
Two zones by the grace of God, and a path was cut through both
Where the slanting signs might march and counter-march. The world
Rising steeply to Scythia and the Riphaean plateau,
Slopes down in the south to Lybia.
This North pole's always above us: the South appears beneath
The feet of darkling Styx, the deep-down Shadow people.
Here the great Snake glides out with weaving, elastic body
Writhing riverwise around and between the two Bears –
The Bears that are afraid to get wet in the water of Ocean.

As I was working on the play I happened to see, at the Royal Academy Pompeii exhibition, the many images of holy snakes, guardians of houses in Roman times – clearly the snake played an ambiguous role in Roman culture as well as in Virgil's own art. But I cannot help feeling that there is something private too in Virgil's almost compulsive concern with snakes.

The second crucial image, more complex than that of the snake, was that of Orpheus. In the forth *Georgic* Virgil beautifully recounts the Orpheus legend and helps to fix it for all time. He only hints at what Rilke was to pick up twenty centuries later, that the power of the Orpheus story lies in its ambivalence: the singer is finally destroyed, torn to pieces by the Maenads, but it may be that this was his final triumph. In the phrase which so fascinated Kierkegaard (who got it from Hamann, who claimed he got if from 'a Greek'), *periisem nisi periisem* ('I had perished had I not perished'). The Orpheus story was to play a central role in my play and to become, for me, the key to Virgil's life and art.

And now for two minor points. The first, which I learned from two American scholars, Duckworth and Brown,[2] had to do with the role of number symbolism in Virgil. What I was particularly struck with was Brown's analysis of the role of the Golden Mean and of the Fibonacci series (1,2,3,5,8 . . .) in *Georgic* I. In a brilliant analysis Brown shows how the series functions to hold the poem together, and how it can be discovered by working from the centre outwards. I do not know if Brown is right. Scholars seem divided on this, as far as I can make out, as they usually are with any demonstration of number symbolism in familiar works of literature. To me it does not matter very much. One takes what one can where one can. I had for some time been feeling that if my play was not to be hopelessly loose it would have to be based on some kind of grid or pattern, which would not be obtrusive, but which would give me something to work with apart from my overt themes. The discovery that Virgil's own rather open structures might themselves be underpinned by something as rigorous as the Fibonacci series gave me a great boost. I sensed the play beginning to take off.

The second minor point has to do with my title. Why *Vergil* and not *Virgil*, since the latter is the accepted modern form? Again the early lives and legends about Virgil guided me. It is said that Virgil insisted on a link between his name and the words *verus* and *ver*, True and Spring. This suggests that Virgil was quite conscious that he was writing poetry that was neither wholly new nor wholly traditional, as Spring is both a yearly occurrence and new each year. At the same time Virgil recognised that it is the task of the responsible poet, the poet dedicated to Truth, to be clear in his own mind about his relation to the work of the great masters of the past and to the age in which he writes. This I take to be the substance of Brooks Otis's important work on the *Aeneid* as a study in 'civilised poetry'; in its emblematic linking of

2. George E. Duckworth, *Structural Patterns and Proportions in Virgil's Aeneid: a study in mathematical composition* (University of Michigan 1962); Edwin L. Brown, *Numeri Vergiliani: Studies in 'Eclogues' and 'Georgics', Latomus, Revue d'études latines* (Brussels 1963).

the man and the work the name was too good not to use.

IV

For a year then I read, took notes, and felt my way into the piece. I then went away by myself for a few weeks, realising that the moment of truth had arrived: now I would know whether I really had a play or not.

To my amazement I discovered that not only did I indeed have a play but that it seemed to be falling by itself into a beautiful palindromic pattern. I had seven scenes, the last three mirror images of the first three, revolving round a central scene which was to contain the single action of the play. This was Virgil's attempt to destroy the manuscript of the *Aeneid* and his failure to do so. The period of the play was to be the same as in Broch's novel: Virgil's last night as he lies, weakened by the illness he has caught on the way from Athens to Brindisi, in Augustus's palace. Elsewhere in the palace celebrations are in progress for the Emperor's birthday, and it is precisely to have him read from his epic poem about Rome that Augustus has forced Virgil out of his retirement in Athens to return with him to Rome. Virgil, however, is not destined to reach Rome; but he is not to die in Athens, the city of pure philosophy, either. He will die *on the road*, in a room that is not his own, in a way he has not chosen. The play will show him coming to terms with this and recognising in the end that it is right that he should die like this, that in a sense it *is* the culmination of his whole life and work, that if he has anything to say to his fellow men it is this, that there is nothing we can with assurance call our own, neither field nor house nor language nor even life.

The first and seventh scenes are called 'The Threshold' (1) and (2). The first is a kind of overture, which pre-echoes the central theme of the whole play in the way a Mozart opera overture does. It would be the threshold of the play, but it would also be Virgil's realisation that he himself is on the threshold of death, that he only needs one more step to go over. At this moment he also starts to realise that all his life he has only ever been on the threshold – of life, of power, of reality. In the last scene the same insight will return but with the realisation that this is how things are, that it is not a particular failure of his own, something to be lamented or fought against, but something to be accepted. At its first appearance though this new awareness brings with it a realisation of the abyss, a feeling that even now, in what he senses are his last moments, he cannot escape from the labyrinth of contingency, of doubt, of self-torment.

In many of my works I like to incorporate my earliest images about the work. I am not quite sure why, but I feel that this brings things to a close and in some obscure way provides justification both for the initial insight and for the final result. In *Vergil Dying* I incorporated at the close of the opening section the very first stirrings of the play within me:

> You move forward. Slowly. You are inside. It is dark. A dark wood. Dark belly of the snake. It winds. It curves. You are inside. But it is not a snake. No. It is your own entrails. You are inside. You look for the light, the entrance, you look for the way out, the way in. You recall the voice, telling you always to turn left, left, left again and again. You look about you for the dove, the branch, you are inside the belly, it heaves, it sways, nothing stays still any more, there is nothing to hold on to, nothing, desert, stone, stone and scrub, stone and scrub, swaying, swaying, moving, inching forward, turning over, turning round, you are inside, outside, inside, outside, nothing, nothing . . .
>
> Yes. There is nothing at the centre.
>
> No man-faced bull. No father.
>
> There is no centre.
>
> And you – where are you? You call and no-one answers. Is it night? Day? What is this room?
>
> You wander through the dark wood. By the broad river. The bank is full of reeds. They bend before you as you walk. Your feet sink in the mud. You turn, you walk more quickly. You are tired. Nothing has changed. The same grey light. The same river with its belt of reeds. The same dark wood. The same voice saying left, turn left, but there is no left, no right, just the heaving desert of stone and scrub and the sun beating like a hammer on your head.

> You are inside. The scaly belly moves gently, rhythmically. Where is the throat, the mouth, the passage to the light? There is only the voice, telling you to move, to walk, to turn left and again left and again and again.
>
> And now where are you? Where is this voice that says turn left? Where is the voice that says where is the voice?
>
> Where?
>
> Where?
>
> Where?

The second and sixth scenes are called 'Orpheus' (1) and (2). The second, starting with Virgil's proud claim to have done something quite new in poetry, to have beaten Homer at his own game and to have written the epic of the new Roman empire, modulates, by means of the Orpheus passage from the fourth *Georgic*, into an awareness of failure, loss and disaster:

> For Caesar's sake you helped perpetrate a lie. You sang of history as if that was the way it had to happen . . . You gave history a meaning: Rome, destined to belong to Aeneas and his descendants. But there is no meaning. Except for the iron will of Rome. Of Caesar. Crushing. Forcing all into his mould.

The balancing sixth scene leads him up again into the realm of acceptance as, finding himself once more meditating on the fate of Orpheus, he realises that it is necessary for Orpheus, for the poet, for every man, to be torn, fragmented, to have his limbs float upon the waters of life. We cannot hold on to ourselves or anything else; we must accept that to sing is to be torn, to live is to let go.

The third and fifth scenes are called 'Into the Depth' (1) and (2). In the third I make use of a Kafka letter, and show Virgil finally coming to terms with the fact that his betrayal of art was not the result of Augustus's bidding, as he had tried to make himself believe, but had to do with the very nature of art itself: to write an epic is to make a pattern; it is therefore to justify – the ways of Rome to the world, of God to man, of man to life. But this is precisely what is wrong: writing is a way of trying to make yourself immortal;

it is as much an attempt to force the world to fit your wishes as is the overt bid for immortality of a Julius Caesar or an Augustus. When he finally recognises this Virgil realises that he must destroy his work. It is the only thing that will redeem his life.

But, in his weakened state, he can neither find the key to the metal casket in which the manuscript is kept nor break the casket himself. The hysterical effort to do so with his bare hands pushes him beyond the point at which he still clings to himself. Out of the totality of despair a genuine acceptance can come. This acceptance of oneself as good simply because that is how things are was what I felt Dante understood when he invented the first encounter between himself and Virgil at the foot of Mt. Purgatory in the first canto of the *Commedia.* There in answer to Dante's query: 'Who are you?', Virgil describes himself not as the author of the *Aeneid* but simply as a Mantuan, born under Caesar at the time of the false and lying gods. It is left to Dante to exclaim: 'Oh are you then that Virgil, my master and my author, that fount of living speech which ever nourished me?' Acceptance, as it develops in my play in the course of the second set of three scenes, is just that: acceptance of himself as having been born in a certain place and time, and having lived a certain life. There is an end to it. There is no point in destroying the manuscript, for it is there, it is done, and who is he, Virgil, to say he knows best what should and should not exist?

The play is about Virgil's re-assessment of his life and work in the most extreme conditions possible: the moment of death. It is right that it should itself be in the form of repetition, a repetition in which the material of the first three scenes is taken up again but newly assessed and understood. The first three scenes are in a sense false versions of the last three, and yet the final recognition of all is the necessity of both versions: reality is not the dismissal of what is false but the recognition of multiple viewpoints, of the fact that every element changes when it is taken up into a new context. Spring is not something quite new, it is a renewal, and that is the final truth.

From the first I sensed that the play would be written in the second person. It is a monologue, but it is not a speaking out of what is already known, but rather an exploration and discovery. That is why from the start Virgil asks himself: 'You – where are you?' The second person stresses the central theme of exile: from the start Virgil is exiled from himself. Only in the end does he arrive at himself, so to speak, and he does so not by an act of interiorisation ('you' returning to 'I', which is a giving up of 'you' as well). The play moves, in the end, from Virgil addressing himself in puzzlement as 'you' to Virgil merely speaking a line from the first *Eclogue*: 'Longer falls the shadow cast by the mountain heights . . .' Then even his voice stops and the only sound is the sound of a flute, and then that too is silent. I thought of this flute as a rough reed pipe, played perhaps by a boy below the window of the room where Virgil is dying, and Jonathan Harvey provided me with a perfect bit of music, beautifully played in the radio version by Sebastian Bell.

The play then is Virgil's coming home to himself, his *nostos*. Yet if I am right what Virgil has to teach us is this: in the *Odyssey* Odysseus does eventually come home; but for Aeneas no return of this kind is possible; there is always a gap between the self and peace, the self and truth. Virgil had hoped to spend his last years in Athens, devoting himself to philosophy, free from the lies and labyrinths of fiction, from the daily labour of polishing verse which can never be, like a diamond, merely neutral. He hoped to devote himself to the study of truth after a life-time in the service of poetry and the state. But life teaches him a harsh lesson: there is no Truth beyond the labyrinth of words, beyond service to some secular power. We are always in the realm of fiction, of poetry, of possibility, of uncertainty, so long as we live. The Platonic *idea* is a beautiful myth; it corresponds to something man does yearn for, the feeling that you can rise above the contingent, above time and its traps. But in the end he recognises and accepts it is not a cruel fate which has dragged him back to die in the backside of Italy, nor is it a ruthless master. That is simply how things always are, that is what life is. And he realises that his poem is not a failure because it is broken-backed, unsure whether it supports Dido, Aeneas or the dying Turnus. On the contrary, its doubts are its deep truth.

Home, for Aeneas, is always a new place. Perhaps in recognising this I was only doing what readers have always done with the great classic works of the past, bending it to my own concerns. But (as readers always feel) I believe there is an objective truth to what I discovered. I did not read it into Virgil, I found it there. (When I say 'discovered' I do not mean to imply that no-one had ever seen this in Virgil before but only that we each have to discover these things for ourselves in the great art of the past, and my work on the play entailed a confrontation with this poem such as I had not undergone with any other.) I saw, as I emerged from the writing, how deep were the links with my novel, *Migrations*, with its epigraph from Micah: 'Arise and go now, for this is not your rest'. The Hebrew word for rest, *m'nuhah*, appears several times in the Bible: the dove sent from the ark finds no rest for its feet, the Jewish people find no rest, Ruth finds rest in marriage at last. And the *Aeneid* tells the story of another people who find no rest, and of a man who can find none either. And as Aeneas, so Virgil. His homecoming consists in his discovery of a new land, as does Aeneas's. But for him that land is not on any map, for it is nothing other than his own body. The play is a celebration of that homecoming, but the paradox is that he can only discover what it is he has been seeking at the moment when he is to part from it. With death comes understanding. But we could also say: 'To understand is to die':

> Yes. Now understanding comes. How the poet, limbs torn and strewn on the waves, sings on.
> That is not heroism. He can do nothing else. For there is no song without tearing. No true song. For the tearing is the truth.
>
> And the song is the response. And that too is the truth.
>
> From the rotting flesh emerge the bees. Without the carcase there would be no bees.
> Swarming. Swarming.
>
> From the waters, from the snake, comes life itself, destructive and creative. We cannot avoid it . . .
>
> Accept. Accept.
>
> Perhaps there was a purpose but you could not fathom it. Who are you to say that you knew better?

Accept it all. As it happened. As it is. Accept. Accept.

But the pain of it . . .

And now: nothing more. Nothing possible any longer. Petrifaction.

This room. This bed. Hardest to accept.

And yet . . . is that not part of the pattern – the pain of failure, loss?

Perhaps that was really the substance of your poem. That history must be accepted. Recognised and accepted. Not justified. For nothing is ever justified. But recognised.

And the poem must stand. It exists now. It is there. It must be accepted . . .

My life too. Its failures. No house to enter as my own.
No children. Grandchildren. Dust. Dust.
Accept. Accept that too.

Carry him. Carry the father. The household gods. Carry them on your back . . .
As Daedalus carried his son
Not as an effort of the will but out of love . . .
Because that is what we are: creatures of sympathy . . .
It is *ourselves* we carry! . . .

The city destroyed. The farm left behind. Lost paradise – always an illusion. We are never one with the land, the river, the flocks – with the Mother or the Father. We have always to set out, to leave the sacred places, the dark wood . . .
Stone labyrinth . . .
Be torn be torn be torn!

Daedalus crying for his son . . . He could not look, could not bear to fashion again the image of those wings . . .
And had there been no Eurydice, what would Orpheus have sung?
She was there. Existed. That is enough.

Yes . . .

And can a man love language as I have loved you, my language?

I followed where you led. I did not try to restrain you, only to give you shelter, a place where you could grow in the sunshine and be strong . . .
The protection of a line, a page . . .
Where I could nurture you in the warmth . . .

My language.

And now even you can go. You were not mine, even at the end. I only gave you shelter.

Gone.

Gone . . .

Accept.

And so we move into the last section, 'The Threshold (2)':

And yet . . . One last time . . .

The unconsenting spirit fled to the shades below.

Yes. The unconsenting.

To let go.

Let go of all. Even the name.

Spring and Truth. *Ver* and *verus*.

What is that sound? That music?

(Lights start to dim. In the background, over the sound of the fountain, a flute has started to play.)

No boundaries any more. Round the city. Round the self.

Gone. Finished.

No Truth. No Spring.

Accept. Accept it all. Sympathy with all.

A fish. A bird.

Bird swimming in the waters of the sea.
Fish flying in the firmament . . .

Ashes. Warm in the hearth. Warm in the urn.

Yes. At last.

(He listens. Then cries out suddenly) Oh! What? You? Mother?

Venus! Mother!

Must you too be cruel? Must you make a game of your son now with shapes of sheer illusion? Oh, why may we not join hands and talk together? Why this? Why?

Gone.

Gone.

The final folly. Wanting to understand it all. To talk face to face. If only for a moment . . .

Gone. She's gone.

And that's right. Accept that too. Accept. Yes. Accept.

(It is quite dark now. The fountain and the flute still play. He is no longer a body, no longer Vergil. He is a voice, speaking fragments of the work of a poet, chasing his own echo, but in a kind of game now, no longer in anguish and despair.)

And longer
falls the shadow

Where?

Longer falls the shadow cast by the mountain heights
That voice . . . You? Or you? Or you?

Falls
falls the shadow
longer falls
longer
the shadow

(Whisper) AT LAST!

(The fountain. The flute.
The flute fades.
The fountain fades.
Silence. Darkness.)

THE END